The New History

The New History

ALUN MUNSLOW

PEARSON
Longman

Harlow, England • London • New York • Boston • San Francisco • Toronto
Sydney • Tokyo • Singapore • Hong Kong • Seoul • Taipei • New Delhi
Cape Town • Madrid • Mexico City • Amsterdam • Munich • Paris • Milan

Pearson Education Limited
Edinburgh Gate
Harlow CM20 2JE
Tel: +44 (0)1279 623623
Fax: +44 (0)1279 431059
Website:www.pearsoned.co.uk

_____

First published in Great Britain in 2003

© Pearson Education Limited 2003

The right of Alun Munslow to be identified as author
of this work has been asserted by him in accordance
with the Copyright, Designs and Patents Act 1988.

ISBN 0 582 472822

British Library Cataloguing in Publication Data
A CIP catalogue record for this book can be obtained from the British Library

Library of Congress Cataloging in Publication Data
A CIP catalogue record for this book can be obtained from the Library of Congress

10   9   8   7   6   5   4   3   2   1

Typeset by 35 in 11/13pt Bulmer MT
Printed in Malaysia

The Publishers' policy is to use paper manufactured from sustainable forests.

Once again, a book for Jane

Contents

Preface to the series

*H*istory: *Concepts, Theories and Practice* is a series that offers a coherent and detailed examination of the nature and effects of recent theoretical, methodological and historiographical developments within key fields of contemporary historical practice. Each volume is open to the idea of history as a historicist cultural discourse constituted by historians as much as it is reconstructed from the sources available about the past. The series examines the discipline of history as it is conceived today in an intellectual climate that has increasingly questioned the status of historical knowledge.

As is well known, questioning of the status of history, indeed of its very existence as an academic subject, has been seen in several recent scholarly developments that have directly influenced our study of the past. These include the emergence of new conceptualisations of 'pastness', the emergence of fresh forms of social theorising, the rise of concerns with narrative, representation and the linguistic turn, and a self-conscious engagement with the issues of relativism, objectivity and truth. All these are reflected in the appearance of new historical themes and frameworks of historical activity.

In acknowledging that history is not necessarily nor automatically authorised by one foundational epistemology or methodology and that history cannot stand outside its own genre or form, all volumes in the series reflect a multiplicity of metanarrative positions. Nevertheless, each volume (regardless of its own perspective and position on the nature of history) explains the most up-to-date interpretational and historiographic developments that fall within its own historical field. However, this review of the 'latest interpretation and methodology' does not diminish the broad awareness of the 'challenge to history as a discipline' reflected in the tensions between referentiality, representation, structure and agency.

Each volume offers a detailed understanding of the content of the past, explaining by example the kinds of evidence found within their own field as well as a broad knowledge of the explanatory and hermeneutic demands historians make upon their sources, the current debates on the uses to which evidence is put, and how evidence is connected by historians within their field to their overall vision of What is history?

Alun Munslow

Introduction

This book is intended to serve both as a critical introduction to and an engagement with the theory *and* practice of a new conception of history, one that has increasingly become sensitive to its narrative-linguistic form. This, I shall argue, suggests the need to re-think history at its philosophical and epistemological level – specifically as an act of representation. My argument is that history is best understood as what it plainly is – a narrative about the past. In explaining why, in this book, I think it is useful to view history in this way, I will clarify the philosophical bases to historical understanding and, in the process, explore history's nature as a form of knowledge through a consideration of the historian's capacity to think in and through language. As a description for this activity I shall refer to history as primarily an act of 'narrative-making'. This is convenient shorthand with which to describe the whole of the history production process. I conclude that the architecture of historical knowledge has, at its centre, the philosophical, epistemological and the narrative choices made by the historian.

Further, I shall be suggesting that in acknowledging the role of the historian's linguistic consciousness, expressed variously as 'figures of thought', 'root metaphors' or through the use of the 'tropes' (the adjectival form would be 'tropical thinking'), we have located the fundamental mechanism through which historical explanations are generated. In this sense history is an intellectual activity that is very much a product of and subject to human beings' normal figurative thinking processes. Hence, the way we think as creatures of language influences the history making enterprise *as a whole* including the character of our engagement with the evidence and the theories, conceptualisations and arguments we deploy. My position is that history is not simply an observational and reconstructive activity, the function of which is to locate empirical (sometimes called synthetic) and/or analytical truth. History is a mind- and discourse-dependent performative literary act.

Working from the belief that historians ascribe meanings to the past rather than discover its inherent or given meaning, my basic pre-supposition is that the positioned historian through his/her historicised (ideologised, gendered, class-based or whatever) situation, constitutes the meaning of the past as he/she narrates it. In other words, the historical consciousness is as much tropical or narrative-linguistic as it is a synthetic empirical-analytical undertaking. This is the perspective, founded on the work of key philosophical, literary and historical thinkers like Stephen C. Pepper, Paul Ricoeur, Hayden White, and Frank Ankersmit that informs my view of history. In pursuing this vision I shall also note those historians who have self-consciously, in their work, acknowledged their own epistemological choices. These are historians who recognise the narrative-making character of what they do and who willingly accept that writing history does not simply conform to a logic of discovery and reconstruction. As I have argued elsewhere, there are four key aspects of historical thinking and practice which are essential to an understanding of how historians come to terms with the past (Munslow 1997; 2002 reprint). They are:

- The *epistemological* foundations chosen for historical knowing
- The role of *referentiality* (the 'reality of empiricism') in constituting the discourse of history
- The deployment of *theory* and *concept* in creating an understanding of what the past means
- The figurative processes of writing and *representation* that constitute meaning

To explain how these four elements constitute the design of history this book consists of four sections, each of two chapters. The first chapter in each section is a historical introduction, the second an assessment of how each constituent element 'fits' into the overall narrative-linguistic and empirical-analytical approach to 'doing history'. In this Introduction I begin by outlining my general position and the key ideas to be explored in greater depth in subsequent chapters. In this Introduction I will clear some preliminary ground by explaining the key ideas and concepts that will arise later: epistemology, reality, referentiality, inference, facts, truth, imagination, narrative and representation. These concepts are central to any understanding of what is history.

In the first section I will address how historians choose their epistemology that informs the character of their 'historical knowing'. This will be done through a brief survey of the development of historical thinking and how conventional modes of historical analysis create the meaning we give to the past. In the second section I will examine the connections between the observation of the evidence and historical practice by reference to the correspondence theory of knowledge, objectivity and seeking truth. In the third section I will deal with the historian's use of theory and concept and explore how histories are self-consciously authored or 'made'. In the final section on writing 'the-past-as-history' I will consider the centrality of language and representation in historical understanding, as well as the nature of the connections between the historian and the past. My argument is that history is a discursive process in which the creation of meaning through the linguistic nature of our thinking is at least as significant as empirical research and its rational analysis. What does this mean for historical knowing? To start with we need to acquaint ourselves with the concept of epistemology.

Epistemology

The most interesting feature of how we can justifiably 'know something' – technically called the epistemological process – is that at some point we are free to interrogate that process itself. That we are free to believe in certain procedures and principles for knowing rather than others is one of the key features of our present epistemological condition in the arts, humanities and social sciences. Hence, we can legitimately talk about different epistemologies: race epistemologies, feminist epistemologies, gay epistemologies and Marxist epistemologies. The implication to be drawn from the existence of such 'situated knowledges' is that we can 'take apart' the basic assumptions of the modernist or as it is sometimes known the historist epistemological model. To point this out is not to endorse irrational thinking but it does present a challenge to some of historism's more dubious assumptions concerning the nature of representation, the correspondence theory of truth, the knowability of the past and the possibility of objective or non-positioned knowledge of it, the separations of subject (the historian) and object (the past) and content and form, and the generally misleading equation of 'descriptive statements of fact' with 'truth'.

For the discipline of history, the present widespread epistemological self-consciousness – sometimes referred to as our postmodern condition – can be seen in the spectacular explosion of books, articles and even new journals, dedicated to precisely this activity of re-thinking how we 'know the past as history'. Our modernist Enlightenment-inspired epistemology allows us to ask whether the way of knowing we started out with has remained adequate in an age when the status of knowledge is now always challenged. For most of us the original way in which we justified our beliefs was through empiricism. The evidence of our senses reflected what was 'out there' (what you see is what you get). The benefit of questioning this naïve version of empiricism means we also confronted its associations with the male, white, Western European, bourgeois property-owning knower. But our self-reflexivity also allows us to ask whether naïve empiricism is still up to the job of generating satisfactory knowledge under rapidly changing epistemological conditions. Of course, as increasing numbers of historians have realised, and as we shall see, such questioning does not have to stop even with more sophisticated versions of empiricism.

Historians are always worried about whether they are acquiring knowledge adequately. The basic question is what is the most appropriate epistemological position for historians to adopt today? Take, for example, Simon Schama's book *Landscape and Memory* (1995) in which personal history and his own 'mind's eye' mix with 'straight' historical analysis. Schama attempts to situate his monumental study of the interaction of humanity, culture and nature within human consciousness and perception. The reason for doing this is to make a key point about how we create history. Schama early on uses the metaphor of René Magritte's 1933 painting *La Condition humaine* in which a painting has been placed over the view it portrays through a window so that 'the two are continuous and indistinguishable' (Schama 1995: 12). The point Schama (and Magritte) is making is that what we see as being outside ourselves is really only a mental representation of what we experience inside ourselves. In other words, we need a design or form before we can grasp what we are observing. As Schama concludes, it is 'culture, convention, and cognition' that makes that design for historians. It is this presumption, so Schama argues, that upsets so many landscape artists when they try to represent the reality out there rather than recognise and work with and within their own artistic intervention. I would suggest much the same has to be said about historians and the past. Historians cannot represent the past as it truly was. They can only take control of it through their preferred theory of knowledge and/or perception.

So, is one theory of knowledge rather than another more adequate in achieving what we want in the study of the past? What this kind of question asks us to consider is not just that we choose our epistemology but what outcomes flow from it in terms of how we might rethink the nature of the historical project? This is the intention of this book. I want to suggest we replace the epistemological contradiction that lies at the heart of modernist history thinking, that of 'the truthful interpretation', with the much more helpful notion of history as a form of representation. To do this we need to remind ourselves of the three primary epistemological positions that exist side-by-side in historical thinking and practice today.

Three epistemologies of history[1]

The first epistemological position or historical genre is the crude reconstructionist or unreflexive 'modernist' approach that can trace its origins to the naïve interpretationalism of the kind of nineteenth century Anglo-American empiricism that Schama was criticising. The reconstructionist or modernist historian maintains an absolute belief in empiricism and the capacity, through the close scrutiny of the sources, to produce the most likely historical meaning of the historical event, action or human intention. The reconstructionist historian claims to fair-mindedly discover the 'truthful interpretation' in the documents and write it up in an essentially unproblematic representational way. The argument underpinning this is that the real intentions of the dead can still address us today thanks to the historian's professional practices. So successful has this realist-representationalist position been – in large part because of its supposedly 'common sense' approach to understanding reality – that it is seen in the popular imagination as the only way to re-animate the past and, therefore, know what it means.

Reconstruct.
obj. empir.

The second approach is the positivist-inspired, twentieth century position defined as constructionist or 'late-modernist' history. The constructionist or late-modernist historian opts for a self-consciously social-scientific and theory-laden style that practitioners believe produces the most likely meaning of the past. This is done by moving beyond the description of the event as 'found' in the sources to the 'discovery' of the underlying structural character of historical change. The use of sophisticated theories and concepts thus, it is assumed, 'opens up' and allows us to access the 'real patterns' that exist behind the accidental to 'see the pattern' that would remain hidden without the benefit of sophisticated theorising. For constructionists the well thought-out use of political, economic, social or a variety of cultural concepts (e.g., race, gender, imperialism, class) is basic to an appreciation of the structures that fashioned

Construct.
theoretical
modeling of
patterns

[1] I have previously explored these epistemologies at greater length in two other books, *Deconstructing History* (1997) and *The Routledge Companion to Historical Studies* (2000, reprinted 2002). See also Keith Jenkins and Alun Munslow *The Nature of History Reader* (2004 forthcoming) in which these approaches are examined as distinct genres of history.

the decisions and actions of past historical agents. What connects such historians to their reconstructionist cousins is their shared belief that their intellectual intercession, though not secondary to empiricism, must never be viewed
as masters of the evidence. Historians who adopt these genres place empiricism and analysis at the heart of their endeavours.

decon.
narrative
repre.

The third genre is what I have called deconstructionist history. The deconstructive historian maintains the content of history, like that of literature,
derives its meaning as much by the representation of that content, as by
research into the sources, tracing the causes and effects of events as well as the
hidden but discoverable structure(s) of historical change. This approach
maintains that history, rather than discovering the most likely meaning to the
past either by virtue of the evidence and/or its theoretical underpinnings
can, rather, only offer a representation of pastness. The main disagreement
among historians within these three epistemologies, which I take to constitute distinct genres of historical writing, clearly concerns the extent to which
any individual historian (such as yourself) holds to empiricism as the primary
feature of historical thinking and practice.

I have written this book from a deconstructive epistemological perspective. I endorse the view held by deconstructionists generally and Hayden
White and Frank Ankersmit in particular and unlike modernists and late-
modernists, that history is the product of the evidence of the content of the
past, our theories and concepts, *and* the coercion of language (White 1973,
1978, 1987, 1998, 2000; Ankersmit 2001). In claiming to obtain knowledge
of the past to generate truthful narratives, reconstructionists tend toward
allowing only the necessity of evidence (content), while constructionists
interpret the data as informed by what they judge to be the most appropriate
theory and concept (content plus theory). However, what radically expands
our understanding of the nature of the historical enterprise is, I believe, the
deconstructionist acknowledgement of the effective collapse of the distinction
between the historian and the object of their study which, in effect, brings
about a mutuality of content *and* form in historical explanation (content,
theory and literary form). Most historians (i.e., constructionists as they now
constitute the large middle ground of historical thinking and practice) have
thus moved beyond viewing history as just content for which considerations
of narrative form have no relevance. I would ask historians to reflect upon the
argument that the form of history is itself part of its legitimate content and,
therefore, a matter for the kind of serious consideration conventionally given
only to sources or theories.

The fact that history is primarily a form of literature determines how
historians come to terms with the nature of the past. This is dependent upon

the nature of the connection between our existence(s) in the present (our subjective 'being' or ontology), the ways in which we come to know the reality of the past (our epistemology or 'knowing'), and its representation as history (our 'telling'). These constitute three reciprocal and co-equal key features of the history project – being, knowing and telling – and should be recognised as such within any vision of what is history and what it is that historians do. As both the French critic Roland Barthes and Hayden White argue, when we write history we transcend the subject/object duality through the act of writing. Because this is unavoidable, historians should explore what it means for their work rather than try to avoid or circumnavigate 'the problem' through a total and, hence, unrealistic reliance on empiricism and inference. How do historians thus make the connections between these three elements? Invariably they begin with what they take to be past reality.

Reality

To insist, as reconstructionist historians do, that knowledge is independent of our minds and what we write, is to take a 'realist' position. This is their foundational epistemological orientation. It is, they claim, 'common sense' for all proper historians to hold a realist position. Without a belief in the reality of the past, they argue, how can you reconstruct it? So, what is the nature of this realism? Realism holds that the objects of our knowledge possess an independent existence. In other words, they exist whether or not we perceive them directly. Thus, when my dog Rosie leaves the room and I no longer see her, a realist would maintain she does not cease to exist. When I am at work, my house does not disappear. At this simple level virtually all human beings are realists. What follows from this position isn't quite so simple, however. It follows for realists – and this is the first error they make – those objects (dog or house), if they can exist independently of the observer's mind, must also be independent of any written or verbal descriptions of them. Reality does not change as we describe or represent it. This is translated into the notion that the past can be reconstructed and be accurately represented. Those historians who would dispute this naïve belief that what we say or write can correspond with reality as it actually is, are variously called sceptics, relativists, anti-realists, and occasionally, lumping these various positions together, postmodernists.

So, the realist argument runs, it must go against 'common sense' to argue we cannot have a very high degree of certainty about the reality we all inhabit, and over which there appears to be a great deal of everyday agreement. We all 'know' there are buses, televisions, politicians, aeroplanes, teacups, computer disks, books, bank statements, bills, bottles, and wristwatches. To perceive and know these objects for what they are is to be 'in touch with reality'. It follows that, at least for everyday purposes, we all share an objective and truthful knowledge as to the nature, function, and purpose of such 'real objects', that is, what they are taken to 'mean'. Thus, few people will attempt to stir a cup of tea with a book, look at a politician to tell the time, or deny the fact that bills printed in red tend to mean you owe money. But, unfortunately for unthinking realists, most historians do not operate at what is, in effect, a banal intellectual level (although it may be perfectly adequate for everyday life including paying bills). It is all rather more complex when it comes to 'doing history'.

But this is not a new debate. Going back to the nineteenth century, various philosophers like Georg Simmel (1858–1918) denied the 'common sense' notion that what we think and write *corresponds* to what we think we have perceived (and thereby experienced) through the historical sources. The reason is not very difficult to understand. The historian imposes his/her own categories of analysis on the sublime (i.e., unknowable) past in order 'to make sense of it' and then 'tell it'. The idea of simply trying to reconstruct it as it actually was according to the available sources would, at worst, result in chronicle rather than history. Hence, the belief in reality is actually a belief in its knowability, that is, what it really means. It seems to be common sense that if we know the nature of physical reality at the level of everyday life then the same basic process not only does but also has to apply to the study of the past. How this is achieved is through the nature of our referentiality.

Referentiality

So, just how do unreflective realists derive historical knowledge? Their primary epistemological concern is that their historical beliefs (beliefs about the 'real nature' of the past) are measured and verified only by reference to the data-stream. Hence, 'what the past means' is primarily derived from evidence of 'past experience'. The immediate question that now arises is how do concepts and ideas fit into the process? At this point a little basic philosophy can help. Philosophy tells us we have at least three broad avenues to knowledge. The first two are rationalism, which denies that knowledge must ultimately derive from experience and empiricism that, as we now know, aggressively asserts it does. Rationalists maintain ideas do not bear the imprint of experience. They argue, in general terms, that concepts pre-exist in the human mind. Rigid empiricists, however, deny ideas exist before experience. They maintain our knowledge of reality emerges through our perception of the world 'out there'.

In other words, to know anything is to be referential. Beliefs about reality can only be established by engaging with and exploring reality through its evidence. For such a historian this means that holding a belief about the content of the past and what it means must always be justified 'by the fact of the matter' (McCullagh 1984: 1). The third road to knowledge is idealism, which holds what we know about reality cannot be disconnected from the mind. Put at its most basic, our being (present or past) reflects back on how the mind and its language and representational mechanisms work. This is most definitely not the same as saying reality is simply imagined. Idealists are concerned to emphasise that in accounting for the physical nature of reality we have to recognise how the mind operates, conceptualises and narrates what we perceive and observe.

Hans Ulrich Gumbrecht has made this point in his book *In 1926: Living at the Edge of Time* (1997) arguing that only if we cut ourselves off from 'old and worn out' ideas about 'learning from history' will we be required 'to think seriously about different ways of using our historical knowledge' (Gumbrecht 1997: 414). His main point is that it must be, and remain, an open question whether we can and should assume the existence of reality beyond discourse. He concludes that what we think of as reality might be best understood as social construction. This acknowledges, as he claims, the inventiveness of our historiographic writings. Gumbrecht complicates our historical understanding by inserting the issue of subjectivity at every turn using, for an example, the invention of class-based society as an illustration of the belief that such realities are the results of human actions. This, he argues, confuses writing history with making historical reality.

For the idealist, then, our *only* cognitive engagement with the reality of the past is through the intervention of 'thought up' models and which can only be expressed through our language-based narrative representations. Realists deny idealism by saying the past must exist regardless of whether there are any historians just as mountains exist regardless of whether there are mountaineers or geographers. Idealists will respond by saying that any characterisation or description of the past must be mind-built because our only contact with the data of the past is through the mediation of thought, that is, our powers of conceptualisation and imagination. Quite simply, the past cannot be compared to a mountain or any other physical object. Certainly this is very persuasive for deconstructionist historians like Gumbrecht and

Schama who judge that our knowledge of the past must be constrained and directed by the use of our mental images, concepts, figures of thought and how we give a form to our narrative representations. But this is not the last word. The rejoinder of realists and referentialists is to note the power of inference as the analytical logic of history. History is not just empiricism, it is also analysis. *and representation.*

Inference

If at this point you are thinking that I am in danger of ignoring the empiricist-based procedures for *attesting to* and thereby justifying knowledge, then your hard-core realist position is demanding I address the role of inference often called 'explanation to the best fit' or simply explanation according to the evidence. As I have just said, the beliefs the reconstructionist has about the past are founded upon his/her sources. What the constructionist believes about the past is also founded on sources but, with the application of a conceptual lever, their empirical study is claimed to shift to a rather more complex analytical level. I cannot imagine any historian denying the power of inference in a general sense. What seems indisputable, on the other hand, is that historical beliefs though referentially based are always second-hand and profoundly mediated knowledge. The way the universe is made there cannot be any first-hand experience of the past in the present. Even though we may have 'lived through' a past event or process, our beliefs about our experience are reliable or true dependent not only on the credibility of the evidence (memory?) but the other non-inferential mechanisms we choose in order to provide a meaning for it.

Nevertheless, the basic instrument for providing a meaning for events in the past is inference. Among the best explanations of how inference works was provided by the early-twentieth century English philosopher-historian R.G. Collingwood (1889–1943). What is particularly helpful in Collingwood's understanding of inference is that it makes room for the exercise of the historian's imagination. Although I shall return to Collingwood later in this chapter and again in Chapter 7, it is immediately necessary to note his singular contribution to historical thinking. Technically inference is a form of logic whereby we connect the premises to the conclusion of an argument. The important point for both reconstructionists (who usually prefer to talk of their 'assumptions' rather than their premises) and constructionists (who would prefer the language of 'premises') is that whether the assumptions or premises imply the conclusion is independent of their beliefs. But, as Collingwood recognised, the important point is that of belief in the adequacy and consistency of the assumptions or premises. Is there more to inference than this?

Briefly, there are three kinds of inference: deductive, inductive, and abductive. Deductive or 'logical inference' is that form of analytical thinking where, from a given set of premises, a certain conclusion *must* follow. For example, assume all the students in your class are either male or female. The person sitting next to you is female (these statements constitute two premises). *Therefore*, the person sitting next to you is not male (the conclusion). In his *Critique of Pure Reason* (1781) the German philosopher Immanuel Kant reflected on this by distinguishing two kinds of truth: analytical and empirical. Analytical truths are guaranteed by the necessary connection between premises. Thus, all spinsters are unmarried. Clearly, the premises imply the conclusion. This is rarely the form of logic that historians use, not because it is rationalist but simply because it makes no 'reference' to empirical reality.

The second form of inference is the one that produces Kant's empirical truths. While less certain because it is not guaranteed by logic, such thinking is much more useful to historians. Inductive inference does not guarantee the truthfulness of its conclusions (hence there is no concept of proof in history) but, through its appeal to the sources, can produce truth-conditional statements of a high level of probability. Induction works, as Collingwood noted by observation (of the sources) and inferring a possible explanation for the data and what it probably means. This is normally done by reference to other data (the context). The historian's assumptions or premises are usually constructed out of the connections they imagine they see among the data. Obviously there is a constant movement between belief, data and premise otherwise the historian's beliefs may turn out to be based on their preceding belief in the conclusion. This is what Sir Geoffrey Elton, the British Tudor historian, once called 'question begging'. Given this loop of data-inference-data-inference the eventual 'final' interpretation is always provisional, awaiting the discovery of fresh data or better inference by a smarter historian, or both.

There is a special form of inductive inference, however, that applies to individual events. This is called abductive inference. This type of inference does not aim to make historical generalisations based on comparison but still involves setting up premises but, because it tries to explain single events, the conclusion can never have a general application. Thus, historians may (using abductive inference) try to account for the assassination of President Abraham Lincoln. They can do this very satisfactorily by explaining it was the result of the act of John Wilkes Booth, who was a deranged defender of the South. But clearly, this explanation has no general validity. Deranged people do not invariably assassinate heads of state just as people who have been known to lie can sometimes tell the truth. But what both induction and abduction have in common is the exercise of the imagination of the historian – as Collingwood suggested – to make connections between premises and conclusions. These imaginative connections are then 'tested' in the evidence.

The conclusion that realists reach is, if the available evidence amply supports a historical description, it is very likely to be closer to the empirical reality than other, less well-supported referential statements. Few people would deny this as far as it goes. The compulsion of evidence is very strong in making justified factual historical statements. In most cases there is no need to question the validity of a particular historical statement simply because it is derived second-hand. However, inductive thinking for historians tends to move beyond simple conclusions. By this I mean the conclusion moves inexorably toward an interpretation. In other words, the conclusion is in effect amplified into an interpretation – the historical interpretation or large-scale inference moves beyond the claim made by the assumptions/premises. The mechanisms for this tend, of course, to be linguistic in nature, that is, they are arguments made by comparison, connection, analogy, contrast, similarity and difference. But what, you may ask, is the link between the justified statement of belief, and fact and truth in history?

Facts and truth

There is no agreed definition of a 'fact' among historians. In their more thoughtful moments they talk about 'truth conditional statements' or, in the words of the realist philosopher of history C. Behan McCullagh, they offer 'justified historical descriptions' (McCullagh 1984: 4–8, 38–40). As I have suggested, in everyday life we may deem that which we perceive to be is what is out there. We can, for most common or garden purposes, accept that our concepts parallel the nature of reality and we can agree inference works well enough. Nevertheless, all historians admit that it is never possible to prove the truth of any historical description beyond all possibility of error. Rather, and in support of the view of most of the profession, McCullagh argues that historical descriptions can be safely regarded as probably true given empiricist assumptions and the inferential conditions that have to be met to produce the 'truth conditional' statement or description.

A reasonable historical explanation is one where we can be justified that a statement is true if it is supported by similar statements that refer to the same observable data. In addition, such statements are required to explain more than other statements. This means it is more probably true, is more plausible, and is less likely to be disconfirmed or 'disproved' by other competing beliefs or statements. With the possible exception of reconstructionists most historians would agree with the view of another realist philosopher of history, Michael Stanford, that historical facts are always uncertain because the historian's statements are inductively derived and cannot 'reflect' reality in any obvious, much less scientific, way (Stanford 1998: 7). History is not, as a result, just a recapturing of the empirical reality of the past, but it is about how the facts are derived *and* presented in order to give them a meaning. Assuming the historian is not just out to 'discover the facts' about an event in the belief that this will reveal their true story, but is more interested in telling *a* story that plausibly explains what the data (documents, artefacts, etc) mean, then the truth conditional statement ceases to be central to the 'big picture' of doing history. This is not to dismiss empirical truths or arguments to the best fit/explanation: they have their role and function, but they are not the 'be all and end all' of what it is that historians do. Unfortunately and prematurely, the epistemological thinking of many historians stops at this point.

That this does not have to be the case is exemplified in Natalie Zemon Davis' intensely personal book *Women on the Margins: Three Seventeenth Century Lives* (1995). Davis' book is heavily referenced, archivally based and inferential in all the right places but the aim is to create and intertwine the lives of three women who occupied different seventeenth century places and worshipped different religions. Davis' aim is to extend the theatre of women's history – and she sees her history as a performative act – through her personal commitment to these women. She does this by emphasising the autobiographical writings of the three women and engaging effectively in a continuing conversation with them. She starts, indeed, with an imaginary conversation between herself and her subjects in which, under questioning from the three women, she admits she anticipates that they share her hopes for the world.

The deconstructionist assumption is that the meaning of the past can only be properly obtained by taking into account the historian's organisation of the data into a coherent narrative in the form of 'this happened, then that, because'. Now the crucial issue is whether the narrative pre-exists in the data-stream or is imposed by the historian. Is past reality already shaped into a narrative – do events and human actions carry within themselves an intrinsic narrative shape? Do events unfold according to the story form? But equally important, perhaps, is the question what happens if we argue that the truth of a historical statement originates as much within the outlook and interests of the historian's own ontology – his or her own existence in time and place? If we do argue that then we can produce books like those of Schama, Gumbrecht and Davis.

Arguably, as those authors indicate the intellectual milieu of the historian is just as important in generating historical facts (justified historical descriptions) as the data itself. In the matter of whether or not Tokugawa Japan was a patriarchal society the data is in only one (though a conspicuously important) sense important. The rest of the job also has a great deal to do with the present early twenty-first century intellectual climate in which the historian finds himself or herself. In other words, our contemporary interest in the role of women in history, in effect, pre-programmes the historian of Japan to seek out certain patterns in the data by asking particular questions that have been prompted by his/her or the profession's specific concerns. In addition to these 'professional' and 'personal' interests, are those theories and arguments, concepts and ideologies they choose to endorse. What I am saying should be plain enough: that those historians of Japan who are interested in patriarchy will come up with factual, that is, truth conditional statements that reflect their ontology as much as the data.

Let me be clear what I mean by ontology. By their ontology I mean the historian's commitments to certain theories of life and living. It is reasonable to assume like Schama, Gumbrecht and Davis we all have our ontological commitments. We all assume that certain relations exist between objects in the world, and between our theories and ideas. Some of us may believe in God, others in Marxism, astrology, the supernatural, hedonism, feminist political philosophy, Korean Buddhism, Narrativism, parapsychology, agnostic materialism, etc. What I am suggesting is that the historian's ontological commitments, whether they choose to acknowledge them or not, are always the filter through which their epistemology works and their factual statements and narratives are written.

The American historian Marjorie Becker has, like Gumbrecht, Schama and Davis written history from a pre-positioned personal perspective and this has directly influenced the form she has chosen. In two recent articles, one in the experimental history journal *Rethinking History: The Journal of Theory and Practice* and the other in the somewhat more establishment *History and Theory* though in a themed 'unconventional histories' issue, Becker has explored her own ethno-historical relationships with the characters in her histories (Becker 1997: 343–355; 2002: 56–71). Her efforts to respond to the connections that exist between the historian's being and their historical choices are mediated in her own experimental forms using a variety of techniques borrowed from journalism and fiction as well as classic empiricism.

Understanding our ontological commitments is important because, as the example of Marjorie Becker illustrates, they provide the nexus for our knowing and telling. Our ontology provides the circuits between the explanatory theories we wish to use and, very importantly, the 'ontology of our theories' by which I mean the things that we take to exist in order for a theory to be true. Similarly, historians need to be aware of the ontology of their narratives. Crude realists would wish to exclude such commitments as much as possible. Hence we have the desire to be 'objective' and the congruent belief that bias is a fall from a state of referential grace. For myself I doubt that the recognition of subjectivity does very much harm to our understanding of what we think the past means. Important as the 'truth of the facts' is in the sense of deriving justified or truth conditional statements, of equal importance is how we see as meaningful the connections we draw between them.

Theory, concept and historical explanation

How do historians who have taken the overtly 'analytical turn' explain the past? The historical theorist Peter Burke, who has examined the connections between what he calls 'history' and 'social theory', concludes that 'empiricists and theorists are not two close-knit groups but two ends of a spectrum' with 'conceptual borrowing' taking place only among theorists (Burke 1992: 164–165). As he points out few historians deploy theory as a sociologist or economist would, but most use hypothetical models (of past reality) that they test in the evidence and, of course, all historians use concepts of varying complexity. Constructionists generally are aware that their narratives do not automatically mirror the reality of the past and that objectivity (at least as understood by reconstructionists) is impossible. To put it somewhat differently, bias in terms of method and theory is normal and objectivity an abnormal state of affairs in historical work. The important thing is not to avoid such bias, which is impossible, but to recognise the impossibility of the kind of objectivity that demands theory free knowledge.

Hence, there is no uncritical endorsement by constructionists of the correspondence theory of knowledge. However, constructionists do share their reconstructionist colleagues' belief in knowable past reality, referentiality and the possibility of remaining separate from the object of their knowledge. The separation of knower and known is a bedrock assumption having the same level of epistemological importance as the truth conditional statement. Unlike reconstructionists, however, constructionists accept that getting at *the* story is not assured by a detailed knowledge of the sources. For them the probable truth of the past (the most likely story) can only be known because history is engineered using the tools of sophisticated conceptualisation and social theory. Unlike for advocates of naïve reconstructionism empiricism alone is never enough. Appeal has to be made to the social, economic and other laws of human behaviour that 'cover' or explain a variety of general processes if not the individual events and actions that make them up.

As the theorist of history Clayton Roberts argues, the use of concepts and explanatory frameworks borrowed from the social sciences should be regarded as necessary to understand the structures that brought about social processes and directly influenced if not determined the actions and intentions of historical agents (Roberts 1996: 135–137). In effect, theory intrusions by constructionist historians do not automatically or necessarily spawn a fake past reality. This is because their covering laws and other forms of conceptual and theoretical mediation are always couched as a proposal to be 'tested' in the evidence. Taking their cue from nineteenth century social theorists like Comte, Marx and Weber, constructionist historians are informed by a desire to discover *the* underlying structures of history, *the* structures that underpin events and which, when they are known, will go some way to explain them. It is this effort to understand *the* connection of event and structure that is at the centre of mainstream or constructionist history today.

For deconstructionists the empirical-analytical methodologies of both reconstructionist and constructionist kinds are unable to bridge the gap between knowing and telling, between the source and its meaning. For the deconstructionist, a proper understanding of history requires that it cannot be simply reduced to data and/or concepts. For them history is about exploring the consequences that flow from the fact that all the events, actions, intentions and processes that occurred in the past have to be 'turned' by the historian into a 'historical narrative' though this narrative can be black marks on a white page, or as theatre, or on film. Although he was no deconstructionist, William B. Gallie over forty years ago argued that history's primary cognitive mode was that of the story. More recently, the philosopher Louis Mink has argued that telling stories is a way of knowing. As we shall see it is the American historian and philosopher Hayden White who has been central to the further argument that history and fiction must share – because they are both narratives – the same formal structure. This inevitably casts doubt on the primacy of the empirical-analytical truth acquiring and, hence, the representational status of history.

In another book, *Slaves on Screen: Film and Historical Vision* (2000) Natalie Zemon Davis, for example, examines the ways in which film connects knowing and telling. For Davis it does so by comparing film as a historical form to the thought experiments increasing numbers of historians are making. At best film is normally regarded as a déclassé history and at worst an inventive entertainment that can only do permanent injury to our understanding of the past. After all, so the argument runs, film is there not to serve the past but serve it up as diversion and distraction. The point of addressing the past in a form so radically different to the book, article or lecture is to simply show up that all of them are moral and symbolic constructions though in their different ways. It is not to ask can film *be* history (because it does not employ the paraphernalia of archival research demonstrated in references at the bottom of the screen) but in what ways might it be more convincing *as* history given the fact that film and history are both forms of narrative rather than reflections of reality. It seems we end up fudging the issue by claiming film can only give us *a* visualisation of the past rather than thinking about the fact that history is also only doing that. Why do I claim this? Well, it is because of the thing both forms have in common: a historical imagination.

The historical imagination

When I introduced Collingwood and his thoughts about inference I noted his emphasis on the historian seeing connections between data. Prior to any examination of the linguistic-narrative dimension to 'doing history' we need to be clear, as Collingwood was, what we mean by the term 'the historical imagination' and its role in producing historical narratives as forms of explanation. There are two important points to note immediately. First, as most philosophers have argued from David Hume (1711–1776) and Immanuel Kant (1724–1804) onwards, the power to represent any thing, object, or process depends on the ability to create a mental image or picture of it (these days it might be film?). Second, for the creation of knowledge every image has to be represented (verbally, aurally, written, or in a visual form). Fortunately, human beings share the ability to mentally construct objects and processes and the connections between them, none of which is directly perceived or necessarily real, and then describe them (more or less adequately dependent on their communication skills). In order to produce interpretations about the meaning of the past, historians apply this common human faculty that, in effect, gives a form to ideas. They do it by imagining possible connections between the traces of the data-stream to see how it might all fit together. In other words, like film-makers, novelists and other creators and writers of realist fiction, they construct mental images of objects in particular relationships to each other in order to tell *possible* plausible stories about the past based on the available evidence (although film does not have to obey this latter stricture). This is what I meant earlier when I said historians (and film-makers) infer. They are drawing conclusions concerning the potential causes and effects between past events when they use the human ability for comparison, connection, analogy, contrast, and difference.

Collingwood had what, from a narrative-linguistic perspective, is a much more complete and balanced view of history than many historians have today. Most important was his attempt to balance the empirical with the imaginative, the empirical-analytical with the narrative-linguistic. He did this by recognising that history is as much a literary as an analytical way of knowing. Nevertheless, Collingwood was no proto-deconstructionist or postmodernist. Even as he argued in a vein similar to that of his great contemporary, the Italian theorist of history Benedetto Croce, that history is historicist (contemporary) and never final, believing 'every new generation must re-write history in its own way', he still insisted this was not an argument for (what some might consider today to be a postmodern or idealist) historical scepticism (Collingwood 1946 [1993]: 248). He believed in the compulsion of reality *and* the power of inference while admitting the fundamental role of imagination in creating links and connections within the data-stream, and which thereby generated historical knowledge and understanding.

For Collingwood the simple difference between the narrative of the historian and that of the novelist is that the latter is not constrained by the real. As far as Collingwood was concerned the historian's mental picture was meant to be true. Hayden White, as we shall see, takes a different tack, concerned as he is to argue that modernist literary writing is more fully 'objective' than historical writing in that it self-consciously features its own modes of production as elements of its 'contents'. However, as Collingwood says, the 'novelist has a single task only: to construct a coherent picture, one that makes sense. The historian has a double task: he has to do this and construct a picture of things as they really were and of events as 'they really happened', (Collingwood 1946 [1993]: 246). To ensure the fulfilment of the second task the historian must stick to a real time, a real place, and appeal to the evidence. But, because Collingwood believed that historical thinking must be an act of imagination, history is never solely determined by the real. The consequence of this is that the historian must offer an 'imaginative reconstruction of the past' but one that 'aims at reconstructing the past of this present, the present in which the act of imagination is going on, as here and now perceived' (Collingwood 1946 [1993]: 247). Collingwood is thus making the point that historians do not just rummage in the archive, and do not scissors and paste data together. They have a central and active role in imagining what the past was 'really like'.

In imagining 'the reality of the past' we are getting closer to the work of Paul Ricoeur, Hayden White and Frank Ankersmit. They argue that the most convincing way to turn the past into history is to accept the idea that the study of the past is as much a narrative-linguistic as it is an empirical-analytical activity. They maintain that our narrative representation is as significant in determining our understanding of the past, as are the sources, the historian's ontological and epistemological position as well as his/her skills of inference. This constitutes a view of historical explanation as an all-inclusive reciprocal structure of representation in which the interplay of ontology, epistemology, data, concepts, ideology and language interact to generate historical meanings. In other words, no single element in this process has priority over any other. History does not start in the archive nor does it remain there. This view clearly challenges the epistemologically privileged position conventionally given to source-based empirical-analytical explanations of the meaning of the past. Not conceding to the empirical-analytical priority over the narrative-linguistic allows us to view history as what it plainly is, the linguistic product of the connection between the nature of our 'being', the processes of our 'knowing', and our 'telling' of the past.

Narrative-thinking/narrative-making

Defining narrative as 'this happened, then that, because' demonstrates how a story is told regardless of whether it is fictional or referential, written or filmic. It should be clear that all narratives contain causal connections. For the historian like the novelist, a narrative is the telling of an event/events, actions, intentions, and/or decisions and their consequences to the reader/listener/viewer/hearer. Before the construction of the narrative the historian/author arranges the events as an emplotment based on what they imagine and then feel justified in believing to be the correct causal links with the aim of producing a truthful explanation of what really happened and why. What is usually neglected in this, however, is that the repertoire of narrative construction and emplotment is actually quite restricted. There is, moreover, another matter. How does the *choice* of emplotment fit in with the idea of the narrative *reflecting* reality as it actually was? Surely historians can't have such flexibility? My position is, of course, that historians do and always have had that flexibility. And they exercise it.

As the French cultural critic Roland Barthes argues, narrative cuts across most boundaries that shape our existence, how we know and how we tell, it is just there, like life itself (Barthes in Heath 1977: 79). As most historians would accept, they can only explain the events of the past and understand what they mean by locating them in the form of a narrative. Invariably their 'narrative representation' contains copious references to 'what happened' and possesses rational argument and they may openly lard it all with concept and theory. They may also choose to occupy an ethical or more overtly ideological position that reflects their ontological presuppositions about what is right and wrong, moral and immoral, just and unjust. In other words what they perceive to be the nature of their being in the world is informed by certain principles upon which they call to help them navigate their way through it. However, because history is plainly a narrative-making activity, we need to pay more attention than has hitherto been usual to how historians deploy the specific figurative process of troping as well as emplotment in their rendezvous with the past.

As I have suggested, it is unconvincing to argue that history can explain the meaning of the past by insisting that a historical narrative is truthful because it is referential. To claim this leads to the strange idea that the history text can recapture the 'true meaning' of the content of the past. This common but crude kind of representationalism assumes we can 'verify' the meaning of the narrative according to the evidence defined as the truth conditional sentence. In other words, the statement of fact is assumed to remain completely insulated from and wholly unaffected by its eventual location or placement within an interpretative narrative. In effect what is being claimed is that our descriptions are not only accurate but that what they represent (as descriptions) is unaffected by their further representation in narrative.

Representation

To better appreciate the connection between knowing and telling, historians might be advised to come to terms with the structure and functioning of the figuratively engineered history narrative and the variety of ways it can *represent* the past. The point is simply that as language use is an intellectual activity, it is the historian (the historian's mind to be precise) that endows meaning and understanding *in and through* metaphoric language, i.e., as the reality of the past is 'linguistically turned' or troped into the narratives they write. The consequences of this for doing history are, I believe, ignored by reconstructionist and constructionist epistemologies that insist on a 'realist/referentialist' and then a 'representationalist' view of language rather than recognise the consequences of the mind-language connection.

There are at least two important considerations that result from the situation of the historian's mind determining meaning and understanding of the past through the troping function of language. The first is that if the intellect allocates meaning to language-use then language, in turn, provides the means for the intellect to express itself. There is a clear negotiation between mind and language. The second consequence concerns how language represents the world, in our case past reality. As language is the instrument for our representations and explanations of experience and reality, historians are right to be concerned about what makes for truthful descriptions, i.e., truth conditional statements about the data, the famous 'facts of history'. Such considerations are important for how we think history works epistemologically as well as in terms of method.

If insecurity as to historical meaning cannot be remedied by recourse to the sources or, for that matter, a covering law, it suggests that narrative-making, as the complex form of representation, should also be regarded as central to the historical imagination. In other words, the act of narrative-creation takes the historian irrevocably beyond the anchor of the sources. This suggests that change through time can only be properly understood when it is cast into a narrative representation. Hence it is that narrative takes the form of 'this happened, then that, because'. What is more, to understand the nature of representation, i.e., to understand how the historian 'makes history' as a structure of explanation, we must also explore how meaning and truth is created by narrative.

The best way to approach the issue of the past cast as a representation – as a narrative – might be by questioning the notion of imitation. Conventionally this is how we are brought up to think about history. History is popularly regarded as the narrative imitation or very accurate simulation of the past. But to fully grasp the issues involved in this belief we might simply ask whether the question of historical narrative is not just confined to how we construct a written emplotment of the past. The leading film historian Robert Rosenstone looks at film in a way that compels us to rethink what we mean by history as an imitation even though be it usually written. In his book *Visions of the Past: The Challenge of Film to Our Idea of History* (1995) Rosenstone examines the parallels between history in words and history in images. He forces us to ask why we really think words on a page are up to the job of showing us the true nature of the past. Indeed, is it too outlandish to ask whether language is rather restricting as a medium for engaging with the past? The fact that people had to

Why film is a better way to serve our desire to find the past.

ride horses before the motor car was invented does not mean we still privilege the former over the latter as the only way to get from A to B.

What I am saying is that the meaning and truth we may wish to 'find' in the past might be better served by a medium that is more empathic like film even though it isn't heavily larded with debates between historians, seems light on data, lacks numbered references, doesn't have a bibliography, a contents page or a heavy duty index. What is more, film is a heavily fabricated and director-ially intrusive affair which (we are still usually told) history is not. As we all know the construction of the film-maker resides in his or her emplotting of the action, shifting and cutting scenes, directing the actors, and attempting to create their own vision on the screen (of what might be real or fictional events). At first this sounds pretty much unlike the work of the historian. But is it? After all, both the film-maker and the historian create narratives. Both render their subject into representations that organise an explanatory struc-ture and, crucially, produce narratives that never existed as representations before. As Rosenstone says, just as film is shaped by genre and language in order to imbue its content with meaning, so is history. The danger for his-torians is not to think of film as ersatz or déclassé history, but to consider history as an accurate representation of the past pretty much as it happened and, therefore, knowing what it most likely means. Historians might do better if they thought that, just like film, history is subject to many different forms and strategies of representation and intrusion. If we forget that we cannot hope to progress beyond the prosaic level of reconstructionism.

The-past-as-history

The implication of what I have been suggesting, and which I examine in more detail in the rest of the book, is that the past is always already constituted as an object for narrative explanation even before it is empirically observed (and not that different to how the film-maker does it). The reason is because it must become the subject of the historian's process of narrativisation before meaning can be ascribed. This process is, I believe, inescapable. Even for those historians who say they do not write narrative(s) because they work the-matically or conceptually in a 'problem orientated' fashion, their claim ignores the linguistic nature of their thinking. From a deconstructionist perspective, while the historical narrative is 'about the past' it can only ever be approached through 'history'. As the philosopher-historian David Roberts says there is 'nothing but history' (Roberts 1995). The fundamental principle of the deconstructive view of history – and one which clearly demarcates it from both reconstructionist and constructionist history – should by now be clear: it is that any meaning the historian ascribes to 'the past' can only be achieved through the imaginative and representational processes characteristic of narrative discourse.

There is at least one very important consequence of this. Regarding the past as unknowable except through the made-up discourse we call history means giving up on the possibility of understanding its true meaning even if we like to assume it has one. To the deconstructive historian this is unproblematic. Indeed, it is liberating. There is nothing to be concerned about in the belief that the content of the past acquires its meaning through our representation of it. That history cannot guarantee the most likely meaning of the past, but only generate alternative plausible meanings within the confines of its textuality, is just the way it is. I am suggesting that the main disagreement within the three epistemologies hinges on the extent to which they are committed to empiricism as the primary element in 'doing history' but it also depends on the degree to which they are willing to accept that, as the philosopher Wilfred Sellars argues, all awareness is a linguistic and a social affair (Sellars 1997 [1956]: 4).

Conclusion

The empirical-analytical approach alone is inadequate in and of itself in creating our meaning for the past. It is this challenge to conventional reconstructionist and constructionist views of history that I want to examine now. In so doing I will argue that historical knowledge is still possible and can be useful. This is not, however, because it has an empirical foundation and that meaning can only flow from such a foundation. It is, rather, because it is a narratively self-conscious endeavour that while it must put any claim to the priority of empirical-analytical approaches to truth in jeopardy it makes our understanding of history one that is more inclusive and more realistic. In addressing the empirical, analytical and linguistic nature of history we become much more aware of our epistemological choices, the nature and role of referentiality, the use of theory and concept, and how our narrative-making produces the meanings we ascribe to the past. In the next two chapters that comprise the first section of this book I will examine in more detail the development and nature of history cast as an epistemological enterprise.

Epistemology and Historical Knowing

Chapter 1

Epistemology and historical thinking

In this chapter I offer a short review of the key thinkers that influenced the structure of historical thinking between the seventeenth and late nineteenth centuries. I do this to establish the basis for the historian's engagement with the concept of epistemology surveying its development from the Enlightenment to its expression as Positivism. The reason I do this is to establish how and why the empirical-analytical model became the dominant modernist framework for study of the past even though it was constantly challenged by a metaphysical inclination toward emphasising the role of the mind and aesthetics in turning the past into history.

The epistemological problem in history

Deriving from the Greek *episteme* (knowledge) and *logos* (reason), epistemo-logy is that branch of philosophy that deals with the origin, character and boundaries of knowledge and belief and, most importantly, its justifications (Audi 1998: viii). Beginning with the French philosopher René Descartes (1596–1650) and his wish to know the basis of true knowledge, the 'modern age' has been characterised by a willingness to engage in the process of self-doubt. Modernist thinking is auto-critical. It questions its own nature and explores the limits of its ability to know and represent knowledge accu-rately. Arguably what has defined the 'postmodern age', or what is a new phase in modernism, is a widespread scepticism about knowing truthfully or true meaning.

This scepticism about knowing has been promoted and facilitated by events in the last century, particularly recurrent and massive economic dislocations, famines, dictatorship, war, genocidal mass murder, and the advances in technology, global communication and new forms of representation that have brought such modernist events into the lives of ordinary people. As a result many of the 'foundational' assumptions and principles that have undergirded Western thought, culture and social existence – progress, science, truth, honesty, meaning, and the political, economic and intellectual forces that promoted these concepts – have been doubted and in some instances rejected. If it is not postmodern, the practical consequence of our late-modern intellectual scepticism has been to question the fundamental 'principles of knowing' – the epistemologies – that came to govern many disciplines especially within the arts, humanities and social sciences including history and which, arguably, provided the intellectual climate that has permitted the horrors of modernist existence.

Generally, since the Enlightenment, philosophers of history have tended to ask the same epistemological question, namely, what is 'appropriate' as a structure of historical explanation? This question prompts two further questions. First, can the study of the past be in any way objective (value free) and truthful? Second, what is the role of narrative in expressing historical knowledge (Mandelbaum 1938; Walsh 1967 [1951]; Gardiner 1959 and 1974; Collingwood 1994 [1946]; Atkinson 1978; Danto 1965; Dray 1985 and 1997; Mink 1978; Goldstein 1976; Ricoeur 1984 [1983]; Stanford 1998; Burns and Rayment-Pickard 2000)? That there is no complete agreement as to the most appropriate structure for historical explanation is evidenced in the three distinctive approaches of reconstructionism, constructionism and deconstructionism. Although reconstructionists and constructionists agree there is a past that is accurately knowable and thereby share a belief in a modernist epistemology with its ability 'to know' and represent such knowledge accurately, they do not share an agreement over the most appropriate methodology to be pursued in that endeavour. Deconstructionists, however, have doubts about epistemology, believing there is no way of knowing (and hence no method best suited to its attainment) that can reveal the truth of the past and, therefore, what it means. They are unconvinced there is a way of getting back to past reality once the unavoidable move is made, as it must be, from the actual event to its location in a narrative, from being, to knowing, to telling.

Because all three epistemologies can be legitimately viewed as story-making forms, as history genres, each accepts the importance of narrative to creating historical knowledge, but they do not agree on either its nature or its purpose. It is Hayden White's assertion, for example, that no story exists in the past hence it is the function of the historian to provide one through an emplotment. Louis Mink, on the other hand, sees the functioning of narrative as the tracing of patterns in events. For Paul Ricoeur the emphasis is different in that he views narrative as the mechanism that enables our understanding of time itself. With the role of narrative in the forefront of our minds it is an essential preliminary step to review the development of historical thinking up to the point in the late nineteenth century when constructionist history in the shape of Positivism became its dominant form. For the purposes of my own emplotment I will start with the two central presuppositions of Western philosophy – the 'logos' and 'logocentrism'.

The logos and logocentrism

The desire 'to know' goes back at least to the Pre-Socratic Greek philosophers of some 2,500 years ago with their wish to understand the fundamental character of the cosmos without reference to myths and magic. This 'natural philosophy' tradition continued in its epistemological direction after Socrates through Plato and Aristotle in the third and fourth centuries. Greek philosophers were concerned with big issues like the nature of universality and the particular, the character of continuity and change, reality and its expression, being and non-being. Ultimately the aim was to grasp (if possible) the essential nature of the cosmos that rules all its apparent diversity. From the outset, the recognition of and accounting for similarity, resemblance and difference produced the desire, which continues up to the present in the empirical-analytical epistemological scheme of things, to discover the nature of reality, or accept that there can be no adequate and ultimately convincing explanation of it.

All this may be summarised as the endeavour 'to discover' or 'to know' the 'logos' or structure that permeates all objects and their representation. The dual controls of knowing were defined as empiricism and reason. Eventually the effort was made to harmonise them. This, in effect, generated the empirical-analytical way of knowing. The success of this endeavour, reinforced as it was by the onset of the Enlightenment with its scientific revolution, is seen in the empirical-analytical foundational belief that the human mind has the capacity 'to know' the structure of reality through the investigation of the data (empiricism), the inference of its meaning (analysis) *and* its accurate report (representation). Its success reinforced what present-day French deconstructionist philosophers, especially Jacques Derrida, have criticised as 'logocentrism'. This is defined as the belief that accompanies empirical-analytical epistemology that there is a 'natural' order of priority as between truth, meaning and language. Advocates of the empirical-analytical take it for granted that language (especially the verbal or spoken variety) is up to the job of accurately representing ideas, concepts, theories, and above all data. What this means is that, in its form as a written narrative, language is seen as a transparent medium of report with its form being determined by its content. Thus, the hierarchy in knowing as emphasised by both reconstructionists and constructionists is that narrative is cognitively inferior to description of the sources and their subsequent analysis. The upshot of this is the belief that we can know the nature of reality outside the realm of language although, of course, we can only represent it in language.

The Enlightenment: rationalism and empiricism

Philosophers up to the seventeenth century Enlightenment and later, shared the empirical-analytical logocentric desire to discover the true nature of reality through empirical investigation, the application of inductive and deductive reasoning, and then represent it accurately. Enlightenment philosophy is early on divided between rationalism and empiricism. Rationalism holds to that aspect of the Platonic view that it is feasible to discover truths about the character of reality by the application of reason. The mind can grasp that which is outside itself but we must always distrust our senses because they can only tell us about the chaos of particulars 'out there'. The strict rationalist insists that while there is an obscured reality, it can be understood by the mind alone. It is the shadowy reality that through the action of the mind produces our concepts that reflect the true and objective nature of reality. This is not just a matter of sitting and thinking, of course. Rationalists (or, as they are some-times called, conceptualists) like Descartes, Dutch-Jewish Benedict (or Baruch) Spinoza (1632–1677) and German Gottfried Leibniz (1646–1716) believed there are ingrained ideas or concepts that exist independent of our experience of the material world.

Such concepts or ideas exist *a priori*. They result from the basic nature and workings of the mind (epistemological questions are often related to the philosophy of mind – how it interacts with material reality). Alternatively, one may choose to believe that they have a substance separate from the mind but are grasped only when it achieves the capacity to discern them. Rationalism (also called 'apriorism') thus insists on the role of reason in the derivation of knowledge and thereby opposes the priority of sensory experience. The rationalist presupposes the mind's power to deduce connections between objects and imagine or intuit knowledge apart from that grounded solely in 'factual experience'. Truth emerges ultimately from intellect, not the unreliable perception of experience or factualism.

The strict empiricist, by contrast, rejects this apriorism, the idea of concepts existing prior to experience and insists that, apart from mathematical and logical truths, all knowledge results from our perception of the 'real world' exterior to us. The 'empirical turn' was made by the first widely recognised English empiricist John Locke (1632-1704), and then doggedly pursued by his two most famous successors, the advocate of 'common sense' the Irish cleric George Berkeley (1685-1753), and the Scottish sceptical philosopher David Hume (1711-1776). In essence, both argued that justified beliefs must be established by 'the given' (i.e., prior to the mind) experience that is observed neutrally and objectively though sceptically, according to its evidence. Indeed, the root of the term empiricism is the Greek word *empeiria*, which means 'experience'. However, as Locke, Berkeley and Hume recognised, the problem with a purist or foundational empiricism is that being reliant on sense data *alone* is somewhat constraining if the aim is ever to move beyond knowledge of 'the given'.

Immanuel Kant (1724-1804)

The empirical-analytical assumptions upon which justified beliefs are founded, therefore, (see Chapter 2) on several important additional principles, those of induction, causation, the existence of a knowing subject, the distinctions of subject from object and form from content, and agent-intentionality or rational action theory as it is sometimes called. What makes Hume particularly important to reconstructionist and constructionist historians alike is his blend of rationalism and sceptical empiricism. As Hume argued, when historians are confronted with the evidence of the past they can only be sure they are mentally receiving bundles of perceptions. In other words historians (like all humans) can never be sure about the knowability of things beyond the mind because human beings can't step outside it to 'see reality as it actually is'. As philosophers like Immanuel Kant and later Ludwig Wittgenstein (1889-1951) argued, without being able to judge meaning through the exercise of the imagination, genuinely useful knowledge cannot arise from referentialism alone. The mind, so they argued, is an active element in knowing, not just in organising the data, but also in organising the process of data input.

However, the good news for realists is that, as Hume has it, our ideas are imitations of our perceptions and experiences. Our consciousness never misleads us. Such mental copies of reality (ideas) exist because of his definition of cause, which is the constant conjunction of impressions, or the repetition of presuppositionless events. Hence it is that the evidence of reality and its repetition must mentally stimulate concepts. So, while we can never be sure about what empiricism is telling us, our impressions and the concepts that are their after-image are not misleading us. They are there. Unfortunately, while Humean empiricism is useful (in its scepticism about crude empiricism), as Kant pointed out, it somewhat still over-simplifies knowing. It leaves no room for knowledge beyond the empirical. As Kant argued, perceptions of the real are only the start of the process of knowing rather than the end. As he argued concepts only *refer* to reality, they are not produced by it. In this fashion Kant attempted to reconcile empiricism and rationalism and connect reality and referentiality.

Kant resolved Hume's scepticism about knowing (at least to Kant's own satisfaction) by arguing we are mentally pre-programmed (*a priori*) to understand how reality works. This is because everyone has a 'transcendental idealism' (given to humanity by God/Nature) with categories and concepts that enable us to construct our understanding of the world *as* it actually is. The concepts given to us are found in a grid of four essential though broad categories: quantity, quality, relation and modality. Under each of these, Kant argued, are further concepts such as plurality, negation, necessity/contingency and cause/effect. With this grid in our minds we can understand reality because these categories and concepts govern it. Understanding is thus provided, so Kant claims, by that compromise, so wonderfully convenient for constructionists, that our mind meets reality half way. Indeed, the universe is so made that 'how we know' matches 'what we come to know'. In other words, the correspondence between mind and world is not just possible it is unavoidable. Kant is thus not taken in by the crude notion that reality determines concepts. He holds to the rather more sophisticated notion that our mind is the source of the laws of nature – at least in the sense that our mind makes sense of nature because it equates with it *a priori*. Thus when we think of causality, for example, it is as it is.

Kant can be useful for both constructionist realists and non-realists or idealists as well. Like Hume he accepts there is a reality 'out there' but we cannot know things in themselves. All we can be sure of is that the objective world appears to be organised according to our categories and concepts. In other words we can never be sure the objects we perceive are in fact arranged by our categories although we believe they are. However, we must take this on trust, as we cannot break out of the categories (the categorical form) of our knowledge into the content of empirical reality to find out. For postist anti-representationalists and non-realists Kant's denial of foundational empiricism is highly significant. It suggests that it is only through an understanding of both 'forms' as well as 'contents' that we may more plausibly think about the historical enterprise.

As Kant suggested (in his *Critique of Pure Reason*, 1781) we must reverse the 'common sense' notion that our knowledge conforms to the world of objects. Instead we would do better to think of objects as compliant with our modes of knowing precisely because all we know of objects is their appearance rather than what they 'really' are. Hence, the objects of history are 'thinkable' but not 'knowable'. This means our knowledge of the past is unavoidably mind-affected or subjective, and cannot be objective or truthful in any strict empirical sense. It follows we cannot accurately represent what we do not know. As deconstructionists tend to point out, in Kantian fashion, the power to narrate is best thought of as an integral part of this 'thinkability'. It then becomes reasonable to assume that at a very basic level it plays a significant role in the creation of historical knowledge and meaning.

thinkable not knowable

It follows that it is only when we muster content (reality) through its form (a narrative) that we acquire knowledge about the nature of the world. And, of course, the key word is *about* – as the work of Gumbrecht, Schama, Davis and Becker clearly indicate. History exists in a prepositional sense to the past in that it can only be near or close to it. While a few historians may have an acquaintance with Kantian thinking, most usually neglect his views on history. Kant's transcendental idealism led him to believe that human beings conceive of the past through one of three forms that, unsurprisingly, are forms of emplotment. This means that the form of our narrative consciousness imposes an order on the past in much the same way as we impose an order on reality generally. So, it is the historian's connection between the content (event, process, action) and the narrative form of history (our chosen emplotment and figuratively inspired arguments) that 'informs' our understanding about the past. In Kant's judgement the three conceptions we can choose from to describe the past and its direction toward the present and (who knows?) its future, are progress, degeneration, and stasis. These forms approximate to the emplotments of Comedy, Tragedy and Epic. History is, for Kant, the result of the mind's ability to manage past reality through these 'formal' choices. Hence, in the Kantian world of historical knowing, we already possess a range of narrative conceptual capacities through which we make sense of the past's transition to the present and the future.

Perspective, presupposition, theory and Friedrich Nietzsche (1844–1900)

It is important at this point to note that if his ideas and assumptions are correct, Kant's theorising about the nature of understanding and the past (like all theorising) must be undertaken within his (the?) process of formal categorisation. As both he and Hume acknowledged, you can't escape the categories even when 'doing philosophy'. Thus, if we were to invoke the theory of tropic or figurative thinking, Kant's theory of 'doing history' has to be seen as such an exercise, that is, the characterisation of an object (in this case history as a key way of engaging with the past) within a chosen figurative discourse. For Kant, history (like everything else) is lived and conceived within the universe of thought, language and the world, and so the next issue should be plain. It is the place and role of our perspective, our presuppositions and intellectual preferences in generating truthful knowledge about (but not of) reality. Not surprisingly many philosophers, especially the 'Neo-Kantians' at the close of the nineteenth century (there were many varieties of Neo-Kantianism) returned to this question, debating whether we could know the past in a presuppositionless (or as I have suggested a non-prepositional) fashion, that is, 'scientifically'.

There was a precursor to Neo-Kantianism in the Neapolitan historian and lawyer Giambattista Vico (1668–1744) who believed truth was essentially historical and imaginative rather than scientific. Vico's ideas were historicist to the effect that they were cast within the notion that we can only be sure about what we have created through the exercise of our own minds. This has a particular resonance for most historians because it is often said that only by entering into the imagination of other people (having an empathy with them and the conditions of their existence) may we understand what motivated their actions. Thus, true historical knowledge came to be recognised toward the end of the nineteenth and in the early half of the twentieth century, in the work of Croce and Collingwood in particular, as that generated through empathy. However, re-thinking the thoughts of historical agents for realists and positivists is just plain wrong. They would argue it is perfectly possible to know the nature of reality with a fair accuracy – even with objectivity – even though such knowledge is processed through the historian's mind.

The case for the most basic challenge to modernist epistemology and for the perspectival and/or subjective element in knowing emerged with the opposition to Kant's argument that the world of experience is shaped by the universal and *a priori* categories of thought. That did not convince the German philosopher Friedrich Nietzsche. Nietzsche rejected Kant's transcendental categories, claiming they were neither necessary nor valid, refusing to accept the idea of a mentally projected real world. Equally doubtful to Nietzsche was the correspondence theory of truth that holds knowledge is a reflection of reality. Nietzsche argued instead that truth, while it may or may not reflect reality, certainly always advances interests and values. The Nietzschean insight is that all assertions 'to know' are at best interpretations or value judgements that originate from differing perspectives. From Nietzsche's own perspective, truth – because it exists within a cultural framework – can be measured only on a sliding scale of interest and power. It cannot be calculated according to objective facts, which for him do not exist outside values (inter-pretation) and present existence.

Because there is no universal means 'to know' the world, for Nietzsche the split between its material existence and its representation disappears. As, according to this position, there is no way 'to know' past reality we cannot compare it with what it seems to be as history. At best we would only be comparing representations. By his own logic, of course, Nietzsche's views are just another interpretation or position (a representation that he has opted for) to cope with what he presupposes to be the nature of existence. So, it is quite possible his perspectivism is specious. When he says there is no truth can this be regarded as true? So we can only choose to believe that as yet another interpretation. Hence, everything – the world, our culture, our concepts, our histories – are seen from a standpoint. Hence 'the past' is empty until we fill it with our positioned stories and situated representations (interpretations), i.e., create a history or histories.

We should be clear that Nietzsche like his deconstructionist progeny has no quarrel with the concept of reference in itself, only the perverse idea that reference (particularly in the arts of which history is one) can be independent of a point of view, a cultural position or the nature of language use. He wants us to accept that all referentiality exists within interpretations. There is, for Nietzsche, no ground upon which we can stand in order to compare our interpretation with reality. We cannot appeal to the facts as the final jus-tification for knowing anything, because facts are just descriptions caught up in our own nets of interpretation. This leads him to a full-blooded attack on the logos and logocentrism. Nietzsche rejects the desire in Western philo-sophy 'to know', to determine the 'logos' (form) that organises objects and their representation (in the form of empiricism and reason). He denies there is a fixed world of subjects/agents with predicates/actions stuck to them, or 'objects' that 'interact causally' that can be 'observed' by the distanced and objective subject, the 'I' or 'self'.

As the key critic of logocentrism Nietzsche believed it to be very unfortu-nate that such a naïve belief is so firmly embedded in our intellectual culture.

For Nietzsche no belief is actually the result of objective causality based on the repetition of events, as Kant would have us believe. In the chaos of existence events are never exactly the same but humans choose to imagine they are to impose an order, 'to explain', 'to disclose', 'to make plain', 'to clarify', ultimately just to cope with the chaos of existence. We invent convenient conceptual and theoretical fictions with which to deal with unknowable and sublime existence. If these conceptual fictions 'work' then fine, if they allow us to hack it through life then good, but don't believe they truly reflect knowable and objective past reality. In effect (and paradoxically being more realistic), as Nietzsche puts it, humanity addresses the material world in a perpetual state of 'as if' that, to which our concepts refer, is real.

Our 'as if' intellectual orientation provides us with an arresting answer to the problem of knowing useful things about the past because Nietzsche denied the existence of a historical process if, by that ,we think we can be led to truth. Historians, so Nietzsche thought, always judge the nature of the past by their own motivations and what they think it should, could or does lead to (teleology). According to Nietzsche historians can only constitute their perspectives within their narrative-making. Nietzsche warns historians against a view of understanding that only arrives at the end of the epistemological process, historically as it were, as a narrative that is grounded empirically and, thereby, given and discoverable. In a Nietzschean history all we can know about the past is that it cannot be a closure through an appeal to the empirical alone. What historians should learn above all from Nietzsche is to welcome uncertainty of meaning and not imagine it as a 'problem' that can be rectified through an intimate association with archival 'empirical reality'.

For Nietzsche content, form and meaning are aesthetic rather than empirical in origin and, therefore, history must be art. As a result the scientific pretensions of the empirical-analytical model are rejected. In a series of complex arguments published over several years, Nietzsche tried to both provide an explanation of what history was from his perspective and the role played by myth, art, poetry and metaphor in its construction. All this led him, in one of his most well-known phrases, to define truth as a

> . . . moveable host of metaphors, metonymies and anthropomorphisms: in short [truth was] a sum of human relations which have been poetically and rhetorically intensified, transferred and embellished and which, after long usage, seem to people to be fixed, canonical and binding. Truths are illusions which we have forgotten are illusions; they are metaphors that have become worn out . . . coins which have lost their embossing and are now considered as metal and no longer coins (Nietzsche, *The Birth of Tragedy*, quoted in Burns and Rayment-Pickard 2000: 150–151).

Nietzsche's judgement on explanation, objectivity and narrative is significant for interpretational disciplines such as history. His view, that it is history's
metaphoric structure which provides its power to explain, suggests that what
historians take as knowledge is perspective, and historical knowledge is not
attained solely by the reciprocity of empiricism and analysis, but also through
linguistic construction and narrative composition.

'As if'

Thanks to Nietzsche, the idealism (a strong element of which we have seen in
both Kant and Hume) that took us beyond both rationalism and empiricism
has yet more mileage in it. Reality must reflect or at least be mediated by the
mind. This does not have to be defined, as Nietzsche pointed out, in 'objective
idealist' Kantian terms. Most idealists do not go so far as to say the mind
creates the material world but, in a much weaker version of idealism, argue that
in explaining the nature of reality we must always take into account the way the
mind works. This is not particularly important when addressing everyday
matters of 'this happened rather than that', 'I am here rather than there', but
it becomes far more significant when historical judgements about value, good-
ness, legitimacy, right and wrong, are required.

Idealists come in many (post- Neo-Kantian or Nietzschean) varieties and
deconstructionist historians are often accused of being, if not actually rationalists, then idealists of some kind. Such a description reflects the affront
experienced by realists upon hearing the Kantian message that the only reality
we can have knowledge of is as we conceive it to be. It is even worse to be told
it also contains a heavy dose of perspectivism. And when we get to history
being a story imposed on the past by the historian, fights have been known to
break out. For constructionists seeking a way out of this dilemma what is
required is a return to a non-Kantian and pre-Nietzschean universe of explanation. In other words, they have to believe they can work out the underlying
structure of empirical appearances. This, they think, provides them with a
mechanism of investigation that, if done properly, can pretty much guarantee
the objectivity of their constructed narratives.

For the historian who prefers to pursue the Kantian insight that history is
as much about the forms of narrative emplotments as the evidence, the issue
ceases to be simply one of knowing through empirical and rationalist epistemologies. If we assume histories result from our figures of thought, those
figuratively inspired models of explanation upon which we all rely, then the

idealism of post-Nietzschean philosophers like the German Hans Vaihinger (1852–1933) has a persuasive logic. Vaihinger's reading of Kant and Nietzsche (in his book *Philosophy of 'As If'* published in 1911) led him to the conclusion that while our perceptions are real everything else consists of a jumble that we subjectively make sense of through pragmatically justified fictions and useful fabrications. Vaihinger accepted Kant's judgement that knowledge cannot reach back to things-in-themselves (as content or bits of reality) and the resultant chaos (so familiar and disconcerting to Nietzsche) could be coped with only by creating fictional explanations of the material world 'as if' there were good reasons for believing our fictions reflected reality. So, in writing and researching history the historian can usefully proceed in several ways, but all of them in an anticipatory fashion. Thus, they can proceed 'as if' the past is knowable or 'as if' it is not. The path they elect to follow is that which convinces them intellectually and which best fits in with their belief in a pre-existing order in the past, or choose to impose on it. This is not to exist in a state of relativism much less is it scepticism, but it is a practical response to the problems of knowing (or, rather, not knowing) the reality of the past under our present conditions of post-epistemological uncertainty.

Conventionally, so far as the status of knowing is concerned, empiricism will deny 'as if-ism' along with its rejection of the Kantian belief that the object conforms to the mind as well as the perspectivism or subjectivism of Nietzsche. Thus, for the empiricist, thought and representation must correspond to reality as closely as possible and must exist outside the 'here and now'. Hence Kant's transcendental idealism (subjectivism) that, by its very logic denies humanity a doorway to the material world, must be rejected. Reconstructionists, for example, will not accept the Kantian exclusion of knowledge of things-in-themselves and that knowledge of objective reality is unobtainable. To grant a transcendental and anticipatory basis for knowing seems to be offering too constructionist a role with respect to experience. Of course, for those who have substantial doubts about the knowability of the 'true meaning' of the past this turns into a history that can be viewed deconstructively. Deconstructionist history assumes our anticipatory acts must be fictive enterprises where 'facts' are seen as narrative creations, as events under a description. The past becomes knowable only when viewed as the narrative story assembled by the historian for a purpose. If, contrary to this, we choose to believe that concepts are produced by the association of particular real occurrences, then Kantian categories (like his emplotments) can still be denied. In other words, form ceases to be the horizon for our knowledge and the 'as if' view of history is firmly rejected.

G.W.F. Hegel (1770–1831)

Vaihinger also owed a debt to G.W.F. Hegel who provides one of the most striking examples of idealist 'as if' history. Hegel's vision of history grew out of the question, how does the historian's subjectivity (his or her mind) connect with the past? The greatest of the idealist philosophers, Friedrich Hegel, put the study of the past at the centre of his thinking about knowing. Indeed, it could be argued that Hegel more than any other philosopher constituted 'history' as an epistemological issue. Following Kant, Hegel argued in his *Lectures on the Philosophy of History* that every historian – even the most factualist – has rational categories of analysis and sees the data through them. As he argued, we only have a tenuous hold on the reality of the past and what we know about it is as much the result of our being a part of it as standing outside and observing it. For Hegel the material world and the mind are all part of the same reality and, furthermore and very importantly, we can only judge by the standards of our own time. He then takes this a step further. By assuming reality follows the model of the mind, the universe must not only be knowable but also it must be rational. Hegel ends up with what seems, to postmodern or late modernist eyes, the rather odd notion that the whole universe is one Idea.

The Idea works dialectically, overcoming opposites not least universals and particulars, arriving at the truth through question and answer. This vast dialectical effort is directed toward the Idea (the Absolute or World Spirit) knowing itself through reason. This abstract system reveals the historicist (historically conditioned by time and place) nature of our thinking and Hegel's personal belief that the history of the world discloses its inexorable rational drive toward freedom. It was being convinced by this Hegelian belief that persuaded the American political commentator Francis Fukuyama, for example, to declare in the early 1990s 'the end of history' consequent upon the dismemberment of the Soviet Union. What Fukuyama did was to confuse Hegel's definition of freedom with the classic liberal notion of personal choice. Hegel's freedom is actually much more concerned with recognising the rational community acting collectively rather than individually.

The 'as if' in the Hegelian system is history operating through the Absolute or World Spirit, the Idea, coming to know itself by the elimination of conflict and thereby producing the rise of a progressive and harmonious world. The mechanism for the purposive creation of this non-chaotic existence is the 'mind', 'spirit' or *Geist* in German. Hegelian history thus demonstrates a movement from alienation to reconciliation that, along the way, disposes with the distinctions of subject and object, and form and content. Like Kant before him Hegel accepts that the empirical cannot be grasped other than through the form of our understanding. In other words, the Kantian notion that the mind creates reality because we can only know it through a framework of our own creation continues with Hegel. How this works for historians Hegel described in his *Lectures on Aesthetics*. Like Vico, Kant, and later Nietzsche, Hegel stresses the metaphoric basis of historical writing and knowing. Facts have to be expressed and are thereby given meaning figuratively. The way content is matched to form makes history. As he said

> However much [the] historian must endeavour to reproduce actual historical fact, it is nonetheless incumbent upon him to bring before our imaginative vision this motley content of events and characters, to create anew and make vivid the same to our intelligence with his own genius (Hegel, *Lectures on Aesthetics*, quoted in White 1973: 89).

It was Hegel's epistemological decision to view history as determined by the historian's working out of the nature of events and actions in one or a combination of the four modes of emplotment. Hegel regarded history as tragedy or comedy dependent upon the particular event or action one is considering (White 1973: 94). Hegel's history is not the logical demonstration of what happened, it is actually a part of the content of the past. Hegel seems to be saying the referent (event, action) as located in the discourse of history is never just what happened but is the emplotted connection made by the historian between the present and the past because he or she is located spatially and temporally between the past and the present. In other words, there is nothing but histories, that is, narratives organising events assembled in the present, as well as those assembled by actors in the past as they created narratives about their own lives. History is, then, not just what happened but its narration by the subjective historian. In Hegel's case history was the narration of what he thought of as the true but dramatic and often tragic history of politics.

Empiricism and science

Given the logocentric legacy of the Enlightenment, the empire of science struck back very successfully against all these deviationist varieties of idealism, subjectivism and relativism. It did so in the late eighteenth century and throughout the nineteenth with its own version of rationalism couched in terms of its own logocentric 'big idea'. This was that we could discover explanations that reflect the rational structure of nature through empirical research, the inference of its meaning and the representation of its findings as the truthful descriptive statement. For this reason science, from the end of the eighteenth century up to the present, has proclaimed that true knowledge derives from empiricism coupled to rational thinking: the epistemology of the empirical-analytical. These ideas were no better exemplified than in the work of the British clergyman, geologist, astronomer, and philosopher of history William Whewell (1794–1866). In his *History of the Inductive Sciences* (1837) and *The Philosophy of Inductive Sciences* (1840) Whewell provided a brilliant rethinking of the connection between the facts as 'found' by the scientist and the concepts he or she contrives in order to organise and thereby explain them. He argued that fact and concept are opposites but must always work together. He suggested that all empirical inquiry must be based on certain concepts or general laws of science. In other words, theory can, and often does, precede empiricism.

This was certainly the view of other scientifically inspired historians like the Dane Barthold Georg Niebuhr (1776–1831), French historians François Guizot (1787–1874), Jules Michelet (1798–1874) and Alexis de Tocqueville (1805–1859), the English historian T.H. Buckle (1821–1862), the German Leopold von Ranke (1795–1886), the Swiss Jacob Burckhardt (1818–1897) and the American historians Frederick Jackson Turner (1861–1932) and James Harvey Robinson (1863–1936). In spite of their many and substantial differences in attitude, style and topics of interest, these critical empiricist historians took their cue primarily from Niebuhr's vision of history as a hermeneutic (interpretational) *and* science-inspired project. The aim and practice of such a vision of history was to reconstruct the past, as Ranke later famously described it, as close to how it actually happened as possible through the interpretation of its sources, and without presuppositions or grand Hegelian-type designs.

In the nineteenth century science became the key perspective through which human beings came to terms with the natural world. Scientists obtained such a remarkable understanding of it that the regimes of knowledge with which we are all familiar today as the disciplines that organise the physical and life sciences as well as the social sciences and humanities were founded. Most importantly for the study of the past the procedures of scientific method appeared to offer a dedicated model of critical inquiry. By the exhaustive deployment of analytical techniques of authentification, comparison and verification the basic methodology of evidence-based historical research was quickly established. The late nineteenth century use of documents to map change over time rapidly became the preferred method of the empirical-analytical model of historical work in the universities in both Europe and America. With a plausible epistemology and a dedicated methodology through which the meaning of the unique event might be discovered, history very rapidly became a profession that happily modelled its thinking and quickly its practice on scientific thinking.

Positivism

Although not early on in the mainstream of the new late nineteenth century profession of history, an important part of the investigative activity of one group of realists at least was the effort to move beyond the event, to discover the scientific laws that governed social and human behaviour. This 'social science' or 'positivist turn' emerged as a response to German idealism particularly in the wake of the mid- to late-nineteenth century growth of capitalism with its free market inspired mass industrialism, urbanisation, technological and scientific innovation, and Darwinian evolutionism. Positivism presupposed that human existence (and its manifest horrors) could be explained through the discovery of general laws of human social behaviour. Knowledge of such laws allowed historians to recognise and categorise human activity and locate the structure and function of such activity. This was undertaken (inductively) by noting regular historical circumstances. In this way the observer-historian-social scientist was able to infer the hidden patterns of human behaviour objectively.

Inevitably, perhaps, the growing popularity of positivist ideas slowly infiltrated the empiricist world of history. Working beyond the single occurrence/event the positivist epistemological turn prompted early fore-runners of constructionist historians to track down the laws that they believed influenced or determined the progress of social development. The French sociologist Auguste Comte (1798–1857) (who coined the term positivism) and the German materialist historian-philosopher Karl Marx (1818–1880) both endorsed the general notion that the application of scientific procedures (as then understood) could generate increasingly precise explanations about the proper organisation of political society. And both delivered complex stage theories of historical change derived (so they argued) from a detailed study of empirical reality based on and reproducing the (theoretically informed) facts. With the exception of the empiricist-scientific historian T.H. Buckle none of this convinced dyed in the wool English empiricists.

Comte is best known for his three-stage theory of human history in which society passes from a theological, through a metaphysical to a final positivist stage. This kind of speculative history seemed an unlikely model for historical thinking and practice given the difficulty of fitting facts into pre-determined schema. Comte defined positivism as the methodology of observation of 'the facts' conducted with hypotheses. He did not entertain any thoughts about knowing the true nature of reality, preferring instead to study phenomena. Although there were no big meanings to be found, social scientists could know, through empirical observation, the laws that governed events and human actions. This epistemological process, which depended on the discovery and confirmation of repeatable occurrence, reinforced the belief in facts and factualism, particularly the existence of 'social facts'. Such guiding laws were called and popularised as 'covering laws' (the notion of 'covering' an event with a law that explains it) by Carl Hempel in the 1940s, although the philosopher Karl Popper originally put the idea forward in the mid-1930s (Dray 1966 [1957]: 1–4).

As the successor to rationalism, positivism served as the springboard for the social science constructionist turn in history that emerged and became dominant in the social history of the 1930s through to the 1970s. It was certainly one measure of the success of the modernist desire to throw light on the world, and our understanding of past reality. The metaphysical opposition that stressed historical knowing free of, if not exclusive of empirical work, seemed to have been routed once and for all. Although a few British early Victorian historians like T.H. Buckle aimed to write history with general laws after imbibing the positivist message, and from a later generation J.B. Bury who claimed history to be no less and no more than a science, the Anglo-American empirical tradition remained largely inured to the positivist turn (indeed Bury later recanted). Nevertheless, epistemologically, while positivism seemed a scientific step too far, the heroic model of science was accepted. The basic principles of 'the scientific method' – observation, inference, theory formulation, empirical testing – could and must be applied to the study of the past. According to Arthur Marwick, the leading British reconstructionist historian writing at the end of the twentieth century (Marwick 2001: 81–82), the French historians C.W. Langlois and Charles Seignobos in their famous 1898 history primer *Introduction to the Study of History* had pretty much got it right when they declared history was not literature, but was an empirical and analytical science. They meant that painstaking empirical research in the sources and according to the rules of evidence and inference was the only way to truth.

Conclusion

The nineteenth century by its close had welded empiricism to inductive forms of analysis. Despite a variety of modifications and the emergence of many trends, shifts, and turns the empirical-analytical model of historical knowing was to dominate historical thinking throughout the twentieth century. However, for the historian who, late in the twentieth century, returns to the questions of form and representation first raised by Kant, Hegel, Nietzsche and Vaihinger, other considerations are as important to historical knowing as the sources, inference and accurate representation. The present fissures among historians are deep because what seems to be at stake is the very existence of the empirical-analytical model itself. However, before we can fully grasp the significance of the rift in historical studies at the present time, it is necessary to explain the central epistemological features of historical analysis as the overwhelming majority of the historical profession currently practises it. I shall do this in the next three chapters.

Chapter 2

Reality and correspondence

At the close of the last chapter I suggested that before we can understand the arguments about the nature of history, we should be clear how most historians think about what they do. The aim of this chapter, therefore, is to address the most basic conventional beliefs held by historians – specifically the belief in the reality of the past and the possibility of the correspondence of history with it. The expectation that flows from the empirical and inferential method is that of being able to objectively separate our ontological state from how we generate and represent historical knowledge about 'the real past'. This is not, of course, to claim that the majority of historians believe in the complete separation between history (as a written discourse) and historian (as an author) although there are still relatively few Schamas and Davises around. Notwithstanding the reasonableness of this belief and before dealing with inference and explanation in the next section there is a fundamental assumption that needs to be addressed. This is the realist presumption that historians can escape the confines of representation into the once real world of the referential, evidence, 'facts' and 'factualism'. It is this belief that, as I noted, has been threatened by idealist thinkers since Hume and Kant but which is an epistemological position that realist philosophers and historians have tried to defend and support through their belief in the knowability of the past via its evidence and the correspondence theory of truth.

Historicism and hermeneutics

In the last chapter I argued that the empirical-analytical model of knowing had become accepted as the dominant way to think about and practise history and its success was due to the popular victory of modernist science. In Western Europe and the United States it had become culturally imperative that the scientific method could prise open the reality of the past as it did the reality of nature, with the secrets of the past discovered and delivered up like those of the natural world. With science as the model history quickly became a guarantor of social progress through the disinterested discovery of truthful knowledge about the past. The power of scientific knowing from the mid-eighteenth century was located in institutions like the museum and library and the emergence of publications such as the dictionary, catalogue and encyclopaedia. The careful organisation and the forensic investigation of phenomena (undertaken experimentally as appropriate) became the new route to truthful knowing. Even primary or source texts (like ancient documents and the Bible) were soon analysed for the truth (and to dismiss the myths) assumed to exist in their words. The scientific critique of texts, sometimes called philology and sometimes hermeneutics, became a popular nineteenth century scholarly activity.

As we know, the Enlightenment effort to apply scientific method to history was always accompanied by its idealist challenge. The basic objection came from that metaphysical perspective I have described as historicist (Stanford 1998: 155). This is the view, popularly associated first with Giambattista Vico, and then with the German philosophers Johann Gottfried Herder (1744–1803) and later Friedrich Hegel. From these thinkers we get the idea that history is a unified process capable of explanation only by reference to itself. In other words, the truth of the past can only be found self-referentially.

Historicism turned out to be a troublesome concept thanks to a variety of awkward re-definitions. For the German historian Friedrich Meinecke (1862–1954) historicism was a reflection of that change in Western thinking away from the idea that truth is universal and exists regardless of time and place. For Wilhelm von Humboldt (1767–1835) historicism meant understanding the role of language as the basis for and medium of all knowledge. Most significantly Humboldt took language to be the expression of human nature 'an involuntary emanation of the spirit' believing that 'language is the formative organ of thought' (quoted in Burns and Rayment-Pickard 2000: 78–79). The idea that thought is the product of language and they are inseparable means, of course, that understanding is very much dependent upon, or relative to, how individuals use words and language. The historicist thinker Friedrich Schleiermacher (1768–1834) also pursued this idea to explain how the historian could achieve an understanding of the meaning locked in primary source documents. He developed the science of hermeneutics or interpretation of texts, arguing the historian-interpreter (of the text) can and must place him or herself within the mind of its author. This can be done, as later Croce and Collingwood agreed, only because we all share the basic building block of thought and knowing, i.e., language.

The recent late twentieth century acknowledgement of language as the vehicle for the study of the past – the so-called linguistic turn – while it has now begun slowly to sink into the professional consciousness it still remains a problem for most historians because of the difficulty they have with the historicist idea of 'linguistic presentness'. To be reflexive about one's practice is all well and good and to be encouraged, but to expect that historical understanding begins with the historian's language rather than the past takes a heart in mouth epistemological leap. Most historians can't do it and won't do it. That a journal collection called 'Is An Experimental History Possible?' published in 1996 (*UTS Review*) was – coincidentally – followed by the founding of another journal dedicated specifically to confronting conventional history thinking and habits (*Rethinking History: The Journal of Theory and Practice* which started publication in 1997) and the imminent publication of a book collection to be called *Experiments in Rethinking History* (2004 forthcoming), is in all likelihood highly disconcerting.

The fact that the latter two developments were and are the result of the work of only two historians and two perspicacious history editors indicates the state of play in the profession. For many professional historians such developments sound too much like a celebration of historicism rather than a cool examination of it. And so it may turn out to be. That 'experimental history' seems like a contradiction in terms is testament less to the adventuresome (reckless?) nature of a handful of historians and editors than to the lack of reflexivity within the profession of historians as a whole. That so many historians would probably baulk at this accusation of a lack of originality may only serve to further indicate that the self-conscious pushing back of the frontiers of history is still mainly restricted to new methods and themes while they remain ensnared within the envelope of modernist epistemology.

One of the main (and dangerous?) implications of historicism is that truth in science and truth in culture (and history) must be different. This conclusion led toward the close of the nineteenth century and primarily in response to the rise of the Comtean positivists, three German philosopher-historians, Wilhelm Dilthey (1833–1911), Heinrich Rickert (1863–1936) and Georg Simmel (1858–1918), to produce a new scientific history. Aware of the historicist message, they did so without giving in to a crude scientific approach that they felt was inappropriate to the study of human beings. This took the form of a re-vamped and redefined historicism. Dilthey, in particular, argued that the human or cultural sciences (*Geisteswissenschaften*) could not be understood by methods derived from the natural sciences

(*Naturwissenschaften*). Unfortunately he had a false start with his *Intro-duction to the Human Sciences* (1883) in which he promised, but did not deliver, a fresh epistemological approach to the human sciences based on his notion of the psychology of inner will. His early dalliance with psychology, which he judged to be the most appropriate means for historical explanation, was moderated in the late 1890s by his reflections on the logos and the im-possible dream of knowing the actual nature of reality. Nevertheless, Dilthey still wanted a factual knowledge of the past. In trying to ride two horses at once – the recognition of the subjective nature of knowing and the desire to objectively establish impartial facts – he was setting out the guidelines for all later constructionist history.

Dilthey's, like Rickert's and Simmel's rejection of the Enlightenment-inspired mirror of nature or correspondence theory of truth underpinned his belief that a dedicated epistemology must exist for understanding change over time. Dilthey returned both to Kant and to hermeneutics (now more fully developed as the theory, practice and technology of the interpretation of written records). Following Kant he accepted that knowing the meaning of texts is a process that exists in the cultural sciences only through the mind and reality operating together. Dilthey, like Kant, accepted that the knowing subject (the historian) acquires his or her knowledge by mentally and concep-tually processing traces of the data stream. But what must be remembered, so Dilthey argues (echoing Kant), is that the data stream cannot be transcended by the mind to discover the reality behind it. In the case of history reality is its traces. Here we return to the prepositional nature of history. For Dilthey historical knowledge can never be more than a consciousness about the reality of the past. Dilthey's conclusion is that the historian cannot escape his or her mind or life in order 'to know' the past thing-in-itself whether it be an event, action, decision, or a large-scale process of change over time.

For Dilthey historical knowing can only occur through the conjunction of the three processes of inner experience of life (*Erlebnis*), its outer expression (*Ausdruck*) and empathy/understanding (*Verstehen*). In other words, historical knowledge can only be derived through a combination of the psychological state of inner directedness (the will), ontology (the experience of being) and epistemology (the desire to know and explain). For Dilthey history must be as much about our lived experience as it is about the content of the past. Like the founder of hermeneutics Friedrich Schleiermacher, Dilthey acknowledged the unavoidable 'hermeneutic circle' that characterises cultural understanding that knowledge comes only from the knowledge we already possess. The historian, therefore, uses categories (following Kant) but they are not *a priori* (unlike Kant's categories), but they are provided for us by our experience of life, which changes over time and according to place and language (hence the recognition of historicism). So the categories we use in 'doing history' (such as notions of 'truth', 'value', 'progress', 'accuracy') come from our everyday experience and not a distanced understanding of the given meaning in the data. This recognises the unavoidable relativism in historical knowing.

Historicism, history and the documentary form

Despite this mid-nineteenth century historicist counter-Enlightenment backlash, history was established through the process of male bourgeois professionalisation in the emerging university system in Europe and North America. Characterised by written syllabuses, survey courses, special subjects, teaching timetables, the lecture, seminar and tutorial the creation of the discipline of history was intellectually moulded by the scientific and anti-historicist epistemological model. Organised teaching was combined with archival/library research, the dissertation and a formal examination system that tested the historical-scientific method and the understanding it produced. The power of this remains with us today in the outcomes-based learning model of history teaching and, in the UK, the centrally imposed History Benchmarking Statements that provide the officially sanctioned outcomes for all history degrees. These outcomes are cast in terms of the historians' skills and qualities of mind as well as the criteria for content.

The rise of the university presses and the scholarly publication of monographs braced the nineteenth century disciplining of the past. Scholarly journals were established like the *Historische Zeitschrift* in 1859, *English Historical Review* in 1886 and *American Historical Review* in 1895. The period also witnessed the founding of local and national historical associations plus that essential feature of professional esteem and self-propagation, the history conference. As a consequence, the growing collective reverence for documentary 'facts' found a home in highly researched and deeply referential conference papers, research seminars, monographs, and scholarly journal articles. The undergraduate dissertation or extended essay in the UK has now become the bedrock of undergraduate and postgraduate history teaching. While reflexivity about the nature of historical study is officially encouraged the form is intrinsically assumed to be empirical-analytical. Thus, it would be somewhat unusual for a student to be allowed to experimentally mix 'fact' and 'fiction'. There is a right way to do it and only when mastery of this is demonstrated might professionals be permitted to experiment.

One of the basic principles of this late nineteenth and early twentieth century professionalised endorsement of the epistemology of realism was its practitioners' 'common sense' separation of the mind and its contents from the outside material world. The realist epistemological position insisted those objects of which we desire knowledge have an autonomous actuality not just outside our perception and our description but also ourselves. It rapidly became self-evident that historians must partition what they think from what they found in the evidence. In other words demarcate the 'imagined' from 'the given'. The early and mid-nineteenth century counter tradition that historians emplot the past primarily as an act of imagination was firmly rejected by what rapidly became the vast majority of the new mid-nineteenth century generation of historians. The basic aim of the newly professional and realist historical fellowship was to discover the 'facts of past experience' in the archive, and then re-tell *the* story of what had happened with as little embellishment as possible of an either conceptual or ideological nature.

This mind-set, of course, was not just limited to historians. Although David Hume had forcefully argued that human beings only had knowledge of sense impressions and must thereby remain uncertain as to the real nature of cause, effect, and truth, in the second half of the nineteenth century the vogue for scientism infiltrated most aspects of American and European culture. While in the discipline of painting the shift from the poetical romance of Eugene Delacroix to the grubby 'slice of life' authenticity of Gustave Courbet may have seemed slow, in opera the displacement of Romanticism with Realism was far more dramatic in effect as it was in other art forms, and especially literature. While the practices of European Realist writers were diverse, the documentary depictions of everyday life of Edmond and Jules Goncourt and particularly Gustave Flaubert and Emil Zola combined with the technological breakthrough of mass printing to create the bourgeois 'literature of reality'. Contemporary settings, commonplace dialogue and often written as a history, the intention of realist writers like the Americans Henry James, William Dean Howells, Frank Norris and Stephen Crane was didactic, to teach the readers, especially the protected bourgeoisie, about 'real life'. The pen like a blade cut open reality and laid it bare. The artist like the historian had become a technician. This techno-artisan self-image continued well into the twentieth century.

One of the most significant of nineteenth century professional historians, and the one taken to be most representative of the technical craft, was the German Leopold von Ranke (1795–1886). He has been described as the first 'international model for the master historian' and, most importantly, his name has 'long seemed synonymous with the goal of objectivity' (Stanford

1998: 54; Appleby, Hunt and Jacob 1994: 74). In the conventional narrative of thinking and practice in history Ranke is best remembered for his 1824 statement that he wanted to tell the past 'as it actually was' (*wie es eigentlich gewesen*) (Stanford 1998: 54). Now, while it is not altogether clear what he meant by this phrase, it is unlikely to be what many reconstructionist American historians in the years up to the 1900s believed, that is, an absolutist defence of an epistemology that depended primarily upon excavating the archive for 'the facts'. Rather, according to the philosopher of history Georg Iggers, though rigorous in his defence of primary source research and critical methodology, Ranke was likely to be defending a substantially more sophisticated idea.

This was Ranke's belief that the role of the historian must be to understand events in their essential terms (Iggers 1997: 25–26). Ranke's aim was to reveal the complexities of change over time by getting as close as possible to, or even inside, the reality of the past. For Ranke the purpose was to reveal the moral nature of society's institutions and practices, specifically the workings of God on earth. So, while Ranke became the model for this techno-artisanal scholarship he was not entirely led by the desire to be objective or persuaded by the metaphor of the historian as a blank sheet of paper upon which the past would imprint itself. Ranke actually prefaced his most famous statement by saying history was about judging the past for the profit of future ages. By that he probably meant the historian should reveal not just what happened and how, but what was its essential meaning (Iggers and von Moltke 1973: xli–xlii; Bentley 1999: 39). He did, however, insist that the way to the 'real meaning' of the past could only be through the critical and elaborate examination of its documentary sources.

Ranke's famous statement was for a very long time (and sometimes is still today) interpreted to mean it is possible to recount the past accurately and more or less objectively in a correspondence sense. It has been concluded, for example, that Ranke may be regarded as having sustained a high level of impartiality because of his scrupulous care in allowing the facts to emerge from the data (Iggers and von Moltke 1973: lix). Such a view tends to ignore the narrative-making and emplotting aspect of Ranke's legacy (White 1973: 167). The Rankean inheritance may be regarded as having two aspects. It is initially one of documentary referentiality as the basis for the study of the past viewing history being about scientific rigour translated as objective evidential and archival study. But it is also concerned with the discovery of the meaning behind the singular event and human action. This is done so the claim can be made that historians may judge the past in its own terms rather than those of the present or by the imposition of their preferred story.

Scientific empiricism

In the face of what became the Rankean juggernaut with its assumption of fact-based scientism, there was soon no room among professionalised historians – especially those of a positivist inclination – for the thought that the meaning of history could be legitimately provided by their imaginative acts of narration. The very notion that metaphoric figures of thought might influence or even direct the historical emplotment would have been rapidly dismissed as dangerous nonsense. Indeed, at the end of the nineteenth and start of the twentieth centuries we can readily detect the authority as well as the richness and variety of the scientific approach to history. Hence, we find the French positivist historian Hippolyte Taine (1828–1893), the American factualist economic historian Edward P. Cheyney (1861–1947) and the English scientific historian J.B. Bury (1861–1927) all believing in the pursuit of the laws of human behaviour through the gathering of facts. Such a pursuit would result in the accurate representation of the past. Each, in their different ways, reacted against the legacy of Vico, Kant, Hegel and the historicists as well Nietzsche and Vaihinger.

The ultimate success of dressing empiricism in a scientific jacket is nowhere better illustrated than by J.B. Bury's declaration in 1902 that history should be viewed as a science, no less and no more. But, having said that, while he thought history undoubtedly possessed a scientific method, it was also still about contingent events and in his mind this militated against the establishment of firm general laws of human behaviour. What Bury seems to have been saying, like the contemporary French historians Charles Victor Langlois and Charles Seignobos, is that history is an empirical science rather than the collection of 'facts' for their own sake. This was not, however, the case in the United States where through the nineteenth century debates on method gave way before the overwhelming desire to collect facts and equate this with objectivity (Bentley 1999: 51). However, despite discussions about method, the important point is that Bury, Seignobos and Langlois shared with most other empiricist historians of the early reconstructionist school the belief that facts were fragments of past reality. Working from this odd presumption reinforced with the application of the mechanism of cause and effect and inductive inference, the new profession came to think that the true meaning of the past not only existed but it could be approached, understood, and accurately described.

If Taine, Cheyney and Bury would not accept that the emplotments of their histories affirmed an allegiance to a particular philosophy of history or argument, or that history was primarily a form of literature, then certainly neither would Seignobos and Langlois. Following the assumed path of Ranke, they maintained that because history was scientific in approach and empiricist in method, it must be factual in outcome. In their joint *Introduction to the Study of History* (1898) they offer a typical picture of modernist attitudes toward historical methods. They argued that professional historians should not draw up general laws, and in this sense they were anti-positivist, but historians should still aim to explain reality in ways that moved them beyond egoism, partiality, and the demands of the present. Both stressed that history, though scientific in approach and a science of observation, was also a science of reasoning. In other words, history was about analytically deriving from often-tainted documentary sources a genuine insight into what actually happened and what it meant. The belief in science, empiricism and referentiality was paramount.

Raw materials

This empirical-analytical belief led directly to the sovereignty of the raw materials, those primary sources or testaments left behind by the historical actors themselves. In turn this produced the powerful idea of 'the facts' as found in the evidence bolstered the idea that the existence (and inherent nature) of objects in the past does not depend upon the character of our beliefs, or our perception or description of them. Belief in the facts accepts not just that the past once existed (would anyone of course seriously deny that?) but it existed in a particular and knowable way. Thus, the editors of the 1876 *La Revue historique* could reasonably demand that their contributors followed scientific procedures of exposition 'where every statement' had to be accompanied 'by references to sources and by citations' (quoted in Appleby, Hunt and Jacob 1994: 75). Thus historians at the close of the nineteenth century saw history as objective because it avoided a variety of assumptions in the forms of theory, laws, ideology, philosophy and dangerously emotive narrative. The rise of the numbered reference in the history text reflected the primacy of the techno-artisanal assembly of sources. It still does.

Given this belief in the possibility of objective knowing, it followed that direct empirical or sense perception became the first step on the reconstructionist path, one that must surely lead to the discovery of past reality, its evaluation and explanation. In other words our perceptions may usefully be regarded as largely unmediated and can be written down accurately once they are properly and systematically referenced. That there can be perceptual anomalies (false data) is taken care of by constantly checking the traces against each other (the comparison and verification of evidence) and thereby relent-lessly and ruthlessly revising explanations according to the dictates of the available evidence. Relativism (the belief that the nature of knowledge depends on the interventions of time, place, and perspective) is kept at bay through this potent mechanism. Hence realists quickly arrived at a method of explanation through investigation and its accurate description, rather than explanation by emplotment or figures of thought. 'The facts' became the basic building blocks for reconstructing events as they occurred. The facts of the past were, and are, discovered. They are not created.

That there are historians today who push the boundaries of history beyond the confines of demonstrable fact directly contests this notion that history cannot be usefully considered a creation. That, for example, Robin Bisha should attempt in her article 'Reconstructing the Voice of a Noblewoman of the Time of Peter the Great' to offer a reconstruction (the title is, perhaps, inflected with only slight irony?) of the thoughts of a historical agent via 'a pseudo-autobiography', is a deliberate (re) creation of the past as it might have been – but is, perhaps, no less 'truthful' for that (Bisha 1998: 51–64). The piece is heavily researched (though the sources in respect of this historical figure are sparse) but construed in a fashion that intentionally highlights the nature of the exercise as much as the content and the difficulties facing Russian women at that time. As Bisha's exercise amply demonstrates, any history that is unaware that it is history misleads.

As I shall argue at greater length in the next chapter, 'the facts' are an unavoidably contested concept. It is something of a paradox that what 'the facts' mean has less certainty than what they are supposed to represent, that is, the reality of things. According to one of the leading defenders of reconstruc-tionist epistemology, the British social historian Arthur Marwick, history is 'a body of knowledge about the human past based on the systematic study of sources' (Marwick 1998 [1993]: 119). Marwick does not accept the idealist challenge to empiricism by arguing it is the sources that count first and last in 'doing history'. Marwick's epistemological position is that the only approach to the sources that will generate proper history comes with a *strategy* but not *a priori* conceptualisation or ideology. Speaking, as he believes he does for all right thinking historians, Marwick is relentless on this point. His argument is that history is not about 'theory' or invention: it is about inferring the real meaning of the evidence (see Chapter 3). The implication is clear. Empiricism is not itself *a theory* it is *the method* for 'doing history'.

'The empirical method' allows historians, so Marwick claims, to determine what questions need to be asked by establishing an inventory of the kinds of primary sources to be interrogated and making the significant distinction between witting (intentional) and unwitting (unintentional) testimony (Marwick 2001: 172–179). The historian's procedure (Marwick's term is catechism) takes the form of a series of questions addressed by the historian to the sources (Marwick 2001: 179–185). Is the source authentic? When was the source produced? What kind of source is it? How did it come into existence? How reliable is the author of the source? How was the source understood at the time? How does the source relate to other sources? Authenticity, dating, comparison and verification are the essentials of this methodology of corroboration.

Through this 'knowledge and method' rather than theory approach Marwick claims he does 'what writers who theorise about what history isn't, or what it ought to be, never do, [that is] categorise the main types of historical source' (Marwick 1998 [1993]: 121). He comes up with thirteen categories of historical source both primary and secondary. These include documents of record (treaties, Parish Registers, Acts of Parliament, Pipe Rolls). There are, in addition, reports and surveys (such as the Blue Books and Sebohm Rowntree's survey of poverty in York in 1897–98). He also lists family and personal sources, studies of folklore, guides, handbooks and directories, media and artefacts of popular culture, and oral histories (Marwick 1998 [1993]: 121–127). With his techno-artisanal belief in the supremacy of the evidence Marwick becomes irrepressible in his attack on what he assumes to be the errors of Kantian subjectivism.

Marwick assaults all historians whom, he claims, approach the sources with pre-conceived theories or ideological positions (constructionists), or who view history as primarily a discourse about the past (deconstructionists) (Marwick 2001: 1–21). He denounces the constructionist theorist Christopher Lloyd (and his book *Explanation in Social History* 1986) for his argument that history is a theory-laden discipline. Post-structuralists like Attridge, Bennington and Young (*Post-structuralism and the Question of History* 1987), and Marxists like Hindess and Hirst (*Pre-capitalist Modes of Production* 1975) also get very short shrift. The point on which Marwick insists is that history is primarily if not exclusively an empirical practice, and that question begging, which is the province of concept and ideology, or viewing history as a presentist discourse, must be fiercely opposed. He argues it is only through an empiricist strategy that the 'serious professional historian' has the capacity to rise above his or her own situation (the present) and be objective. The point he is making whether he acknowledges it or not, is that 'the data' is neutral. It carries with it no epistemological baggage. For Marwick the sources, if treated properly, can lead us ever closer to the factual truth of the past and hence what we write can correspond to what once was and hence, what it meant.

Correspondence

R.G. Collingwood, in a vein similar to Marwick, argued it was not the function of the historian to divine a plan running through the facts, rather his or her interest should be 'in the facts themselves' (Collingwood 1994 [1946]: 58). However, Collingwood was sophisticated enough to realise that 'facts' are not individually surviving things. They are the products of the historian's work on the evidence. It is this that makes history quite different to science and no amount of stress on empirical method should permit the historian to indulge the delusion that they are engaged in finding out what really happened. They are engaged instead in finding out what *possibly* or, under especially propitious but rare circumstances, what *probably* happened according to the available evidence. The limits of historical knowledge for Collingwood are set by the autonomy of the historian in their drawing of possible/probable meanings and their dependence on the evidence. Thus, what actually happened is what the evidence suggests to the knowledgeable and sophisticated historian is likely to have happened.

The realist position associated with historians like Arthur Marwick is a reiteration of the early twentieth century turn against idealism and Kantian subjectivism. Philosophers like the American pragmatist William James (1842–1910), the Spanish-American George Santayana (1863–1952) and the British logicians Bertrand Russell (1872–1970) and George Moore (1873–1958) pursued realism in order to reject idealism and subjectivism. Their aim was to demonstrate how the human mind could transcend its private domain and escape into knowable reality. In their different ways they tried to demonstrate how knowledge could be freed from the perils of subjectivity and while historians might disagree on the real nature of the thing-in-itself most would accept that Henry VIII existed and that he had six wives. Such information does not depend on our personal choices or predispositions: it depends on (our belief in) the existence of a knowable real world that is independent of our thinking and story telling. In other words it depends on (our belief in) the correspondence theory of truth/knowledge. This means that truthful statements are such because of how things are in the real world (Searle 1995: xiii).

What we might call naïve realism holds that objects in the real world conform or correspond precisely to our representation and our understanding of them. As you can imagine, this absolutist version of realism convinces few historians, even reconstructionists. By the same token most historians would reject the reverse argument, that reality is a human creation. That all we have by of knowing things about the past are our *a priori* assumptions, concepts, beliefs, prejudices, desires and personal ontological commitments. The middle ground is graphically summarised by the realist philosopher John Searle as the rejection of the existence of 'brute facts' (Searle 1995: 2). Historians tend to avoid these epistemological extremes. Most accept Searle's position that there is a reality independent of both us and our written transcription of it. In other words the historian believes in a reality that can be accurately and more or less adequately represented. Hence it is that truthful historical statements are possible because they correspond to the facts of the matter.

What is more, the idea of statements corresponding to the facts is in no way contradicted by the fact that languages and vocabularies are arbitrary inventions devised to represent that reality. Whatever form of representation we use it cannot deny reality (Searle 1950: 151). But, not only does reality exist independently of our system of representation, we can also break out of the discourse in which we choose to represent it. The possibility of the accurate representation of a knowable past reality is thus the basic assumption of realist historians and it allows them to reject what they take to be two very dangerous beliefs: that knowable reality cannot exist outside our representation and that true statements do not have to correspond to the facts (Searle 1995: 151–152).

Now, as far as I am aware, few, if any, historians deny the existence of past reality. And the moral corollary also applies. As far as I am aware all my historian friends and colleagues have integrity, do not deliberately tell lies, are willing to have their interpretations challenged in open and mutually respectful debate, and would wish to engage honestly with the past. I am very happy to accept, for example, that had human beings never existed it is highly probable that the earth would have. To deny this would be tantamount to telling lies. By the same token I am happy to believe that when I die my younger relatives, friends and colleagues will continue in existence. So, when I say I was born in Wales I do so believing it to be an accurate representation of past reality according to all the sources to which I have access. Rather than argue about the existence of past reality (which is at best a not very entertaining parlour game) the important point is that correspondence theory depends on a belief in a 'knowable realism' at a level beyond that of the single descriptive statement. Reality and integrity is not the issue. It is rather the ability of the historian to represent the past as it once was accurately in a narrative in order to provide its meaning. As the pragmatist American philosopher Richard Rorty maintains, if all we have is reality and language then we have no grounds for thinking there is some medium for measuring the one in terms of the other.

In other words, it must come down to the question of the capacity of the historian to write narratives that correspond not just to what once actually was but to what they think it means beyond the single factual statement. It seems to me that those historians who talk about 'discovering' the facts reveal their inability to get to terms with how they write the reality of the past 'beyond the fact'. For most historians discovery is used as both a verb and a noun. The idea of 'discovery' suggests history is a collection of 'dug up' facts that, by definition, are not actually written representations but are somehow actual remnants or the debris of past reality and which, when taken together, constitute the unravelling of *the* plot. Only from this perspective can it be assumed the historian is capable of 'knowing' in some kind of narrative-independent way. One's position on this depends not only on whether you think the historian's statements are pictures or copies of past reality, but also how accurate (i.e., representational) they are. The validity and utility of correspondence comes down to your answer to this question.

It still remains disputed, despite Mary Fulbrook's persuasive argument, that metaphor should be best seen as the graphic representation of a heavily researched and testamental truth (Fulbrook 2002: 162–162). In acknowledging that historians use metaphor and simile she argues this is not a substitute for testability in the evidence. But is this really what is being suggested? Her argument that the historian is more than a camera or photocopier, being a creative intermediary, is quite correct in my judgement. But does it still miss the point? What does she think actually happens when the historian moves from the single descriptive statement to the narrative level of what it all means? For Fulbrook, being creative and imaginative still means finding out *the* meaning of it all through recounting what happened accurately even though she acknowledges there is the matter of emplotting the past by the historian. While never denying the general utility of getting the data straight (to show up liars and cheats) it is still, perhaps, unwise to imagine this will tell us what it means 'outside narrative'. Although Fulbrook provides one of the best recent analyses of all these issues, she remains, by definition, committed to the correspondence theory of truth – even though she does not index it. It is only through such a belief that she can optimistically conclude that it is possible to not only rationally investigate the past (which is true I think) but also represent it (which can still be rational, but is not quite so straightforward).

As Ankersmit points out, those who believe in correspondence (as Mary Fulbrook does) must assume little of significance happens in the shift from sentence length descriptions of events and actions to narrative interpretation. But what is more, they also feel honour bound to defend what is despite their awareness of its theoretically and morally saturated nature, in effect, a very crude form of historical realism. This is, presumably, because they think any anti-representationalism must doubt the existence of the real and, by implication, the travails and triumphs of people in the past. This is quite wrong. As Kant demonstrated, we can believe in reality but not know the true nature of things-in-themselves. Nor does it make us immoral to think critically in this way. Where realists do get into dirty and deep water is when they feel obliged to argue that the existence of past reality must mean there is but one way to gain historical understanding, which is, of course, the empirical-analytical mechanism.

The assumption of many realists is, therefore, that any challenge to their way of doing history must mean a denial of reality. As I have suggested this is not the case. It is not a matter of being anti-realist but of interrogating the nature and adequacy of representation within the historian's narrative. My anti-representationalist position means I do not view my narrative of the past as necessarily corresponding with actual reality. When I write about the past I have to choose ways of thinking and writing that will enable me to cope with what I believe is the essentially unknowable meaning of the past (assuming it has one, of course). For the moment suffice it to say my anti-reprsentationalism recognises the importance of representation (by which I mean, of course, its complexities and its failures) in coming to terms with the past.

As Rorty argues, the realist is now pitched against the anti-representationalist rather than the anti-realist (Rorty 1996 [1991]: 2–3). For Rorty the debate on the nature of representation is actually itself fruitless. This is because anti-representationalists (like Rorty himself) by definition refuse to accept either that thought determines reality or reality determines thought (Rorty 1996 [1991]: 5). Rorty is particularly keen to refute the realist argument that it is possible to achieve accurate representation because sometimes objects outside language can and do cause language to be used as it is. No one has any problem with the situation that when a boxer hits the canvass the referee verbally counts him or her out (the event produces a language use). But realists don't stop at the single statement in which reality causes the use of language: they elevate their realism to the level of the explanation of social practices. So, in terms historians might be happier with, realists don't stick to the single historical description: they attempt to elevate their realism to the level of historical interpretation.

The deconstructionist does not accept, from his or her anti-representationalist perspective, that the single 'fact of the matter' descriptive statement can carry its truth to the level of interpretation and the derivation of meaning. In the memorable phrase of Keith Jenkins, 'truthful interpretation' is an oxymoron. While single statements can be very probably true, narratives cannot be in the same way. So, for what it's worth, I believe there are sources upon which – if the historian elects to do it – facts, meanings, interpretations, and histories can be created. But, as I shall argue in more detail in Section Four, while the narrative-linguistic way of thinking about history accepts the evidence must act as a brake on the history we write, it does not exclusively determine the form that history has to take and, therefore, its interpretation and its meaning.

Conclusion

Realist epistemology receives its fullest expression in the notion (still held by a few reconstructionist historians) that only new doses of evidence can change interpretations or meaning. The implication is that representation is of quite secondary importance because description can't alter reality at either the level of the single descriptive statement (Henry VIII had six wives) or the full interpretation (America 'won' the Cold War). Nevertheless, constructionist empiricists from Ranke onwards have never denied the existence and epistemological utility of *a priori* propositions (not just mathematical formulas but other social beliefs, concepts and life experiences as well). Clearly, whether of reconstructionist or constructionist varieties, all realists continue to deny what they see as un-supported or un-evidenced imaginative speculation and hypothetical or theoretical thinking as sources of trustworthy or justified belief. Imagination and poetry, emplotment and figurative language, speculative theorising and value statements have conventionally found no place in professional history.

History from the mid-nineteenth century up to the late twentieth has been viewed by the majority of its practitioners as a process of discovery, the results of which can then be turned out onto the printed page. In other words, the basic assumption has been that our understanding of reality does not and must not depend on how we represent it. The mechanism for demonstrating the reality of the past remains the empirical-analytical methodology of inference and rational argument. Because we human beings can only know things about the past through our perceptions of the evidence, it is crucial that we ensure as much as possible that those perceptions are 'accurate' and our descriptive statements about them are 'accurate'. It is this mechanism of inference from the evidence, which is so central to the justification of belief, to which I will now turn in the next section.

Section Two

Referentiality, Evidence and Practice

Chapter 3

Evidence, inference, causation and agency

In this chapter I will examine how those historians who endorse the empirical-analytical epistemological model and invoke correspondence theory, claim to be able to explain the reality of the past. They assert a methodology that they believe will lead to an accurate historical narrative, that is, truthful written history. This methodology has three key features. These are inference (often called inference to the best explanation), causation, and agency. It is believed that these, when taken together, will lead to an 'interpretative understanding' of the 'true meaning' of the past through the justified historical description. It is this realist empirical-analytical view of knowing underpinning reconstructionist and constructionist notions of objectivity which I shall deal with in the second chapter of this section.

Evidence and inference

As philosophers of history have argued throughout the twentieth century, from Croce to McCullagh, it is only through the empirical-analytical method that historians can be confident they can discover what actually happened in the past (McCullagh 1984: 2). This has become so basic to modern historical practice that writers of popular primers like the British Marxist historian John Tosh regard it as axiomatic. As Tosh says, most of the historical facts historians derive depend on inference (Tosh 2000: 112). He describes inference as 'reading between the lines' or working out 'what really happened' from a number of contradictory indications – the effort to establish that the author of the data was 'probably telling the truth' (Tosh 2000: 112). As he says, 'formal proof' may be beyond the reach of historians, so 'what matters is the validity of the inferences' (Tosh 2000: 112–113). He maintains that 'refining the inferences that can be legitimately drawn from the sources' is what historians do most of the time, and only then can the facts of history 'be said to rest on inferences whose validity is widely accepted by expert opinion' (Tosh 2000: 113). He concludes, who 'could reasonably ask for more?' (Tosh 2000: 113).

Most historians would accept that it is only by the inferential method that the status of historical facts can be established. This means history is always the end product of the historian's selection of evidence and choice of appropriate sources. Most historians would draw back from the belief that given the nature of inference and the unavoidable presentism in the study of the past (history is constituted or 'known' and written in the here and now), historical knowledge must be discretionary and, perhaps, even ultimately unknowable. However, most historians have a firm professional commitment to the idea of plausible knowability. Through a critical attitude toward the evidence (sceptical empiricism) it becomes possible they would argue to convey historical discoveries in an accurate narrative. Indeed, it is such a bedrock belief that to abandon it would leave the past, it seems, to the plunder of liars, cheats, deniers of reality, irrational relativists and propagandists. Truth, through the accurate description of the evidence is, and must be, the watchword of all proper historians. How do historians believe they can achieve historical truth? The only legitimate way seemingly is to maintain the highest possible standards in justifying sentence-length historical descriptions. As realist philosophers of history explain it, it is accomplished by recognising those conditions that warrant a truthful description.

It is usually pointed out that in spite of the desire to be accurate and reasoned in their judgements, historians acknowledge history is not a hard science in the strictest sense of that phrase. Unlike physics history deals with the meaning of events and people's intentions. It does not study molecules and chemical reactions in laboratories, or conduct tests that will generate repeatable results. This is not to say that historians do not try to achieve the highest possible standards of justification for their beliefs. The model of scientific study defined in broad terms, as an objective and coherent logic of inquiry whereby its results are tested according to the available evidence and explained as honestly and dispassionately as possible, legitimates the historical enterprise. Of course, it is also acknowledged science's discoveries and how they are made are subject to wider cultural and social forces. This is no different in history, which is itself subject to society's desires and demands as well as the preferred theories, models or paradigms of historians. But what seems very clear to the majority of historians, science and history with their shared aim of locating the truth, cannot be allowed to be blown off course by such cultural or what is worse, political forces. Historians must start by acknowledging their own interests and that not just what they do is imperfect because of the demands of language, ideology, and the selection of evidence but also that history writing is an authorial act. But the defence of history continues to rest on historical practice whereby telling the truth about the past is possible if you scrupulously follow history's technical and methodological rules.

At its most straightforward, resolving these problems comes down to rational inference. This is that mental process whereby a thinker draws a conclusion from a set of assumptions or premises. The historian, for example, might claim that from the mid-eighteenth century in America the 'reform impulse naturally found an outlet in the care of the insane' (Tindall 1988 [1984]: 521). This descriptive and interpretational statement is the inference drawn from a reading of the available evidence about social reform and the treatment of the insane at this time and in this place. This description is a generalisation from a specific instance. In this example it is a statement that interprets the general direction of social reform from one key archival reference. The reference is the 1752 charter of the Philadelphia Hospital that it should care for 'lunaticks'. Clearly, the inference is less certain than, say, a more strictly referential description such as 'The Philadelphia Hospital (1752) had a provision in its charter that it should care for "lunaticks" ' (Tindall 1988 [1984]: 521). These two statements indicate the complex and indirect nature of inferential or historical knowledge. Clearly, the inferential knowledge of the statement of interpretation is based on the other foundational statement. In this example it is the historian's belief that the charter of the hospital is actually an accurate representation of reality in as much as the hospital did, *in fact*, care for the insane. What we have here are two levels of historical statement, referential description and its interpretational representation.

As the leading realist philosopher of history C. Behan McCullagh suggests, the truth of single referential statements, such as that about the contents of the hospital charter, can rest on one or more of several kinds or conditions of justification. These include first, arguments to the best explanation or fit, second, descriptive statements based on analogy and finally, statements of statistical probability. The first form of justification is also sometimes referred to as a hypothetico-deductive explanation. As the preferred method of constructionist historians, like the scientist they set up an explanatory hypothesis and then infer its reliability as an accurate explanation by reference to the data. Such historians justify their judgements, and hence their descriptive statements of fact based on what they believe the evidence is telling them. The reference to 'lunaticks' is the data upon which the inference is made. This is why there are so many competing interpretations among historians. Historians do not always refer to the same body of evidence. While this might dismay you, it reveals an important point. Historians do not trust each other's descriptions. Rather, they trust their data and the 'empiricism plus inference' methods they use to handle it just, well, naturally follow. If a historian's description seems incompatible with the data as observed (as debates over Holocaust denial show), other historians will go back to the evidence. They will then seek out – after the event as it were – false inferences (or deliberate lies). They will never just accept the historian's description (which may involve the denial or omission of evidence). Hence it is that most historians prefer the hypothesis that plausibly explains most of the available evidence. In other words, the hypothesis that best fits observable reality and thereby explains its given meaning and which, by definition, can only be rendered in the justified historical description.

Arguments to the best fit

In procedural terms inductive inference aimed toward providing the best explanation, demands the historian first observes the evidence of an event or action and then offer an explanatory hypothesis that can launch him or her beyond the single statement into the generalisation and, finally, into the causal explanation. As we shall see again in Chapter 6, this is what most constructionist historians would do except that in this instance the overall approach is to rely on the documentary evidence as both the source and justification for the interpretation without the initial aid of more or less complex theorising. Let me use the example of the historian Deborah A. Symonds' description of how she discovered the story of a Scottish widow, Agnes Dugald who, in the late 1760s, was indicted for the murder of her own daughter (Symonds 1999: 166–173). This story is founded on Symonds' deployment of the first form of inference. Symonds begins with the assumption that 'history, whatever it may become, begins with the materials of history' and that it is only by facing such materials 'that questions of belief, intention, falsification and truth have to be confronted and resolved' (Symonds 1999: 166). As she says, 'theory comes later, after one has decided what one is, in fact, at the most empirical and scientific level, theorising about' (ibid.).

Symonds first glimpsed the story of Agnes Dugald in a dusty volume of circuit court records in the Scottish Record Office, Edinburgh. Symonds uses Dugald as an example of how the historian 'verifies and evaluates' the event and its story. This approach is different epistemologically to that of constructionist historian Mary Fulbrook, who starts with an entirely different assumption. Fulbrook assumes that all history is 'intrinsically a theoretical enterprise' and historians cannot start work without some kind of theoretical framework, which 'construes the subject to be investigated' (Fulbrook 2002: 86). As we shall see, Fulbrook is close to Hayden White in this assumption, the only difference being that the theoretical framework of Fulbrook is the literary constructionism of White.

According to Symonds, in his court testimony Glasgow apothecary (druggist) William Rutherfurd stated that he had been walking along a footpath with a Walter Stirling when they saw the body of a child recently killed by a wound to the throat. They found a boy nearby herding cows who pointed to a woman in the distance and claimed she had 'just murdered a Child' (Symonds: 167). Rutherfurd ran after her, and with another man, James Cleland, she was caught and held. She had blood on her hands. Dugald was taken back to the body. Dugald admitted she had been forced into the act because as a widow she was on the verge of being placed in the Correction House and so she had 'taken revenge' on the child. Eventually the knife was found by a group of neighbourhood women who had gathered. Stirling later told of his role in the event: how he asked the sheriff substitute to issue a warrant and how he obtained the name of Dugald from her neighbours. His testimony confirmed that of Rutherfurd. Other witnesses included the cowherd who testified that Dugald had told him she had murdered her child.

Symonds goes on to explain how 'Dugald's story' is more than just the court record. It is rather about an act of inference that encompasses a 'network of records that corroborate and constantly enlarge her very small story' (Symonds: 170), and that other knowledge about the geography of the area and the adjacent towns and the local ways of dealing with poverty, verify the event. Symonds is keen to point out that it is the empirical-analytical model that allows the story to emerge. It is not the construction of Deborah Symonds but 'Dugald's story' results 'from a logical mapping' of the available information 'against other information' (ibid.). As Symonds insists, what she takes to be history's turn toward 'the methods of literary criticism' is unconvincing 'hell-bent as its authors are on abstractions and jargon' (ibid.). Symonds prefers Dugald's tale to reading that history results from the clash of categories of sexual and gender difference and ideology. While ideology is real, for Symonds it cannot exist in isolation from human existence. But what is equally important for Symonds is that Dugald's story reveals 'some shreds of free will and responsibility and human agency . . .' (Symonds 1999: 172).

As I will discuss in the next section there seems to be reconstructionist 'either/or' operating here – agency/choice or theorised determining structures? Symonds' preoccupation is with dangerous literary constructionism. Her point is that 'the literary critics, in their various disciplinary manifestations, have burnt all the bridges between the signifier and the signified, the word and the thing, the words "Agnes Dugald" and a once living Agnes Dugald' (ibid.). She concludes that to read the trial record through that lens would render it as just a text in which only ideology is real.

Analogy

Despite Symonds' empirical preferences, the reasonable criticism can be made that just because one historical explanation is better than others in accounting for the available data – the best fit – this does not mean it must be the truth. The response to that, in turn, is simply that there is a widespread and conventional acceptance among historians that explanation, for which there is a great deal of supporting evidence, are most likely to be true. And they can be held to be such until new data is discovered and the explanation no longer best fits. But it has to be noted, that not all inferences are descriptions that best fit the data. There are, in addition, also justifications for single descriptive statements rooted in analogy. This, the second form of inference or explanation by analogy actually is very common among historians. Once again there are certain conditions to be met for accurate and justified historical statements using analogical inference. A term like 'revolution' is clearly elastic and may be applied to an economic process of industrialism or to political, social or cultural upheaval. To qualify as an accurate statement, however, the descriptive term revolution must fulfil certain criteria: in this case revolutions demand rapid and massive change. If these are taken to be its key characteristics it is accurate and, therefore, justifiable to use the term in the description of the British Industrial Revolution in the years from 1840 to 1890, or the Glorious Revolution of 1688. But if the term is more tightly defined with the aim of including different aspects or properties then, clearly, it may be inaccurate and it ceases to function as a form of explanation based on analogy.

Analogy in historical description in effect works on some very simple principles. The historian assumes the object of their study, say the Anglo-French Entente Cordiale of 1904, possesses certain distinguishing properties. These properties might include the desire of both countries to agree to disagree over certain matters. They agreed, for example, to stop quarrelling over the British occupation of Egypt. The historian then assumes another object of their study, say the détente reached between the Soviet Union and the United States in the aftermath of the Cuban Missile Crisis of 1962, shares similar properties (of agreeing to disagree but not quarrel) with the situation in 1904. Equally, a historian of the 1838 Cherokee trek along the 'trail of tears' westward might choose to compare its essential properties with similar events elsewhere and at other times. Giving in to superior forces, signing away their land, and suffering neglect and cruelty by the government are accurate descriptions of their experience. Similar descriptions could plausibly be written about the experiences of other Native American tribes such as those of the Seminoles, Chickasaws and Creeks. Inference by analogy is both legitimate and fruitful in establishing explanations if not guaranteeing their truth.

Statistical analysis

The third kind of inference, as McCullagh suggests, is specifically statistical in nature. Statistical inferences have to meet certain conditions in order to constitute justified descriptions. The most obvious condition is that of probability. Thus, we may infer from all the available evidence that racism was a central feature of everyday life in the Southern states of America in the decades immediately after the Civil War. Hence, in tens of thousands of instances, ex-slaves were subject to intolerable abuse. It follows that it is highly likely that in any individual case of abuse and defilement of, or violence against, the freedmen and women, racism was a factor. Other examples of statistical inference might be the high probability that William Shakespeare wrote the plays conventionally ascribed to him, although there is some evidence that another author might have been involved. Equally, the debate over the identity of the killer of President John F. Kennedy is often couched in terms of probabilities.

High probabilities are usually located in some genres of history rather than others, as in economic or socio-psephological (voting) histories and hence historians will normally use statistical analysis to connect two events or processes that cannot otherwise be readily associated in a causal connection in order to justify a single or general descriptive statement. It might be claimed, for example, that it is possible to determine the character of the links between the ethnocultural nature of a city's population and the history and development of its political institutions. Thus, the historian might wish to test his or her belief that the great majority of first generation Irish in Boston (USA) between 1870 and 1920 consistently voted for Democratic Party candidates for mayor (the hypothesis). To test this it would be necessary to collect both demographic and voting behaviour data. Next, the need would be to establish a measure of statistical association between, say, the numbers of Irish immigrants in individual wards in the city and the votes cast for the Democratic and Republic mayoral candidates over several elections. The analysis in such a study would use advanced statistical techniques. In other words, the historian would try to establish how E changes (where E is an effect) with variations in C (where C is a presumed cause). Hence, the historian would try to determine how changes in one variable are associated with changes in another through the establishment and measurement of a statistical association that may (or may not) be regarded as causal.

The technical procedures of statistical correlation are a relatively straightforward means for establishing how that which is taken to be a dependent variable (voting for the Democratic candidate) varies with the changes in the independent variable (the numbers of Irish in each of the city's wards). Should the statistical association for the period 1870–1920 reveal that when the numbers of Irish in a ward rose so did the vote for the Democratic candidate (and vice versa), then the historian might feel justified in stating that the newly arrived Irish consistently supported the Democratic Party in Boston. Clearly, however, historians are not interested only in justifying their inferential statements about the nature of past events, they are also dedicated to explaining why they happened. So, why did the great majority of first generation Irish immigrants support the Democratic Party over a fifty-year period in one American city? To answer this, and other questions of a similar nature, it is useful to establish how most historians move to the third level beyond that of evidence and inference of justified historical description by understanding the character of cause and causal explanation in history.

Causation and agency

As McCullagh suggests, single referential statements can be true of only one thing at one time (my example was the Philadelphia Hospital Charter). A generalisation (a general descriptive statement) is a statement about that process or series of closely connected events that can have more than one instance (the nature of the reform impulse). At the third level of descriptions, however, are those complex statements of historical explanation/interpretation that invoke the principles of cause and effect. The perennial problem is again, as John Tosh points out, that the evidence is rarely adequate enough to establish a definite causal connection between events (Tosh 2000: 117). At best all historians have are probable or most likely connections.

Once again, according to McCullagh, the association between events is probabilistic rather than deterministic (McCullagh 1998: 172). In other words, causes rarely necessitate a particular outcome. Thus, British sea power, though undoubtedly significant in securing the collapse of Napoleon Bonaparte's ambitions for Europe, did not necessarily bring it about. All the historian could legitimately claim is that had Britain not possessed such naval power, it is less likely Napoleon would have been defeated as he was. Equally, the failure of the Irish potato harvest in the wet summer of 1845 may have had a major impact on Prime Minister Robert Peel's decision to speed up his programme of repeal of the Corn Laws, but other events also had their (longer term?) influence. In very few instances can a definitive causal link be established between several discrete phenomena. Unlike in the natural world, where the regular occurrence between events suggests connections upon which causal assertions can be made, in history it is never so straightforward. Scientists seek out the causes of events according to laws that account for the necessary effects of certain events, processes and actions. In history, as the historian philosophers R.G. Collingwood and later William Dray argued, explanation is not like that. There are few chain reactions in history.

As I have described it, given the nature of inductive inference, historians tend to believe the connections they infer between events are based upon other inferences that might be eventually traced back to a foundational empirical statement such as the Philadelphia Hospital Charter's reference to 'lunaticks'. But in the larger interpretative picture of cause and effect historians tend to aggregate individual causes to build up a picture of the process of multiple causation rather than seek *the* cause. As McCullagh argues, historians are interested in all the causes that brought about an event or initiated a process, as he says 'the whole causal process' (McCullagh 1998: 176). Although historians remain committed to understanding the role of the individual historical agent (see Symonds' comment above about Dugald, and below), they are also very much aware of bigger economic, political, social, cultural and intellectual structures. Knowing the motivations of historical agents does not always illuminate the deep-seated processes that were taking place. These may include changes in population or immigration, rapid economic and technological shifts, scientific developments, or territorial and imperial expansion.

It is at this point that empiricism legitimately gives way to analysis. In order to explain and account for the complexities of the past it is necessary to describe, evaluate, and reveal the interconnectedness of the events that finally make their appearance in our justified interpretations. The 'common sense' understanding of causation is the discovery of regularities. In life this means car windscreens smash when hit by bricks, planes fall out of the sky when the engines fail, water pipes freeze when the temperature drops below a certain level, and students get upset when the teacher writes nasty comments on their essays. Such regularities, however, disappear in history. Usually historians try to connect individual and unique events without recourse to such a common or garden notion of regularity. Thus, a historian might declare that Prince Albert was instrumental in the building of the 1851 Great Exhibition. In saying this, the historian is not depending on a law of regular human behaviour or even a generalisation along the lines of 'consorts of Queens of England are usually so much at a loose end that they end up planning celebrations of national industrial success'. History is clearly the study of particular people and events. Inevitably this 'common sense' has been challenged by those, like the philosopher Patrick Gardiner, who argue that history is also about generalisation and categories of explanation like 'revolution' (Gardiner 1961 [1952]: 80–99).

Gardiner (and McCullagh for that matter) rejects the view that historians only describe unique events and do not make generalisations. Gardiner supports the position of the philosopher of history Carl Hempel in accepting that historians make an appeal, though it is usually unstated, to general patterns of human behaviour through explanation sketches. Because there can be no precise correlations between events in the past, historians invariably fall back on making such sketches in the form of generalisations as 'guides to understanding' (Gardiner 1961 [1952]: 61). After arguing that covering law theory explains the nature of historical explanation through the process of correlation and probability, Gardiner concludes that the historical generalisations that flow from such linking can form the basis of justified historical descriptions. Historians actually address the matter of causation in terms of its *necessary* and *sufficient* conditions. Take the founding, by the American social reformer Jane Addams, of Hull House in Chicago in 1889, the first American Settlement. What caused her to do this? We might answer by stating what we think is a necessary condition, one without which the event could not have occurred. In other words, a thing is caused to happen if, had a prior event not existed and all else had remained the same, the effect would not have happened as it did. The historian would say, therefore, the prior event was a necessary condition for the occurrence of the second event. To be clear, if we believe that the existence of Jane Addams was essential to the founding of Hull House then we have stated a necessary condition for its cause.

In this case there are many possible necessary conditions. Addams would not have established Hull House without the acquisition of the property, or if she had not visited London's Toynbee Hall the previous year and saw the model she was to follow. Either of these could be interpreted as 'the cause'. The historian would actually be most likely to say all of these factors taken together probably provided the necessary conditions for the founding of Hull House (after all, Hull House could conceivably have been founded by someone else). Please remember that I am still talking about conditions for statements of justified belief. Stating the conditions is not to say one or all of them must have caused the founding. All that the historian can say is that a necessary condition for a cause only guarantees that the effect could not have occurred without it.

But the historian is very conscious that this far from exhausts the range of possible inferences of causes for the founding of Hull House. As the philosopher W.H. Walsh argues, the necessary condition for a cause is the historian's choice of what she or he thinks is important or decisive in a given situation. The historian may then go on to think that perhaps it could not have had the effect it did unless another, several or many other things had happened as well (Walsh 1970 [1951]: 190). The fact that Jane Addams was born is, at one level, obviously a necessary condition of the setting up of Hull House. But, like the other possible necessary conditions, it does not explain very much. This signals the shift from necessary conditions to sufficient conditions in understanding the nature of causation. In the example of the foundation of Hull House the historian is likely to examine a variety of factors beyond the necessary combination of which was, in their judgement, sufficient to produce it. The historian has thereby moved from 'the cause' to 'causes'. This is now probably more realistic as a form of historical explanation, but it also introduces a new level of complexity. Out of the potentially vast array of causes of the founding of Hull House, what were the most significant?

The question now is what are sufficient (conditions of) causes? Sufficient causes are those (conditions) that guarantee the result. In the case of the founding of Hull House the range of sufficient causes is substantial. Sufficient causes might include Jane Addams' belief in collective social action, her desire to improve the lot of Chicago's immigrant slum dwellers, her wish to establish a corps of social workers, her feminism, or her inclination to escape the domestic sphere, her friendship with Ellen Gates Starr, etc? Unlike in 'real life' historians don't normally think in terms of one cause producing one effect. You and I tend to think of the alarm clock waking us up, of the keystroke that produces a letter on the computer screen. Historians have a much more complex situation because, by the nature of dealing with the past, they have to pose 'what if' questions. What if Jane Addams had not been the kind of feminist she (seems according to the evidence) to have been? What if she had not been a friend of Ellen Gates Starr? Would Hull House have been established? In other words, the historian puts up a proposition and tests it through the available evidence with the intention of finding the most likely cause or set of causes. They may, of course, find that a single event can be sufficient to make another event happen, yet not actually be a cause of it. Thus, none of the individual causes the historian establishes for the founding of Hull House might, in themselves, be judged to have been sufficient to make its founding inevitable. In other words, there may be connection or correlation, even a functional relationship, but it is probably quite impossible to establish an absolute or necessary condition for causal explanation.

The difficulties experienced by historians in establishing causal explanations can be seen in the arguments between philosophers of history. Such arguments have centred on how useful Carl Hempel's covering laws are to historical explanation. In the 1940s Hempel, working out the logic of the position usually associated with the Scottish Enlightenment philosopher David Hume, maintained that historical explanation is, in the language of philosophy, deductive-nomological. This means historians can deduce facts from the uniformities observed in human behaviour as expressed by general laws. The result of this is effectively to demote empathy or the effort on the part of the historian to rethink the thoughts of historical agents as a form of causal explanation. For Hempel historical explanation is founded upon a universal hypothesis that asserts regularity. So, when C occurs at a certain time and place, an event of a specified kind E will occur at another time and place that is connected in a specific manner to the time and place of the first event (Hempel 1942: 346). This process, claims Hempel, is in effect to say that a set of events described by the historian as C or $C_1, C_2, C_3 \ldots C_n$ is regularly accompanied by an event E.

For some philosophers this means that individual concrete events, particularly individual human decisions, cannot be fully explained as such (the founding of Hull House). However, they may be legitimately viewed as examples of a category of circumstances determined by conditioning explanatory laws. Thus Jane Addams' founding of Hull House might be subsumed under a universal psychological law that states, for example, that when someone has a strong desire to express a commitment to a particular social policy, it might result in such an act as the founding of a settlement house. This is not a complete explanation but it is useful and it does invoke if not a universal law a broad behavioural inclination. Hempel maintained that the historian's use of words like 'therefore', 'because', 'hence', and 'consequently' suggest a tacit acceptance and use of general, though usually implicit and often highly general, laws of explanation. It might be argued, however, that human action or agency – the desire of people to resolve a situation – should be regarded as an alternative to universal explanations or, for that matter, any forms of social theory (Dray 1966 [1957]: 95). So, what is the role of human agency in historical explanation and the justified historical description?

A weaker version of Hempel's covering law model relies on what is probable rather than certain, and it comes down to the explanation sketches historians draw that I noted earlier. This form of historical explanation imagines a series of stages in which events and decisions are assumed to lead to other events and decisions. Hempel argued that such human actions could be couched as justified historical descriptions. Such written descriptions assume human motives that can be accounted for by reference to generalisations based on everyday experience about how rational people might normally be expected to behave in certain specified situations (Hempel 1962). Thus, as Gardiner claims, the explanations of the scientist and those of the ordinary person (including the historian) ultimately depend on 'observed correlations in experience' (Gardiner 1961: 24). In acknowledging the difficulties under which historians operate, Gardiner does concede there is, inevitably, a much greater degree of imprecision in the decisions they make about cause than the physicist would tolerate.

However, William Dray rejected even Gardiner's modest constructionist position. He argued that Gardiner, though temperate in comparison with Hempel, was still wrong even to accept a weaker sketch version of covering law explanation (Dray 1966 [1957]: 19). In abandoning Gardiner's moderate defence of covering laws and even the implicit appeal to regularities in human behaviour, Dray argued in favour of another form of explanation. In emphasising the uniqueness of historical phenomena he suggested historians explain the connections between events primarily if not almost always by reference to rational human actions and agency. In so arguing Dray de-coupled the decisions of people from universal laws of behaviour. For Dray causal explanation in history is determined by the nature of its object of study 'the actions of beings like ourselves' (Dray 1966 [1957]: 118). By this argument historical explanation in the form of the justified historical description relies upon the historian correctly inferring the thoughts that motivated historical agents. The discovery of the agent's purpose or intention is, therefore, central to a justified causal explanation.

Perhaps inevitably in such debates, what goes around comes around. So it is that the historian Clayton Roberts has returned to Gardiner's position to attack the explanatory power ascribed to agency, and defend Gardiner's and, by extension, Hempel's key insights (Roberts 1996). Roberts certainly agrees that Dray's analysis is correct if agency is 'regarded as an alternative to theory in validating an alleged causal connection' and this must be true only 'for a single instance of an event' (Roberts 1996: 30). But Roberts' appeal to W.H. Walsh's notion of 'colligation' to explain events is a way of not privileging human agency and intentionality. By colligation is meant that process of explaining a particular event by tracing the connections between it and others. The underlying assumption is that different historical events may be regarded as hanging together so as to constitute a single coherent process. Thus the Boer War may be viewed as part of the process of British imperialism in Southern Africa. In other words, colligation is the locating of an event or series of events within their context of associated occurrences. But, as Walsh insists and Roberts acknowledges (and just about everyone would accept), because history is unlike the natural sciences, the aim is not to establish a system of rigorous and essentially unchanging general laws, however, generalisations about human behaviour and motivation are often presupposed (Walsh 1970 [1951]: 24–25).

Walsh insists the historian's use of colligation is dependent upon the peculiar character of the object of historical study. As he says, it is only because the historian deals 'with actions' that he or she can think historically at all. Further, he insists it is only the fact that 'every action has a thought-side which makes the whole thing possible' (Walsh 1970 [1951]: 59). He maintains that because actions are the realisation of purposes and purposes find their expression in a series of actions that the historian can say that some historical events are 'intrinsically related' (Walsh 1970 [1951]: 59–60). For Walsh what creates the links between events are the intentional actions of individuals and groups. Thus, Theodore Roosevelt's indecision about the U.S. tariff on imported goods throughout his presidency (1901–1909) resulted in a political explosion for his successor William Howard Taft. Clearly, later events are usually related to former events and decisions (or indecision in the case of Roosevelt) because the historical agent makes assumptions as to the outcomes of their decisions/actions indecisions/inactions. Roosevelt seemed to believe that the tariff was likely to split his party and, therefore, best left alone. This is, of course, not the situation scientists come across. Nitric acid does not think about the consequences of its actions. Of course, history is never quite so tidy as this description might suggest. People do not always act rationally nor less intentionally and they are not always so prescient that they can figure out the likely results of their decisions and actions. In the most recent discussion of historical agency Mark Bevir has revisited this knotty problem (Bevir 1999). He has suggested that a cool appraisal by the historian of the sometimes rational and sometimes distorted beliefs of historical agents 'provides the basis of a form of explanation for human actions' (Bevir 1999: 316–317). Bevir is led to conclude there can be no general theory of social change, and so history becomes the explanation of human action and intentionality.

'Empathy' is a problem for historians as they try to explain people's intentions. Walsh, for example, despite his preoccupation with understanding the nature of human actions does not follow Collingwood's belief in the primacy and desirability of the historian to enter into the mind of the historical agent in order to 're-enact' their thoughts. Working on the principle that every action is an expression of thought, Collingwood assumed the historian must endeavour to think the same thought as the historical agent according to the same rules of thought that operated for them – empathise with them. Walsh is not convinced by Collingwood's method, arguing how can historians know the thoughts of people in the past unless the historian knows how people behave and react in given situations? Historical explanation is thus most likely to demand not just empathic re-enactment but also reference to generalisations about human nature of a conceptual and even theoretical kind. These generalisations directly influence, above all, the colligation process. So it is that colligation also becomes central to historical interpretation because it requires the understanding of actions in the wider context and thus permits the creation of general historical or colligatory concepts such as 'The Renaissance', 'The Industrial Revolution' or 'The Cold War'. Such colligatory concepts thus summarise the facts and provide for their meaning.

Interpretation and meaning

The majority position today has been summarised by the historian Geoffrey Roberts (Roberts 1997). He has argued that what he calls traditional narrative historians view the past 'in terms of the meaning, relations, pattern, and significance of action' (Roberts 1997: 256). Roberts believes action has outcomes (i.e., events) and takes place in descriptive settings (the facts) and, it follows, the action itself provides 'the story'. The important point is that the story in the past is real and not a 'narrative fiction' of the sort provided by the historian. For traditional historians (as Roberts describes himself) historical explanation is the discovery of the agent's intentions/motivations – what he calls the story of action – and this is the story of history. In truth, claims Roberts, there are 'real stories in the past to which historical narratives can correspond', and the narrative written by the historian can, if done properly, 'mimic or resemble the action/story/narrative of past happenings' (Roberts 1997: 257). Roberts is assuming here that factual truth and meaning – what the facts mean – are the same thing and they can be revealed in the historian's accurate narrative. In other words, the historian's narrative can match the real historical narrative deemed to exist in the past. What Roberts is doing is deriving the meaning of the past by establishing the most appropriate form of explanation that will, ultimately, provide the justified historical description. For Roberts this is the discovery in the data of *the* action, which is itself *the* story that is *the* truth and *the* meaning. Roberts insists, therefore, that 'the work of history' is the 'accurate reconstruction and representation of what happened in action terms' (Roberts 1997: 256). Hence, the truth of the past and its meaning can be discovered in the reasoned actions and intentions of past historical agents by the empirically informed and reasoning historian.

Assuming the cornerstone of historical explanation/interpretation is the assumption that stories are lived and they can be discovered and accurately retold, it follows that if the story is imperfectly put together the historian cannot be justified in his or her belief that they have accessed the truth of the past. If they have not done that then their stories must be imaginative fictions or, to be precise, unjustified historical descriptions. The justified historical description thus results from the historian's inference or interpretation as to the most likely meaning of the data. As I have suggested, how historians describe or represent it becomes a particularly important issue when the single historical description is cranked up to the level of general statements that describe cause and effect. According to McCullagh, knowing that our historical descriptions at each level, from the single description through the generalisation to the causal judgement are probably true, justifies us in learning from them. McCullagh is saying that only in this way can historians determine their meaning. Moreover, only through the justified historical description can historical interpretations be regarded as in any way impartial and objective. A meaning or interpretation may be said to be fair if it can be shown to be better than rival explanations according to the conditions for truthful knowing.

Conclusion

In this chapter I have briefly addressed the essentials of conventional history thinking in respect of the justification conditions for single descriptive statements as well as broader descriptions and statements about cause and effect, action and agent intentionality, interpretation and meaning. I have noted how most historians regard all this as adding up to an epistemology with a dedicated methodology founded on inductive inference or argument to the best explanation or fit. This methodology insists that the history we write can connect accurately with past reality because the historian's descriptions can be confirmed (or not) by reference to the evidence and, hence, produce the facts. There are clear conditions to be met for accurate, reliable and justified historical statements.

Acquiring the objective meaning of the past is thereby not only claimed to be the aim of all proper historians, it is clearly achievable. What this means is that there can be no choice between truth and meaning. They are not either/or. It is claimed they must have equal importance to the historian. Of course, as I hope my discussion of the conditions for justified knowing has demonstrated, while truth may be considered a unitary concept, for things cannot be partly true, interpretation and meaning is probabilistic. It should also be clear that historical explanation is not scientific. There can be many possible interpretations and likely meanings in the study of agency and human choice. Nevertheless, interpretation and the meaning it leads to, it is said by most historians, may be taken as the end product of the epistemological process. Once the data in the shape of texts, actions, objects, cultural practices and processes have been interpreted, their 'true meaning' can be determined. The fact that historians may have ideological predispositions, cultural inclinations, theoretical preferences, ontological commitments or life experiences does not mean they cannot reach the truth about the past in the form of the justified historical description. The empirical-analytical assumption that follows from this belief (in justified historical description) is that the historian can be reasonably sure their narrative interpretations of the past are objective and they do not take on a life of their own – or worse – that of their authors. The idea is that once the historian has discovered the actions and motivations of people in the past this will enable him or her to understand why they did certain things and this will lead to an understanding of 'the meaning' of the past. It is this question of objectivity and truth and what the deconstructionist would point to as the unavoidable relativism in historical understanding and knowledge, that I address next.

Chapter 4

Objectivity, truth and relativism

It is now necessary to examine the claims made by historians to the principles of objectivity and truth. This cannot be done, of course, without some consideration of the challenge of relativism. To do this I need to summarise the key principles of the modernist epistemological model of history. As I suggested in Chapter 1, the Enlightenment's logocentric 'big idea' was that we could accurately reflect the structure of the past when we write up our empirical investigations. It should by now be clear that two very important realist claims are being made about history and these claims have a very significant outcome. The first claim is the technical one that we can know the past more or less as it really was thanks to our empirical methods in addressing the sources and by using the analytical procedures of inference. This is the belief in what I call 'knowable referentialism'. The second is that we can describe what we find more or less accurately in our referential statements and narratives. This is the belief in representation. The outcome is that we can reasonably expect to be objective in our history and, therefore, control the relativism that threatens the ramparts of the empirical-analytical approach.

Of course, even the most ardent of reconstructionist historians accepts that history, defined as knowing 'what the past meant', cannot be achieved with unqualified objectivity even though the truth of the past remains the ultimate goal. Fortunately, it is argued, history's methods are said to allow us to approach ever more closely to that ideal. If done according to the available evidence and with sensible inferences being drawn, we may say, like the American historians Appleby, Hunt and Jacob, that we are getting close to telling the truth about the past (Appleby, Hunt and Jacob 1994). However, there are historians who, like me, are sceptical about even the moderate claims of such realists. This is because history is a narrative *about* the past, and is certainly not in any way a mirror of it (though it is said to be always cloudy and/or theoreticised). We need now to consider these empirical-analytical assertions that historians can achieve a modest level of objectivity and truth. As I do not think this is feasible despite a tolerably accurate knowledge of what happened, I think it is also important to explain how historians can and do live with relativism.

Objectivity and the epistemological model of history

Realist philosophers of history defend the possibility of an essentially mind- or discourse-independent historical knowledge while still noting the intimacy between the past and present social reality. Such philosophers believe that the meaning of the sentences the historian writes can be 'reasonably objective' and thereby discover the *real* meaning behind the apparent chaos of reality. As we have seen, historians manufacture sentence-length statements of justified belief (facts) based on their sources from the range of which they select those that they think will generate the correct interpretational unity in their narratives. This process is possible, it is claimed, because they can establish the truth conditions of those sentences from the outset.

How does 'being reasonably objective' fit into this overall picture of 'doing history'? Although he was writing about the experience of the history profession in the United States, the American historian Peter Novick examined at some length the 'objectivity question' in modern historical practice. He described what he took to be the general agreement among historians as to what objectivity means. He concluded (and I agree) that objectivity was a function of the epistemological model. This standard (the modernist) model of history 'thinking and doing' has five elements and numerous procedural outcomes that together are claimed to permit the objective acquisition of knowledge such as the distinctions between fact and fiction, subject and object and knower and known. In summary, the empirical-analytical or epistemological conceptual framework with which we are now familiar maintains that:

- The past once really existed: this is the belief in **Reality**
- That reality can be found, though indirectly, in its evidential traces: the **Sources**
- That which constitutes historical truth is found in the sentence-length descriptive match of the historians' facts/data (as derived from the sources)

to that reality: the belief in the language **Correspondence** of present word and past world
- Such correspondence is achieved through the empirical reconstruction of human action/human agency (as found in the sources): the belief in knowable agent **Intentionality**
- The content of the past ('the facts' or data derived from 'the sources') precede interpretation confirming the process of inductive **Inference** as central to historical interpretation

My doubts about this structure and the state of objectivity that is said to result from it concern the last three principles. This is because I do not think they necessarily follow from a belief in the existence of the past or of its evidential traces (the sources). Although I choose to believe in the reality of the past and its sources, what I don't accept is that correspondence, knowable intentionality, and inductive inference even when taken together provide the only, much less the primary route, to what it means. Put succinctly, my view is that an intimate knowledge of the evidence will not of itself tell you what it all means. My conclusion is that history, as a discursive cultural form, does not depend only on one conceptual framework for knowing – the empirical-analytical. This error is based on the belief that history can be, in effect, the mirror image of the historical thing-in-itself (the past). In other words, I am suggesting there is no means by which we can circumvent what is conveyed to our understanding, as not being as much the result of our mind and language as it is past reality.

Thus, for example, there cannot be historical concepts that are mind-independent. I am suggesting it is through the categories our minds create that we organise our data and, hence, we give a form and a meaning to the empirical. Just as Kant argued time and space are the structures taken by our awareness, so I think the concepts we deploy in our historical narratives result from our perceptions and experiences of the sources, and not characteristics of things-in-themselves independent of our selves. Many realists, most recently Mary Fulbrook, have tried to square the circle of seeking objectivity and truth while still acknowledging or even celebrating competing theoretical and narrativist approaches and perspectives. One common argument is that perspectives in history are not just political or ideological and thus easily dismissed as simple bias, but are coherent, plausible, and are consensually accepted among sensible people. They must also be open to empirical falsifiability and the shared intellectual language of rationality that can adjudicate between competing interpretations.

To 'be epistemologically objective' is not to accept there are many stories in the past or that it is impossible to say which are more plausible than others. It is to aim to be outside both what we are describing and ourselves. It means there is always the strong possibility of locating a historical knowledge that is discourse and mind independent. Hence, even when it is acknowledged it cannot be achieved simply by reference to the facts, or by one's views being open to amendments as fresh evidence arrives, objectivity must assume some sort of unmediated knowledge of the object, the thing-in-itself. The adjunct to this is that it is not good enough to argue that objectivity can arise as the result of the collective efforts of successive generations of historians as they rake the past. Historical practice does not work by building up a cache of verified data and collective wisdom as to what it all means.

To 'be objective' you have to believe in the reality of the object *and* the possibility of knowing it for what it was *and* still is. Constructionist historians would not go this far. They might even find they agree with Arthur Marwick's judgement that 'history is reasonably objective' and 'not *entirely* subjective (my italics)' (Marwick 2001: 45). Clearly, for epistemologists (that is the vast majority of historians working today), 'being objective' is a matter of degree rather than an absolute. I think it's probably fair to say virtually all historians would accept they couldn't hope to be objective simply through their meticulous study and presentation of sources. As Wilhelm Dilthey pointed out, and most history thinkers subsequently have agreed, the historian is a part of the process of doing history, so our knowledge of the past cannot be free of some level of subjectivity. One of the great developments in twentieth century history thinking has been to challenge the logocentric idea that the historian's existence (and their ontological pre-judgements) means they are not outside the world looking in but are a working part of it. Historians are, after all, the authors of the history they compose. As I shall argue later, this has a substantial implication for the kind of truth with which, to be realistic, historians have to be satisfied.

Having said all that, adherence to these five principles gives effect to a set of beliefs and practices that are claimed to establish the basis of objectivity. To the epistemological mind objectivity has three dimensions. First, there is the objectivisation of the past, second the equating of 'knowing the data' with knowing the truth and, finally, that the subsequent object or knowledge can be accurately portrayed in language. In other words,

- The past is viewed as a knowable object (the past-thing-in-itself is objectivised)

- It can be known for what it is through the technical procedures of empirical enquiry (the past-thing-in-itself can be known pretty much for what it is)
- The past (-thing-in-itself) can then be presented for what it is in another form, i.e., as written history

While it has widespread acceptance among historians, this is a misunderstanding of the Kantian notion that the objects we perceive must conform to what we contribute to experience through our category-providing cognitive powers. Although most historians might be unaware of it, this logic of Kant's would probably provide the best grounds for objective knowledge. This view of objectivity does have the very strong advantage of making empiricists sceptical of what the sources may be saying. But it has the disadvantage of seducing us with the suggestion that our explanatory concepts are in some degree facsimiles of our observations, that they are somehow pictures of reality. This follows from the questionable belief that our concepts (with which we explain the meaning of the past by giving it its particular shape or form) are generated almost entirely by the content of the past. Instead, I would argue for my narrativist position, that historical knowledge works through our construction of stories *about* experience rather than being wholly derived *from* experience. Not to believe this is, I think, to run the risk of ignoring what our mental understanding contributes when we go through any process of knowing and telling.

Truth

By now you may be asking yourself what, then, is the difference between objectivity and truth in doing history? I have suggested that objectivity is about what level of mind and discourse independence we may hope to attain in order to make history a worthwhile pursuit of the reality of the past. But while being 'reasonably objective' may be for most a regulative ideal, it is a long way from knowing *the* truth. Truth is the *property* of knowing things 'to be true' cast as what we believe conforming to reality. Hence it would seem we have the (very reasonable to most people) argument that truth is an absolute and cannot be reduced to an attitude or standpoint. There can be no degrees of truthfulness unlike (as most historians seem to believe is) the case with objectivity. After all, is it possible to be '*reasonably* truthful'? Is this like saying you can be *more or less* pregnant, or *almost* human, or your pet is *nearly* a dog or *all but* a cat, or Henry VIII had *in the region of* six wives. Nevertheless, it remains widely held that, as Marwick suggests, a reasonably objective standpoint will be more likely to lead to more truthful knowing than any other attitude.

It is claimed a subjective standpoint, by definition, is unlikely to. So, knowing the truth assumes we are and have been objective to a pretty high degree at least as a profession of people who share a continuing rational conversation about the nature of the past. Indeed, a plurality of perspectives might even bring us closer to the truth. The problem with this argument is selecting those perspectives or the single perspective for that matter that is most convincing or morally respectable and which, as a result, counts more than any other. Perhaps, then, we need some injection of the concept of non-aligned status or neutrality. But how can you be neutral if, for example, you are a historian who endorses, say, structure over agency? Or you are a historian intent on studying the lives of women in the past? Where then is your non-partisan status?

McCullagh has tried over many years to resolve this problem and locate history's neutral ground by claiming two things: first that we can be objective in and through our technical practices and, second, we ignore all other historical interpretations that are demonstrably determined by the historian's interests (McCullagh 1998: 135). McCullagh defines objectivity as the knowledge of what a text means. He argues we can know what it means if it is written according to the basic rules of language and once any indeterminacies in the literal meaning of the text have been resolved (McCullagh 1998: 136). The historian reading the sources must also place the text in its context in order thereby to seek out the likely intentions of the author. McCullagh too notes how historians have to grapple with selecting that cause which best fits the available evidence, one that is more plausible than competing causes. And this can be done objectively. Indeed, the best historical interpretations and generalisations will be arrived at by meeting objective criteria – most notably the deployment of more facts (McCullagh 1998: 130).

Building on his belief in objective knowing McCullagh then goes on to define truth quite simply as the justified historical description. If he is right 'it is reasonable to assume they [historical descriptions] are very probably true' (McCullagh 1998: 16). As I have already noted, the bedrock realist position is that the data derived from the sources must somehow reflect, or so closely resemble the actual experiences, actions and intentions of people in the past that it makes virtually no difference and that, therefore, the accurate description of this by the historian gives us a direct connection with (the truth of) those experiences, actions and intentions. But, being convinced by the Rorty position that we cannot connect world and word through some third mechanism called correspondence and that even if we could the mechanism clearly cannot apply to our narrative representations, I remain surprised not that there is a continuing debate over the definition of truth in history but that it is a matter of debate at all.

Philosophical disputes about What is truth? clearly reflect upon the level of justification needed to claim knowledge of a text to be true. The debate suggests (to McCullagh as well as many other realists) that there are at least four theories of truth available to the historian: correspondence, correlation, coherence and consensus. As I shall suggest in the final section of this book, while I do not believe this is a particularly useful exercise I shall be arguing in favour of what, as we seem condemned to use the term truth, I shall call narrative truth. But for the moment these four definitions may be taken as ways to justify all three levels of historical statement: description, generalisation and interpretation. The first form of justification for truth is the most well known and which I have described already as being at the heart of the epistemological model: the correspondence theory of truth. While it is probably fair to say that correspondence and correlation (a weak version of correspondence) tend to appeal to reconstructionist historians, as we shall see correlation, coherence and consensus hold attractions for the broad band of constructionists. But it is also very important to bear in mind that those historians who endorse these theories, or a combination of them (a situation that is unfortunate for those who like such things more cut and dried) all share a belief in the possibility of accurate (or at least accurate enough) written representation. In other words, to believe in truth defined in one of these four ways means being both a referentialist and a representationalist.

Correspondence

I have already addressed the issue of correspondence at some length in Chapter 2. Suffice it to say here that non-reconstructionist historians are content that they have to work with a weakened version of correspondence because they accept there are innumerable problems with this form of justification. Today very few historians believe their interpretative or generalisation statements (i.e., those beyond the single referential sentence) can be unproblematically truthful in the sense of presenting a linguistic picture of past reality as it actually was. This echoes the point well made by Kant that in the situation where we cannot have knowledge of the thing-in-itself all we do have is knowledge of what we perceive it to be. So, we are ultimately dependent on our perceptual capacities, but they are unlikely to mirror reality 'exactly'. In spite of our empirical procedures for corroborating the data that we have derived from our sources, our perceptions are in some degree language, concept, culture and time bound (our existence or ontology directly influences what we know or epistemology). While acknowledging that it is a matter of degree, it seems unavoidable that the historians' concepts like property, class, race, sexuality, nationalism, or imperialism will not be universally shared and this must affect the nature of the inferences they draw as to what it all means. And, of course, our perceptions are driven by our personal and private compulsions, motives and interests and, hence, so are the concepts and paradigms that we bring to bear. They provide the categories through which we perceive and organise the content of past reality.

However, it would be wrong for me to suggest that correspondence is wholly out of fashion. The philosopher John Searle, for example, has strongly defended the belief that true statements are 'made true' by how things are 'in the real world', a world that apparently must exist independently of what we say about it. Indeed he goes so far as to say that realism and correspondence 'are essential presuppositions of any sane philosophy' (Searle 1995: xiii). Searle also robustly argues in favour of truth as a matter of accuracy in linguistic representation. But even at this hard end of the market he wants to inject a degree of flexibility and latitude in the justification for truth. Thus, saying that the English Chartist newspaper the *Northern Star* was selling 50,000 copies a week in 1838 is to make a roughly true statement (50,000 is, of course, an estimate). An absolutist correspondence theory, by definition, requires the world and the word match exactly and estimates about reality are second best. If the statement is true the past will match it. Put slightly differently, form and content would be the same. But Searle would not say that.

Clearly the choices of concept and social theory (examined in greater detail in the next two chapters) made by the historian are intended to link content and form and cannot but recognise the intimacy that exists between subject and object. But there are also a myriad other complex decisions about the perception and selection of the sources, or how far to 'go back' in determining causes, or what sorts of causes (material, psychological, necessary, sufficient) will be invoked. Correspondence seems to work tolerably well for sentences like 'Abraham Lincoln made his last public address from the balcony of the White House on April 11th, 1865', or 'Richard Wright was a black American novelist who wrote an autobiography which he called *Black Boy*'. Even if we choose to accept that a description of the world can be true in this limited sense (and, as we shall see in the final section of this book, there are genuine epistemological doubts about that as, even at this initial level, we are producing 'mini-narratives'), the correspondence theory collapses utterly when we try to figure out *a* meaning for those events to which our single sentences have referred.

To sustain a belief in correspondence calls for making what I think is the highly implausible assumption that by collecting thousands of referential sentences the historian can mirror the past as it actually was. This is like saying collecting the autographs of rock stars can tell you the history of popular music. So, except perhaps in the everyday sense for explaining immediate sensory input (I am standing at a bus stop, my watch says 9.30am, I rushed my breakfast, I am late for an appointment, i.e., statements that seem to agree with our other statements about the world through its material evidence), the correspondence theory of truth is hardly compelling as a thoroughgoing or complete epistemological position for historians.

Correlation

McCullagh's preferred theory of truth that he recommends to historians is correlation, which is, in effect, a weakened or moderated version of correspondence. McCullagh remains firm, however, in his belief that for a historical statement to be true still requires the sentence to connect with past reality based on the correct perception of the data, sound inference and accurate description (McCullagh 1998: 55). This may sound like the correspondence theory but there is one important difference. Where correspondence requires the word mirror the world through our perceptions and observations of it, correlation assumes the Humean notion that our perceptions are more or less caused by the way the world actually is or, to be more precise for historians, once was. Though accepting that our perceptions can occasionally lead us astray we generally accept that what you see is what you get. In other words, what we are led to believe by our perceptions can be considered as reasonable explanations of those perceptions. The basic reason is that our beliefs generally correlate or stick together with other beliefs about the material world past or present. We can then re-verify or check out our perceptions by reference to a further range of data (visual, tactile, archival). As McCullagh says, for a description to be true it must be confirmable by observation. It is this process that also, so he claims, gives rise to those concepts we use to describe reality. Thus, if the data disconfirms our theory then we ditch the theory and find another that better explains the reality for which we have evidence.

How does this work in practice? If the early twenty-first century historian believes that late eighteenth century Wesleyanism, by promoting prudence and hard work helped to make Wesleyans 'successful', he or she would reach that conclusion after referring to the evidence they had found and from which they had selected. They would not claim either a direct knowledge much less a knowledge that was twenty-first century culture free, but they would claim an honest observational connection with the past via the sources. So, while the early twenty-first century historian would not say that their Wesleyanism corresponded to the real Wesleyanism, if they believed in the correlation theory of truth they would claim that there was something in Wesleyanism (i.e., the promotion of hard work and hence success for many Wesleyans as revealed in the evidence of their lives), which correlates with their historical description and hence their interpretational analysis. In other words, the historian's interpretation two centuries and a culture later, while it remains an interpretation, need not be untrue. Although his or her perceptions could not correspond with the real world of late eighteenth century Wesleyanism, correlationists would argue their present-day interpretation offered truthful information about it as what once, at least in part, caused their perceptions. The correlationists' claim, therefore, is not that the past object or thing-in-itself corresponds to what they write, but that there is something in the past which correlates with their description. The intention with this version of truth is to meet the criticisms of correspondence, while still trying to retain the link between what happened and its representation, and which most historians believe, is absolutely essential to doing history. Clearly, this is a powerful and what is, for the majority of historians, a convincing argument.

Coherence

The third kind of justification for knowing the truth of a description is based on the notion of coherence. Appealing to a different definition of truth this theory probably has its strongest appeal for those historians who perceive an unavoidable relativism in doing history but still wish to maintain the referential and representational link. It appeals to those who think that the gap between what once was and our descriptions of it cannot be overcome by either correspondence or correlation alone nor even collectively. The challengers to Rankean 'history as it really was' such as Dilthey, Croce and later Beard, Becker, Collingwood and especially Michael Oakeshott (1901–1992) recognised (in Kantian fashion) that the past (-thing-in-itself) is always unknowable, that at best our knowledge is second hand and, most importantly, the-past-as-history has no existence separate from the experience and consciousness of the historian. As Oakeshott famously claimed, the historian makes history, and the only way to make it is to write it plausibly and, therefore, coherently (Oakeshott 1990 [1933]: 99). History does not work, he argued, according to the logic of discovery that correspondence or correlation theorists assume. Oakeshott's position echoes what I said earlier, that historical knowledge begins *with* experience rather than being derived *from* it. Oakeshott maintains (in a way not far removed from my own idealist position) that while historical understanding must engage with experience it is the mind that makes sense of it. In other words, it is the historian who takes the clutter of past events, acts and intentions and constitutes them as coherent kinds or story forms of knowledge.

While never losing sight of the fact that history is based on the sources (is referential) and must be an honest attempt at accurate writing (be representational), Oakeshott argued that because the descriptions of the historian must be filtered through their mind (which most historians would, I think, accept), the history narrative that results could at best only be seen within the coherent totality of their explanation (Oakeshott 1933). Discrete atoms of past reality, call them 'sentence-length descriptions', or 'facts' (but never 'bits of reality') individually have no meaning. To pursue the *intrinsic* meaning of a *single* event is, therefore, not just pointless it is also feckless. Such events only acquire historical meaning when put together by the organising mind of the historian. The death of Nelson at Trafalgar has no meaning until it is placed within a bigger perspective. The destruction of the World Trade Centre in New York has no historical meaning until one is ascribed to it (and interestingly the meaning can and has differed considerably between politicians and historians as well as among historians themselves). This process is often referred to as 'placing an event in its context' or contextualisation for short. The historian thus takes the content of the past (event and action) and gives it a coherent form. In one important respect Oakeshott is even tempted to think of history not even as a representation. For him history is not a re-animation: it is a fabricated or constructed re-presentation based on the sources. He even went so far as to claim that no facts as such exist – all the statements of historians are plainly judgements and inferences. Historians, after all, do not observe what happened: they infer what might have taken place from its traces. It is at this point that coherence starts to drift away from correlation, that is, there is more to history than the effort to generate descriptions that connect with high accuracy with what happened.

If Oakeshott is right, and knowledge of data is useless until it is given a meaning by the contextualisation of the historian, how could a historian explain the meaning of a single event? Take the attempted assassination in his office of the American steelmaster Henry Clay Frick by the anarchist

Alexander Berkman in 1892. Most historians would look at the evidence and agree this event took place. But they would say this event couldn't be understood as it is. Its meaning (its reality, its truth?) can only be grasped, they would claim, when it is related to, say, the protracted strike at Andrew Carnegie's steel plant at Homestead in Pennsylvania where Frick was the manager, or Berkman's peculiar place in the currents of anarchism, or his personal alienation in America, or to his poor grasp of the English language which left him unaware of the public debates largely condemning Frick's use of the Pinkerton detectives as a private army, or his sense of destiny, or some further contextual arrangement the historian finds plausible and has put together from the available sources and perhaps their own beliefs about the nature of the anarchist principle of the 'Propaganda of the Deed'.

Though cast as series of individual propositions by the historian, a variety of relationships determine the historical (as opposed to the) truth of this event. So, whether Berkman is a hero or a villain, a misguided fool or a martyr, a sufferer for a cause or a sacrificial victim, depends on the historian's understanding of anarchism, their own philosophy of history and the ethical judgements they make about such an act in the circumstances of the exploitation of labour in America in the early 1890s. In other words, the ontological pre-judgements of the historian are as important in generating historical truth as the range of data (context). Accordingly, truth is no longer defined as either a correspondence or a correlation between a proposition and a real situation. The truth of history will not simply depend on descriptions corresponding or correlating to what once was but, I am suggesting, on their coherence with other descriptions *within the narrative,* and *other narratives* constructed about what once was. The important point about coherence truth is that it is a full recognition and acceptance not merely of referential context, but how the historian 'puts it all together' within the horizon of his or her own wants and needs and their personal mediation of the social reality in which they exist. As we shall see toward the end of this chapter, this opens up the issue of relativism and confronts historians with their creative role in producing history, specifically the conflation of subject and object. It also provides the basis for the discussion of narrative truth that I shall take up in the last section of this book.

Consensus

Those historians who believe in either correspondence, correlation and/or coherence (although I suspect most historians believe in some more or less unarticulated combination) will defend their descriptive statements, as I have suggested, by reference to those 'matter of fact situations' that actually happened and which they can know with varying degrees of certainty. The appeal to some sort of correspondence-correlation-coherence is usually underpinned by a belief in historians as a professional community of rational and fair-minded inquirers. If enough of these rational people agree that an epistemological approach is right and the statements it produces are true, then they are very likely to be thought of as true and epistemology thus becomes the norm. It becomes a self-fulfilling process. While I have been arguing there is no privileged route to truth and no sure method for its attainment, it seems clear that if we rule out a conspiracy then the fact that the vast majority of historians agree that something happened, according to the consensus theory of truth, it very probably did. The most important question then is do they agree on what it means? And if they do, why do they?

In defence of epistemology, for example, it is quite usual for correspondence and correlation historians to invoke consensus when their procedures are challenged on basic epistemological grounds. Consensus becomes a useful tool in their claim to priority for their theories of truth. As they say, all 'sensible', 'fair', 'rational' and 'honest' historians agree on the priority of correspondence-correlation and its findings. Of course we do have to be careful here (as they would readily admit). There can be organised institutional, national and even globalised efforts to create false consensus views of reality. Presumably the members of various fascist communities over the years have held to a neighbourhood view about the nature of reality and the meaning of its data-stream as, indeed, have liberals, feminists, racists, and nationalists or, for that matter, surgeons, motor mechanics and university managers. To the dishonest all things are possible including individual and group self-deception (a knowing group self-deception is often referred to as a collective lie). Clearly, consensus theories of truth do not have to be true defined in terms of correspondence, correlation or coherence. Events commonly described and believed need not 'be true'. It would normally be assumed, however, that consensus truth would probably arise around some solid reference to evidence and rational argument. You would expect, therefore, that historians will not deliberately lie.

The most cogent examination of consensus truth is by the German philosopher Jurgen Habermas and the American Richard Rorty. Habermas describes the consensus theory of truth as emerging from an 'ideal speech' situation resulting in a state of affairs of 'communicative reason' in which we can generate a sort of inter-subjective agreement about reality. The assumption is that sincere, earnest and sober members of a community of investigators would eventually agree about the nature of the object of their study. This is not to claim truth is then fixed in perpetuity and such groups can still be wrong. But by the definition of an ideal speech situation they are agreed on what is most likely true according to the evidence. Consensus thus depends to a large extent on adherence to the correspondence and correlation end of the truth scale and its self-imposed constraint of the available evidence. But, paradoxically perhaps, consensus alone will not satisfy those who closely adhere to correspondence or correlation.

Consensus, according to Habermas, does away with the need for correspondence because of the great problems with it, particularly that it requires that what we say mirrors what is. By the same token, as McCullagh declares, by implication there is no good reason to deny correlation in favour of consensus (McCullagh 1998: 55). The point of correlation is not to assert agreement over what is true but, as McCullagh is suggesting, it is to demonstrate that it *is* true (at least it is reasonable to believe it has been caused by reality). At the correspondence-correlationist end of the market what makes a historical description true or counterfeit is *the* knowable reality of *the* past. Truth conditions are what count ultimately, not general agreement among a body of honest inquirers. Anyway, historians are not by nature herd animals. Most of the time we are loners only persuaded by the data in the archive and not our colleagues' assertions/interpretations. But, consensus theorists, instead of trying to make our statements 'correspond to' the past, or constantly asking have we got closer to its intrinsic nature, would claim it is probably more important and more practicable to ask whether the statements we have got are socially useful and make us better people (so long as they are not self-deceptions or lies). This immediately takes us beyond the territory of the historian as conventionally construed. And, probably, so it should.

Because correspondence and correlation historians say they want demonstration through the evidence as their first priority, not assertion or general agreement (and certainly not a spurious agreement or collective lies), they are very keen to avoid anything that jeopardises that situation, hence their ultimate rejection of the consensus theory of truth. Equally, in order to maintain what they believe to be the fairness of their descriptions of the past, they remain uneasy about the relativism that is seemingly such a risk in the coherence theory of truth. However, the most recent thinking on truth in history, which is that of the British philosopher of history Mark Bevir, is a remarkable attempt to bring all theories together in a logic of history (Bevir 1999). The linchpin of his argument is to fall back on the well-known notion of knowable agent intentionality.

While accepting we cannot know the past-thing-in-itself, Bevir still insists we can have truthful knowledge thanks to the evidence of agent intentionality (as found in the sources) and agreement (among historians) about what constitutes the facts. Truth is thus best thought of as the rational and consensual product of the work of honest historians responsibly investigating human agency (the central element in the operation of past human life). In seeking the correspondence of the past world and the present word and, hopefully, what it all means, Bevir's historian seeks objectivity and truth by understanding the power of agency through generally agreed facts. In this way (by means of the historian's ability to understand purposive human action cast as generally agreed facts) Bevir tries to find room for all four theories of truth. This marriage of the four justifications for what we know about the past is, for Bevir, the ultimate insurance against all forms of relativism. Apparently then, once the historian is in possession of the facts of human decisions and choices, they have an objective knowledge of the past. If this in any way seems implausible to you then you have rejected Bevir's unconvincing logic and entered the realm of relativism.

Relativism

In the epistemological skirmishes among historians, what we might call the referential-representationalists (that is all correspondence, correlation, coherence and consensus historians) believe they have rebutted the sceptical anti-representationalists by a revitalised and recuperated realism that shows how we can be reasonably truthful in our representation of the past. Mark Bevir's is only the most recent attempt to restore objectivity in what he admits is a subjective world. He has done so first by accepting that there are no 'self-evident empirical truths'. But, as I have indicated, he believes the historian can get round this difficulty by addressing the actions and the intentions of the historical actors. In an echo of Roberts, Bevir insists knowledge of action is knowledge of past reality (Bevir 1999: 78–126). In his attempt to defend the middle ground of constructionist history he steers between what he calls the 'extremes of objectivism (epitomised by crude representationalists like Arthur Marwick and Deborah Symonds?) and scepticism' (typified by anti-representationalists like Hayden White and Frank Ankersmit?) (Bevir 1999: 79–80). Bevir's position is akin to the 'practical realism' advocated by Appleby, Hunt and Jacob (Appleby, Hunt and Jacob 1994: 247–251) and the 'real history' and new style realist thinking of Martin Bunzl. Collectively (we have a consensus theory of historical truth here?), it is their claim that while the meaning of the past is never locked onto objects that once existed language *alone* cannot fix their reality. For this reason, they argue, we are not sealed into a universe of discourses piled on discourses. Historians can 'escape into reality' even though it may at times be a difficult and indeterminate one, and even if we can't be sure when we have got there. Mary Fulbrook described this as history seen through a glass darkly (Fulbrook 2002: 185–188).

The effort that Bevir and co have put into saving objectivity and truth is in direct proportion to their fear of relativism. The anti-relativist argument runs something like this: once we cease to believe in the objective pursuit of truth in historical knowledge (though through a glass darkly) we will slip from honest empiricist scepticism, through the veil of idealism into the sink of relativism. Seemingly, if the truth (of a statement) is taken to be relative to the historian's language, culture and time, not only are we questioning the ideal of objectivity and historical truth but we cannot have any firm moral standards, hence we finish up repeating evils such as slavery and genocide because we cannot recognise them as such in the past (Appleby, Hunt and Jacob 1994: 7). This argument suggests that historical relativism eventually produces cultural relativism that reaches its expression in death camps and false versions of history. While it may appear plausible, this reductionist argument actually is a misunderstanding of the nature of relativism.

Believing we cannot get at the truth in a correspondence sense or even in its refurbished variety, i.e., the epistemic relativism of Bevir, Bunzl, Fulbrook, Appleby, Hunt and Jacob, does not mean we must sooner or later become moral drop-outs or fascists, or that we cannot tell truth from lies. To understand the limits to truthful knowledge and its accurate representation (and to try to explain them in books like this) does not mean we ultimately cannot tell 'right from wrong'. The major consequence of the anti-representationalist position is the recognition that no historical descriptions of 'how things were' can of itself free us from our prejudices or our grasp of our own social reality. Even if it were possible to refer directly to something that once existed beyond our own time, minds and/or our narratives – even to knowing what it really meant – it would be no insulation in itself against evil men and women.

In other words, empiricism is not the only route to a defence of democracy or human rights. To believe knowing the truth about the past is always socially useful carries the very doubtful assumption that we can learn from the past and hence we can believe in 'progress'. It must also be worth asking why knowing the facts of a variety of events does not stop them happening time and again and why human beings are inured to 'the' meaning of such events? Human beings, even those armed with an in-depth knowledge of the horrendous events of the past, can still be racist and intolerant. While we can hope it may do no lasting damage to us or anyone else to believe we know the real meaning of the past, it is definitely not the prerequisite to acting decently.

Knowing what is 'more or less true' about what happened in the past is not, therefore, the privileged ground for moral decision-making. Although it may well turn out to be socially and politically valuable to know what happened in the past (to believe our historical narratives), one does not need a detailed historical study of American history from the American Declaration of Independence (1776) to the Emancipation Proclamation (1863) (which the vast majority of people do not have anyway) to choose to believe all human beings have inalienable natural rights or that chattel slavery is wrong. What is *good* for *us* in *our culture* at *this time* to believe might well be practically and usefully informed by our reading of certain narratives about the past (those we select anyway), but it is not a prerequisite. Indeed, judging by the way the horrors we narrate about the past apparently keep re-occurring might we be better forgetting about the past? To put it slightly differently (less polemically?), our moral positions are not verifiable as true or false by reference to things that happened in the past. If that were the case then, presumably, historians would be the most morally informed group of people on the planet.

The difficulty most historians have with relativism is revealed in their use of the term to define the position of anti-realists. According to Rorty, relativism has three meanings as ascribed by realists (Rorty 1991: 23). First, relativism is a term of abuse implying that anti-realists think every belief is as good as any other. Second, relativism holds that 'true' is always a disputed term having as many meanings as there are ways of justification (well, as we saw above there are at least four ways and I will argue later there is something called narrative truth). And lastly, relativism means we can say nothing useful about truth that can possibly apply outside our own particular culture or consensus group. I think we can refute the first realist definition of relativism on the simple grounds that if the second definition is correct and truthful knowing is defined by the form of justification we adopt, it means some beliefs are likely to be more useful than others. In other words, not all beliefs are 'as good as any other': after all, anti-realists can believe robbery with violence is wrong or that being a socially responsible person is good. Believing in duties rather than privileges is not the prerogative of empiricists.

Rorty, as we know, suggests that we should abandon the notion of correspondence (as most historians have at the crudest level) in favour of the well-justified beliefs held by rational people (a combination of correlation and consensus). In other words Rorty does not deny 'reality' or 'truth' as such, but does reject the idea that truth has an intrinsic nature (usually defined in correspondence terms). Indeed he defines truth as, in effect, nothing more complex than the agreement between honest and rational people on what is good for them to believe (fascists and other anti-liberal ideologues are, by definition, excluded from this definition). In this sense Rorty, the archetypal liberal, has also given up on the craving for objectivity and certainty. In so doing he has recognised what in Chapter 1 I said was the long nineteenth and twentieth century tradition of relativism from Nietzsche and Vaihinger through to the American pragmatists (including himself).

Most historians are, therefore, confused over relativism and not least because there are two forms: the metaphysical and the epistemic. Metaphysical (full strength) relativism doubts a reality independent of our minds. It holds our concepts and/or our language create reality for us. All objects are, therefore, mental and linguistic constructs. It means reality can be reduced to that which exists just for the individual (or possibly a group). It is this position that permits the denial of any access to the real and, as a result, all histories have the same weight of conviction. Let me be clear, while unthinking empiricists ascribe metaphysical relativism to anyone who questions the empirical-analytical approach, I don't know any so-called postmodernist historian who is a metaphysical relativist. I am certainly not.

Epistemic relativism, on the other hand, holds that our knowledge of the real world is better thought of as being *fostered* by our mental devices. This is the side of the Kantian argument that knowing is a two-way street – that knowledge emerges from a combination of the empirical (data), the mind's conceptual organisation and our linguistic powers of representation. Epistemic relativists thus place strict limits on knowable reality. The limit is not at the level of empirical procedures and the verification and comparison of sources (getting at the facts if you like), but rather on the level of the linguistic, temporal, gendered, spatial, cultural, political and ideological forces and agendas that unavoidably influence such devices. Recognising the boundaries of truth does not, therefore, make epistemic relativists the puppets of bigotry or incoherence or 'anything goes'. Nor does it mean they wholly reject the empirical-analytical model of knowing. In acknowledging the existence of data *and* the pressures of language as an ideologically saturated discourse, epistemic relativists stop well short of denying there is no truth in history. It just isn't the truth that can *only* be measured by correspondence, correlation, coherence or consensus.

Conclusion

The result of this brief survey of objectivity, truth and relativism in history is unlikely to usher in a victory for my anti-representationalist and relativist position. What is likely to remain is the hold most historians have on the idea of truth obtainable primarily through empirical and analytical means. The epistemological model of constructionist history will, I am sure, continue to control the centre ground of historical practice for some time to come. The reason is because it allows us to fall short of objectivity and truth but continue to regard them as constituting our basic guidelines. For myself I see neither the social need nor the disciplinary necessity to get 'hung up' on the unobtainable ideal of truthful knowing when there is a perfectly workable alternative. This is, of course, the turn from the exclusive privileging of the empirical-analytical to encompass the narrative-linguistic *as well* in doing history. However, before I can get to that – and my discussion of narrative truth – I must address the remaining significant feature of the historical enterprise: the role of theory and concept in producing historical knowledge. As I suggested in Chapter 1, the empirical-analytical approach reflects the realist and logocentric heritage of the Enlightenment. Its constructionist consequence is the belief that even in history there can be no fact without theory. Indeed, to understand empirical reality we must go beyond it by using prior theories of explanation. Indeed, without prior theories there would be no history, only the unexplained past.

Section Three

Theory and Concept

Chapter 5

The history of social theory

My intention now is to begin my discussion of the role of social theory in historical thinking. I will do this by reference to the link between reality and concept, the conflict between science and humanism, the role of the documentary source (the Rankean turn) and the eventual dominance within the profession of social theory constructionism. Having said this, while most historians would not agree that ultimately history is as much a narrative-linguistic as an empirical-analytical undertaking, I suspect most will accept that even the most social scientific history takes the form of a representation. For example, as the realist philosopher of history Georg Iggers says, few historians would flatly deny that history is a narrative prose structure (Iggers 2000: 382). It is plain that histories take the shape of stories. Moreover, these days, most historians would probably admit that these stories do not emerge unproblematically from the sources. Historians generally accept that to be coherent and full of meaning historical accounts require a narrative construction (of a story) that goes beyond the raw data. Indeed, as Iggers concedes, historical narratives demand an emplotment (ibid.). What is more, a significant element in any narrative is its power to explain – this happened then that, *because . . .*. Hence, for the most part, historians accept that they couldn't proceed in the construction of their story without explanatory presuppositions and positions. Apart from, as we shall see in the last section of this book, the implications for 'doing history' of the narrative presuppositions and pre-figurations of the historian, Iggers points us to the conceptual, theoretical and ideological presuppositions of all historians. But what undoubtedly remains important in these debates is that all histories are at least in part built upon hypotheses (sometimes called the assumptions of historians) about why something happened. But what is particularly significant about this, as the

British social historian John Tosh reminds us, is that all 'historical hypotheses amount to an application of theory' (Tosh 2000: 134) and Mary Fulbrook's assertion that 'all history is intrinsically a theoretical enterprise' (Fulbrook 2002: 86).

Clearly, in the past century history thinking and practice was and remains largely under the methodological sway of the so-called social sciences (subjects like economics, sociology, linguistics, anthropology, demography, international relations, political science, and social psychology). But more than their methodological influence has been the manner in which our theories of knowledge – our epistemology – intersect with what we think is the character of our existence: what is society, where are we and where is our society going, also who or what makes 'the decisions' about social change (the historical agent or the social structure?) and what does it all mean? Taken together these considerations and questions constitute our ontological pre-judgements. As the Greek philosopher Aristotle argued, experience and knowledge work together, but it is the tensions between epistemology and ontology, and how individual historians try to resolve them – in the sources they choose, the hypotheses they test through them, and their beliefs about the nature of social and historical change, its degree of knowability, and their own state of being – that produce the key debate in history and also the huge variety in constructionist history. It is the effort to resolve these tensions between the source, the hypothesis, and the historian's own assumptions about life and being that has characterised the historical development of the social sciences and social history. It is with the historical development of, and failure to resolve, those tensions, that this chapter is concerned.

Reality makes concepts

As I noted briefly in Chapter 1, between 1500 and 1800, initially in Europe and then in North America, emerged the birth of the modern era with its belief in science, rationality and the human ability to explain the natural world. I suggested this movement was the start of the modern era's desire 'to know' the logos or nature of reality and then to (assume it is possible to) represent it accurately. In other words, truth can be derived and known independently of its representation. Much endeavour was devoted during this period to the possibilities of rational inference (initially of the deductive kind) and the discovery and scientific explanation of the laws of human and social development. This intellectual process was accompanied (and possibly caused in some more or less complex manner) by the imperial expansion of Europe beyond its geographical boundaries, the rise and fall of its mercantile trading system then the first stages of the rise of industrial capitalism. The period also witnessed the rise of individualism and liberalism, the emergence of nationalism, and the advent of increasingly violent inter- and intra-national social conflict. Usually summarised under the label of the Enlightenment it is not a period to be later distinguished only by the gaining and ordering of knowledge, but also in the epistemological consequences that had a direct and continuing sway over how human beings have created, described and understood the discipline of history.

The period of the Enlightenment, as a convenient description in European history, is usually taken to signify the break with the irrational and/or providential beliefs of the Church-dominated Middle Ages. The period is normally considered to signify the conjunction of numerous beliefs and practices that became foundational to the modern era, i.e., scientific and logical inquiry with its accompanying operational rules such as the principle of the existence of the knowing subject. Also significant was the idea of experimentalism and the various dualities with which we are now familiar (fact/fiction, subject/object, form/content). A whole range of further beliefs can be located in their origins during this period: progress, humanism (white, male, bourgeois) natural and individual rights and the rule of law, the political principles of liberalism and the dominion of 'We, the people', nationalism, and the doctrines of the free market and rational economic choice. All this was presaged in the work and thinking of early scientific and reason-inspired or rationalist intellectuals like Bacon, Galileo and Descartes, and they were followed by Spinoza, Leibniz, Locke, Newton, Hume and Kant. Because truth can only come from the operation of rational (deductive and conceptual) thought, Descartes had no time for history, claiming it was apt to fall into romance and at best (or worst) entertainment.

As we are aware, however, the view of history held by the Neapolitan historian Giambattista Vico had been one of the few voices in the eighteenth century that rose against the predominant scientific mind-set. His pre-Kantian efforts to marry science and empiricism (by creating his 'New Science' of history as an empathic and creative activity) was overwhelmed by the immense popularity, not of the Cartesian legacy of hard-core rationality and apriorism, but of the much more user-friendly and common-sense approach to knowing of first Bacon and then Locke which gave rise to British empiricism. The epistemology at work here (and popularised in Europe by Voltaire who admired what he thought of as the social and political benefits of such an epistemology) depended on the belief that knowledge was derived not from innate concepts and ideas but from a repetitious and soon recognisable arrangement of sense experience that imprints itself on a mind hitherto without concepts, categories, forms or sorting structures. The mind was thought of as a blank and only sensory input could create the regular association of ideas. Obviously, according to this theory, content preceded form. The 'real' generates 'concepts'. In other words, concepts are pictures of reality.

Only when the (too complex and abstruse for virtually all historians) mathematics of Descartes had been wedded to an experimental methodology by the popularisation of the work of Isaac Newton (as well as Voltaire) was the path cleared for British empiricism. Once historians had been freed of (far too difficult) Cartesian geometry they were able to develop their own scientific-like practice. The application of scientific thinking to society now seemed a possibility. The old history of the literateurs and collectors of documents could not stand against the new trends. Despite its echoes today in reconstructionism, the idea that knowing the provenance of a historical source could lead the historian directly to its meaning seemed increasingly ridiculous. Describing the documents was henceforth only half the job: the other half was cultivating and organising the facts they contained according to their dependence on one another. The source became increasingly seen as just that, the point of origin of something bigger and far more complex – its history. Explaining the nature of human action and volition demanded a new approach and science could provide it. Like Newton's mechanics, the rules or laws that governed human society were now (thought to be) discoverable. The key to this knowledge was an understanding of causation.

The eighteenth-century French, American and British philosophers and civic-minded men and women of affairs who espoused the emergent natural sciences, increasingly saw history as a rational pursuit even though it was founded on the second-hand experience of events. The logic that developed to cope with this peculiarity of history was induction. It seemed quite reasonable that extensive research in the documents could provide enough instances of a choice, event, action, decision or process to constitute a viable generalisation as to the nature of cause and effect. Indeed, by expanding their knowledge historians might well discover the science of society. Generalisation through illustration became increasingly recognised as the legitimate methodology of historians. This belief depended not only on the existence of the Cartesian rational subject, but also the further assumption that there was such a thing as human nature, that it was universal and its key feature was individual agency. The common belief was that human beings could and would exercise rational choice (although there were exceptions, of course, like women, slaves, and 'lesser races').

The mechanistic mind-set of scientific empiricism thus 'explained' the reality of human society according to external and detectable features of its existence. Differences in behaviour were 'caused' by environment, means of subsistence, and numerous other 'social influences' like levels of education, political systems, the power of the Church etc, within a state or nation. Here was the move from the earlier obsession with the documents to a much wider appreciation of the possibilities and potentialities of history as a scientific kind of activity. Any 'document fixation' was increasingly frowned upon as society was viewed as understandable only through a sceptical scientific as well as an empirical, analytical, and technical methodology. The first and most influential effort at scientific history (but one that did not neglect archival research) was that of the Neapolitan (and ironically a contemporary of Vico) Pietro Giannone (1676–1748). In his *Civil History of the Kingdom of Naples* (1723) he attacked the authority of the Church in Naples through his analysis of its power over the state. This was history supposedly energised with an objective social analysis but also with a social purpose.

Romance and progress

Giannone's efforts generated one of those tensions, which became increasingly evident over the years within the conflict of justified belief and ontological presupposition. In this case it was objectivity versus commitment (whether political, social or whatever). Such tensions have never been resolved in the study of the past (or the social sciences for that matter). The compatibility between the idea that the historian's job was to reconstruct the past according to the available documentary evidence while scientifically seeking out those general principles beyond person, place and time, was increasingly seen as difficult if not impossible to achieve. The inevitable reaction to the dominance of the heroic model of science began in the mid-eighteenth century. The mechanistic assumptions of the Enlightenment judged to be the values of the present could not, so the counter humanist argument ran, be deployed to understand the past. Under the influence particularly of the German philosopher and linguist Johan Gottfried Herder (1744–1803) what became known as the Romantic Movement (in the arts and history) wanted a way to understand the past and other cultures in its and their own terms. Arguing that language was the key to understanding, Herder's anti-Enlightenment argument was that scientific abstraction was destroying the possibility of a true knowledge of social existence. True history must remain anti-rationalist was the message in Herder's sardonic *Yet Another Philosophy of History* (1774). In an echo of Vico, empathy was the key rather than science.

The conflict between scientificism and humanism thus took an early root in the historical development of history. The effort to overcome this tension produced another idea, however, one that proved very useful to historians right up to and through most of the last century. This was the idea of progress. Despite the efforts of romantics like Herder the success of science was so substantial (given its immense technological by-product in the shape of the European and American industrial revolutions) that it was increasingly regarded as the only way to understand what it had itself generated – massive, rapid and hugely socially and politically disruptive change. The notion that humanity was historically produced received its ultimate reference (or so it seemed at the time) in the cataclysm of the French Revolution (1789). And although historians like Jules Michelet viewed the French Revolution as providing another kind of model for historians – to identify with the struggles of the people they were studying – the transcendence of science was such that it became an epistemological juggernaut. Despite the efforts of romantics like Herder and the events of societies being re-made, science and history were never again to be fully de-yoked.

The notion of linear progress – so central to science – was visibly reflected in something common to both science and history: time. Indeed, Western science's conception of time as linear, worldly and worldwide (as opposed to recurring, spiritual and particular) came to dominate all disciplines and life. An inexorable link between time and progress was made by science, and historians absorbed the scientific conception of time (they had little choice). The modernisation of the West was animated not just by technology but also a sense of movement toward the future, through the fleeting present *from* the past. This constituted the modern sense of improvement that was in part achieved through the study of the past – a past leading up to the present and to the possibility of a better future.

As Appleby, Hunt and Jacob explain, the disciplining of history was only possible once this new conception of time had arrived (Appleby, Hunt and Jacob 1994: 56). They even go so far as to argue that mastering time was prerequisite to the invention of modernity and modernist conceptions of history as a factualised and investigative activity that can allow access to the patterns and meaning of the past and, hence, the future. As the metaphor describes it, time's arrow reveals the meaning of the past in the present. Once the laws of human and social behaviour could be understood, time became a synonym for progress rather than stasis or descent. Indeed, the new conception of time generated new kinds of history. Linear time produced a new conception of history as the 'unfolding' of stages or periods with its suggestion of givenness and trajectory and its discovery not just of what it is, but what it means. This new control over the past was essential to the capacity of human beings (primarily white, male, middle-class entrepreneurs, scientists, politicians and 'men of affairs') to 'engineer' the future. Cyclical change was out, recurrence was passé, and the study of the past – if done scientifically – could reveal the possible yet always progressive direction of the future.

The German philosopher G.W.F. Hegel, who attempted to marry the experimental empiricism of the Enlightenment with the humanism of the romantics, provided one possible way back to the future (or specifically his own peculiar ultimate ideal for knowing: Absolute Knowledge). Hegel's rationalism came in the form of his dialectical argument (defined as thesis plus anti-thesis equals synthesis which equals the new thesis) while his humanism was found in his judgement that (the human) consciousness (specifically of individual independent action) was the answer to understanding historical change. By using the model of the master and slave Hegel established a philosophy that moves us through opposition (thesis [master] and anti-thesis [slave]) to resolution (synthesis [freedom]). This philosophical insight can only be made active, however, in the changes (over time) in actual political institutions and cultures. In other words Hegel's logic can only be seen (for what it is and what it does) in history (i.e., in historical change). Hegel's apriorism became one of the most significant early nineteenth century formative influences in the broader recognition that change over time was generated by conflict between historical agents, and within and between institutions and, most particularly, nations. For Hegel history was only to be understood, as he said in *The Philosophy of Right* (1821), when viewed as the mind clothing itself in the shape of events. To grasp the meaning of the past, therefore, the historian (like the philosopher) has to break through contingent events to 'see' the 'logic' behind them. It is only this logic (rationality or social theory) that can explain the facts and their trajectory.

To illustrate how this works it might be useful to step out of my narrative briefly. You might care to refer here to a disruptive text like Gumbrecht's *1926: Living at the Edge of Time*. Instead of seeing the logic behind the past in Hegel's terms, Gumbrecht deliberately defamiliarises or 'makes strange' our conventional notion that there has to be logic behind seemingly contingent events. Gumbrecht suggests that we approach change over time, specifically the year 1926, through the forms of representation we ascribe to it. As he says, action and agency require 'sequentiality' and the point of his book through its form (descriptions of seemingly unconnected events that simply happened in 1926) breaks with our modernist habit of 'this then that, because'. His aim is for us to 'experience' that past but through a deliberate renouncing of the sequencing we find in narrative emplotment. *1926* is an attempt at an experimentalism that explores what history might look and 'feel' like when we reject one of its key elements. What one should gather from this 'stepping out briefly with Gumbrecht' is that all interventions made by the historian involve constructions. However, some of them are claimed to be social scientific and, therefore, somehow more rigorous and which thereby allow our history to be aligned with the truth of the past. Others, like Gumbrecht's constructive intervention, are just playing around. Is this simply puerile nonsense? I don't think so if it disturbs our conventional understanding of time cast in history.

Materialism

Hegel's view of history (like Gumbrecht's in this respect at least) is not to be confused with the reconstructionist viewing of past events as they actually occurred. Hegel was suggesting that to know the meaning of the empirical the historian must look to that which is hidden from history – the ideas behind it and which determine it. For Hegel, these ideas were immanent in history. They were the motor of historical change. But, from a different perspective (such as Gumbrecht's), the driving force of history could be something quite different. There was no experimentalism for the German historian and social critic Karl Marx. The causational force of history – the mapping of the topography of change over time – was not ideas or national conflict, it was social class. From my perspective, and remembering the efforts of the likes of Gumbrecht, none of this makes much sense if you choose to argue that there is no universal reason or ground causing historical change – that, in actuality, such forces are just the inventions of the historian being the products of their ideals and their chosen philosophy. They are best viewed, perhaps, as the historian's preferred personal resolution to the tension between epistemology and ontology. This is pretty much what Gumbrecht suggests. From this point of view history is that narrative that results from the inescapable collapse of subject and object, specifically the choices the historian makes about the form to give to their history.

If you accept this, what makes for historical change is as much a function of the historian's conceptual and theoretical preferences as what actually happened. Hegel believed, for example, that knowledge does not operate according to the logic of discovery, but is a creation – not specifically of the historian but of men as they live out their lives in their present. But his creationist or constructionist view has to be seen within the powerful post-Enlightenment or modernist framework of knowing and the logos. Knowledge may well emerge empirically and over time and is seen at the time as contingent, but it is acquired 'scientifically' and is rendered in the form of a systematic analysis. In other words history may be believed to unfold according to an inner logic, but it is only the scientifically inspired historian who can reveal it properly even though his knowledge has to be 'after the fact' both literally as well as metaphorically.

The nineteenth-century revolution in history thinking and practice was entirely due to this double helix: entwining strands of philosophy and history. History could henceforth only be viewed as the event rendered through the historian's preferred philosophy and method. None of this precluded, of course, getting the story straight by accessing the facts of the situation that existed in the past. According to a new generation of Young Hegelians in the 1830s and 1840s Hegel's idealism (as the motor of history) was rapidly turned into materialism. Using the debate over religion as universal truth as the convenient vehicle, Ludwig Feuerbach, for instance, argued religion was best seen as a childlike mysticism that obscured the real nature of human culture and society, which could be revealed through proper scientific analysis. Any history that ignored the power of science to reveal the real material nature of society should be rejected. For Feuerbach, concepts were found in the real world.

This view was particularly influential on Karl Marx (along with his friend and collaborator Friedrich Engels). Marx, as a materialist, saw religion as a huge delusional drug that confused our access to reality. True knowledge (of reality) demanded the reversal of Hegel's argument that history revealed the progression of consciousness (ideas) that eventually resulted in the achievement of Absolute Knowledge. Marx's 'Big Idea' in history was no longer a 'consciousness' at all but was the material conditions of existence. Instead of ideas being the determinant of history, they were its product. Ideas, rather than bringing history into being, were its consequence. The material conditions of our existence created change over time. With Marx we have the classic nineteenth century form of scientific explanation. Not only can historical change be explained scientifically but, most importantly, history was itself a scientific act. History was clearly science in action because of its material nature. Marx's theory of historical change thus elevated apriorism beyond the level of theory to the level of demonstrable proof. Change over time was henceforth viewed as the result of successive modifications in the structure of the material world that can be accounted for scientifically. In Marx history and material change were combined.

And so, Marx's resolution to the tension of epistemology and ontology was his historical materialism (as his theory of history is – appropriately – called). It was a massive effort to marry human to social change and explain it all within the compass of a scientific epistemology. After Marx history was no longer about ideas or concepts parading in a temporal succession, but it was generated through stages of material as well as ideational development. Indeed, so powerful was the process of material historical change Marx viewed ideas as the products of a false consciousness created by the conditions of our existence. Of course, the only ideas to escape this false consciousness were Marx's ideas, which somehow were not the fugitive of this otherwise universal condition. But this escape clause probably applies to all theories about how history works once we accept that the 'logic of history' (whatever we think it may be if, indeed, it has one) is imposed by the historian rather than discovered by them.

The past as it actually was

Marxism (aka historical materialism) is, therefore, the paradigmatic illustration of history cast as a science. The unavoidable problem, however, (as it still is) was that science couldn't measure human society with the accuracy of proper science. The physical or natural scientist can depend upon a secure laboratory setting in which to experiment on inert material. There is no passion much less human agency in the structure of Newton's Third Law of Mechanics. The new social scientist, however, must deal with agency and human action (volition, purpose, choice, desire, want) not to mention the lack of evidence and, who knows, their own desire to experiment with the form they wish to construct. But, if the constraints on objectivity and truth (as we saw in the last chapter) can be dealt with as a matter of degree so, it is claimed, can the process of understanding society and its structural change over time. Arguably, inductive generalisation is still possible if the social scientist follows the example of the physical or natural sciences. Their method is 'the model' and, although the results cannot achieve the level of certainty of science, with honest rationality and judicious inference from the available data, a new scientific history 'discipline' (defined as an approach and a subject) can be fashioned.

The high tide of the Enlightenment in the mid- to late-nineteenth century was shaped, therefore, by this desire 'to know' social reality. This desire was manifest not just in Marx, but in the work of Saint-Simon in France and Jeremy Bentham in England both of whom believed in social progress and, moreover, that this could be located and shaped in the new science of man. The desire to explain the origins and character of the *real* social and economic structures of the human world and how they change, came either to dominate (at different times) or have a central role (at all times) in the modern version of the discipline of history as it emerged in the second half of the nineteenth century. But this development could not disguise, much less resolve, the ever-present tension between the epistemological and the ontological. While this tension was always the spectre at the feast, yet another problem surfaced for the would-be social scientist historian. This was how to come to terms with the apparent conflict of social structure and individual event or action. In practice this 'coming to terms' usually meant simply recognising one's own ontological pre-judgements cast as they were as a preferred *a priori* conception of change.

This debate still rages today (see the next chapter), but in the nineteenth century it was only just being realised that the debate about the nature of the past was also likely to mean a perpetual argument about the nature of history itself. This is not just a dispute over what content from the past the historian chooses to examine but how that choice of content reflects the judgement about what is history as a way of knowing. Thus, the most famous of German historians Leopold von Ranke's approach to the documentary sources can be seen as a 'theocratic' and 'political turn' away from an emergent 'social history' while at the same time his declared association with the rise of scientific-like objectivity has been viewed as his greatest legacy to the historical profession.

The Rankean turn

For Ranke, the historian who wished to pursue objectivity really only had one route. This was a dedication to the referential, the cold fish of factualism. It was Ranke who, in effect, inaugurated the mid-nineteenth century empirical turn although the realist-inspired start on developing a critical source-based or referential historical method had actually been made before Ranke by Barthold Georg Niebuhr (1776–1831), a Danish pioneer of hermeneutics. Niebuhr's aim was to dispense with the fictional in the history narrative by the critical evaluation of the sources (through their authentification and comparison). Indeed, Arthur Marwick has argued Niebuhr's *History of Rome* (1811–12) inaugurated modern historical methodology rather than Ranke's religious and political history (Marwick 1971 [1970]: 36 and 2001: 63). The reason Marwick gives is because of Niebuhr's commitment to discovering the truth that he assumed must exist in the documents through his method of forensic philological and textual analysis. Niebuhr also insisted, and Ranke quickly agreed, that to avoid a bad case of anachronism the past must be understood in its own terms. But this was possible only through the closest investigation of its documentary traces in the archive. Only by this means could the pattern that was assumed to exist in the past, be discovered. And, of course, you do not monkey around with its form.

Ranke's importance for the modern historical profession is his emphasis on the factual in pursuing the meaning or pattern he assumed must exist in historical change. This would appear to be a good definition of contemporary constructionist historical practice. But for Ranke an important rider was that the historian had to do this without the distorting lenses of the present or the historians' favourite models or preferred theories or emplotments (or desire to experiment). Yet also, in a characteristic reconstructionist vein, Ranke was also saying let the record speak for itself. In other words, Ranke wanted to demonstrate through the referential (the documentary source) what he believed actually generated change over time. This realist and referential desire to get the story straight makes Ranke the first among those historians who want the evidence to reveal the givenness of the past, but who, in constructionist practice, also wed empiricism to analysis in pursuit of a full understanding of the meaning of the past. Ranke's ultimate legacy seems to be the belief that historical knowledge cannot rely on the study and analysis of individual events alone, but also on the historian's conceptual schemes. It is this legacy that makes Ranke so central to historicist as well as reconstructionist and constructionist epistemological approaches to the study of the past.

While it was increasingly understood by Ranke that writing a narrative was an integral part of doing history – the fact that history is a literary form he did not believe could be reasonably denied – it was still seen as a coherent report of the results of a scientific-like approach and critical procedure. History, though a literature, was not viewed as a literary activity. In other words, the facts were not processed through a literary form that had been pre-selected (as Gumbrecht has done) for their representation. Realist history was explained, as the scientific conviction developed, by understanding the documentary content of the past through the rational inductive inference of its meaning. A form, self-consciously chosen and imposed, could not explain the meaning of the past. The form of history must follow the content of the past (specifically the motivated actions of human beings viewed within a social context). Much less was there any thought that the form itself could be as important as the content in arriving at the meaning of past events or actions. In essence, as the scientific approach gained popularity, there was a rejection of the possibility that language might have a cognitive role in the construction of past reality.

Proper historians, certainly in Ranke's view, have to go beyond the facts of the individual event in order to seek out the power and pattern – 'the meaning' – that surely exists beyond the episodic, the contingent and the unexpected. For Ranke this power beneath the surface of change over time was manifest in the rise of the state, which, in the case of Prussia, he believed was informed by the command of God (Ranke was politically conservative and a Lutheran). Consequently the actions and intentions of human beings in the past were, he believed, ultimately driven by this power that is, as he came to believe, the essence of the state. In his dogged pursuit of his social ontological pre-judgement Ranke still felt obliged to draw upon as many documentary sources as he could find (such as original manuscripts and volumes of ambassadorial reports). He did so, however, to elaborate on and defend what he believed were the two most important aspects of historical study – the development of the state and the emphasis on individuals and events.

The social in history

Ranke's association of close critical documentary analysis with the study of politics can be seen as a turn away from the early manifestations of social history. Though aping science Ranke was no social scientist. The first signs of the social in history are to be found in Britain in embryonic works by John Millar (*An Historical View of the English Government*, 1787), Thomas Malthus (*Essay on the Principle of Population*, 1798), T.B. Macaulay's brief foray into the social (in his *History of England*, 1848) and John R. Green's *Short History of the English People* (1874). But, as in most developments in history thinking even today, it is in mainland Europe that the most radical history thinking occurred. In addition to Vico, Herder, Voltaire, Marx etc, there is a long list of European historians like Niebuhr, Augustine Thierry (1795–1856), Jules Michelet (1798–1874), Alexis de Tocqueville (1805–1859), Jacob Burckhardt (1818–1897), N.D. Fustel de Coulanges (1830–1889), Karl Lamprecht (1838–1917) and others, who allowed the social to force its way into history in a variety of ways. While they did not always agree on how history should 'look', they nevertheless accepted that the Rankean political turn was not history's highest achievement nor its only direction.

There is one British thinker who did make a sustained contribution in the nineteenth century to later history thinking. As I noted in Chapter 1, the British philosopher of history William Whewell in the late 1830s and early 1840s rethought the relationship between the scientist's facts and his or her concepts. Although distinct from each other, Whewell insisted, fact and concept must work in an inferential partnership. Whewell is important because he studied the process of induction as a primary mechanism for knowing. Given that inductive inference is generalisation from specific instances of evidence through argument by parallel, likeness, similarity, attributes, probability etc, its knowledge proceeds indirectly from beliefs which themselves have been inferred from the data. Whewell believed deduction to be inappropriate for the study of the past because its conclusions are determined without reference to the empirical. Rather, Whewell argued that all induction begins with an imaginative act that sees the data in a new way. This can then be formulated as a hypothesis to be 'tested' in the evidence. This leads to explanation. In other words, there is a mechanism for testing knowledge in the mix of data, hypothesis, description, causation, and inference.

This methodological process is seen in the earliest examples of embryonic social history. The 'empirical re-turn' (of the mid-nineteenth century) was famously described some thirty years ago as resulting in the 'poverty of empiricism' that directly influenced British history writing up to the mid-twentieth century (Stedman Jones 1972). This was, perhaps, the ultimate result of the turn toward inference. Much British social history of the late-nineteenth and first half of the twentieth century was often theoretically emaciated, though corpulent in its need to become scientific in its source-based methods. In spite of the crude social history that was John R. Green's *Short History of the English People* (1874) (more Whig, nationalist and progressive than social), there were occasional uses of the concept of class (though not often in the Marxian sense of the term) in the hands of a small group of early economic and labour historians like Arnold Toynbee (*The Industrial Revolution in England*, 1884), the Webbs (*History of Trade Unionism*, 1894 and their multi-volume *English Local Government*, 1906–1929), the Hammonds (*The Village Labourer*, 1911), R.H. Tawney (*The Agrarian Problem in the Sixteenth Century*, 1912), and John H. Clapham (*An Economic History of Modern Britain*, 3 vols. 1926–1938). Although methodologically relatively sophisticated, all these historians remained epistemologically naïve.

In the United States there was even less of an effort to put the social into history until the revolution begun and steered by Frederick Jackson Turner with his insistence on the socially (and politically) formative role of the

American frontier (first articulated in his lecture in 1893 at the Chicago annual American Historical Association meeting). His contemporaries James Harvey Robinson and Charles Beard (1874–1948) also directed Americans to the social origins particularly of their democratic institutions. Indeed, it was Turner who used the famous description of social history as 'history from the bottom up' as early as 1923. However, while the interests of historians were branching out from the political and institutional into the social, its early epistemological and conceptual narrowness resulted not only from the inference fixation, but also because of the inability of historians to resolve the debate over the nature of the relationship between human agency and social/economic structures (in historical change). One answer had, of course, already been provided. The Marxian legacy held that society creates individuals. In other words, agency is determined by the economic structures of wealth creation and its maldistribution. This notion from the political left was to become a central feature of social history from the twentieth century onwards.

The positivist/sociological turn

But there were other developments that took place in parallel with the emergence of the social, not least the rise of positivism. The greatest asset constructionist historians have today is to be able to call upon sociological theory in the pursuit of the structures that it is assumed must have shaped society. The epistemology of constructionism emerged in the mid-nineteenth century thanks not only to Marx but also those other historians who took the 'social turn'. Its theoretical 'bite' was provided mainly through the work of four other key social theorists, the French trio August Comte, Alexis de Tocqueville and Émile Durkheim (1858–1917) and the German social theorist, economist and historian Max Weber (1864–1920).

As a distinct epistemological approach to the past, constructionist history began when it split from the nineteenth-century tradition of naïve descriptive empiricism. Marx with his 'scientific' theory of 'historical materialism', but also Comte with his 'positivism', Tocqueville and his analysis of revolution, Durkheim with his comparative search for 'social facts' and patterns in social behaviour, and Weber with his anti-Marxist examination of the connection between rational action and structure, all argued that to find the truth in the evidence it was essential to burrow beneath the sources to the underlying structures of society and agency.

Such was the sophistication of the turn toward a positivist science of society that there was an acknowledgement of the role of the subjective in establishing the nature of historical change. Weber, for example, accepted the relativism that must always exist as the historian seeks to reach an objective causal explanation of social action through the analysis of cause and effect. For Weber this meant 'understanding' (*verstehen*) agent intentionality. It meant asking how human beings fasten meaning(s) to their social actions and how these are given a material force as 'social norms' (thus raising questions about power in society). Weber argued that social observable facts depend not only on economics but also ideas and constructed concepts. Hence 'status groups' are as historically significant to Weber as Marxian social classes. Equally, the concept of 'charisma' (borrowed by him from the history of the Church) provides an explanation of political leadership.

Durkheim's contribution was to argue that socially derived laws exist beyond the level of the individual, and he tried to understand how social values and norms are created and operate. Within this framework he pointed to the need to consensually regulate capitalist society lest unrestrained it led to social instability and immoral and socially deviant acts. Durkheim's progressive and politically liberal emphasis upon the anti-social results of the absence of moral regulation (*anomie*) worked with his belief in the collective consciousness of society (as opposed to the consciousness of individuals). This led to his notion of an organic society while at the same time recognising the social demarcations of the division of labour. In his most famous text, *Suicide* (1897), he tried to understand the social causes of suicide, specifically its origin in the failure of society to offer a regulatory control over human passion/despair.

The work of social theorists like Marx, Comte, Weber and Durkheim articulated the fundamental problems of social analysis, and helped provide a vast body of social theory with its appropriate models of social change and also produced the key concepts that historians could and would henceforth invoke. The problems of social analysis centred on matters like social structure, function, individualism, consensus, comparison, agency, culture, and the nature of social facts, while the models subsequently fashioned ranged from the general orientations of each of the social theorists – Marxian, Weberian, Durkheimian – to more specific academic constructions designed to prise open certain aspects of past and present social reality. For historians, categories of analysis like capitalism, feudalism, mercantilism, bureaucracy, and revolution are academic inventions that have become essential to our understanding of the knowable reality of the past. Other models have even been developed to describe the complex process of change over time like primordialism and modernisation.

To try to lend the flexibility required in acknowledging the nature of such change over time, highly specific concepts were also developed that could be fine tuned to account for fresh evidence and the altered conditions of time and place: class, status, *anomie*, social norms, collective consciousness, charisma, and in the last century gender, hegemony, ideology, moral economy, socialist humanism, invention of tradition, feminism, etc. As the historian of social theory Peter Burke has pointed out, subsequent generations of social historians have taken these early models, theories and concepts and extended and elaborated on them, hence Durkheim's notion of the collective consciousness has been transmuted into a variety of more recently coined concepts like Mentalité or 'belief system' or 'webs of belief' (Burke 1992: 91, 93). These early forays into social theory have, as a result, provided the bases of later constructionist historical explanations of the processes of modernisation and modernity.

Conclusion

By the start of the last century the social had entered into history or, to be more accurate, historians had injected social theory into their construction of past reality. The problem of the tension between the epistemological and the ontological, however, remained unsettled. In the process of constructing mental models and producing conceptual explanations of past events, it has come to be recognised that history is, despite its referential epistemological character, socially/ontologically constructed and, as a cultural practice, is relative to the historian's understanding of the nature of reality and how it works. It is also subject to the historian's personal experimental choices. Nevertheless, the point of social theory is not to replace the referential. The basic empirical-analytical approach as supported by the theoretical and conceptual still aims to determine the fundamental structures of and patterns to past reality. The question that was left for historians to answer in the twentieth century was how to make history (increasingly understood as social history) more adequate to the job of objectively revealing the truth of the past. While the data remained (and remains) of central significance to the historian, it was becoming ever more apparent that no historical fact can be innocent of theory. In the next chapter I will examine, largely with reference to the historiography of the twentieth century, how historians have gone about constructing the-past-as-history.

Chapter 6

Constructing history(ies)

I shall now evaluate and illustrate the nature of mainstream or construction-ist history as it is thought and practised today. I shall do this by explaining how the modernist epistemological model has been modified through the recognition that the historian constantly makes ontological choices in the effort to resolve the unavoidable tensions that exist within the production process of historical knowledge. This is done by the connections made between human agency and probability, and the structures that are said to result from human activity. The nature and complexity of all this is revealed through the working of covering laws. The basic tension between our being and our knowing, as I suggested at the end of the previous chapter, is not capable of resolution. All that constructionist historians can do is compro-mise: generating meaning as objectively as they believe is possible with truth as their regulatory ideal. The term 'constructionist historian' can only be helpful as a description for those historians who agree with the broad idea that somehow history emerges from the constructive intellectual conversation between their concepts and the content of the past. What this means is that the ways in which they conceptually map, sift and order the evidence has determined the huge variety of approaches that characterise the mainstream of history practice today. What all varieties of constructionist history share is, first, the procedural belief that all their descriptive statements must take the form of propositions and, second, that testing them in the evidence must embody some overall theoretical design, some model that the historian intends to exemplify through the nature of 'discovered reality'.

Consequently, the history of history in the late-modernist twentieth century was as we know characterised by the erosion of the crude modernist reconstructionist notion that written history reflects the past. It was replaced

with the more sophisticated belief that singular events can only be understood by being connected in a structured cause and effect way. It is this
process of developing general as opposed to single-event explanations that
has distinguished twentieth century constructionist historical understanding.
This process recognises that historical knowledge and explanation can be
derived not only inductively, that is, reasoning from the singular instance to
the general, but also deductively, that is, reasoning from the general premise
back to the specific instance. The constructionist twentieth century has,
therefore, seen the rise and rise of propositional and testable history as historians have come to terms with the great dilemma at the heart of modernism:
the dualism of epistemology (knowledge) and ontology (being).

Continuity and transformation

In Chapter 4 I outlined the epistemological model of history as it developed in
the nineteenth century. The model, you will recall, comprises several features.
These are the belief in past reality that is knowable through its sources, that
historical truth resides in the justified descriptive statement that corresponds
to the empirical reconstruction of human intentionality, and the empirical
must always come before any analysis. In this model the aim of history is to
determine the meaning of the connections between events and the intentional
decisions of agents. In the twentieth century historians and philosophers
were engaged in a long debate about the utility of this model. What this debate
produced was the transformation from event history to a social science-
inspired history – what two recent commentators have described as a shift
from an idiographic to an nomothetic vision of history (Fairburn 1999: 15;
Marwick 2001: 4-6, 28, 73, 80, 291, 292).

Idiographic refers to a predisposition to explain the past by addressing
the individual and particular (a person and/or event explicable only in their
own terms), while the nomothetic is concerned with describing the past as a
collection of things (groups of persons and/or categories of events that have
general patterns of connections). As the historian Miles Fairburn has argued,
social historians have tried (with varying degrees of success) to accommodate
both visions of history by trying to include all social categories within the
large aggregates of people in which they are interested (Fairburn 1999:
13-16). Thus, for instance, the historian of the English Chartist movement
might try to include all the kinds of chartists available to him or her through the
sources – not just the elites but the masses as well (including women, regional

chartist movements, and the lower-class chartist orators). The problem with this is how far does the historian want to (is able to?) disaggregate (i.e., select from) the Chartist collectivity and turn them into various discrete categories?

This debate on the idiographic or nomothetic nature of social theory, while it did not force the abandonment of the nineteenth century epistemological model's first three elements, did acknowledge equality between social structures and agent intentionality. In this way the significance of both inductive and deductive inference was established. Constituted broadly as 'social history' its practitioners accepted that history dealt with a real past (real people, real actions, real decisions, real events, real sufferings, real happiness) to which their narrative accounts could and must as closely as possible correspond, even though they were mediated by their mental models, theories and concepts. Objectivity and truth were thereby viewed as unobtainable in absolute terms, but they could still be ideals. A significant distinction thus developed between constructionist social theory-inspired history and, for the lack of a better description, Rankean or reconstructionist history, with its belief that *the* story existed in the events of the past (hence the truer, clearer picture can emerge when we get *the* story straight). Thereafter history was seen as an increasingly complex theoretical as well as empirical process. But, as I have said, while this constituted an advance in history thinking it was not especially radical. The reason lies – as it must – in the tension between the ontological and epistemological.

Ontological pre-judgements and epistemological consequences

Constructionist histories today are eclectic. They possess a wide array of methodologies, occupy a variety of ideological positions, and address a huge range of topics which, when taken together, constitute an enormously rich and complex intellectual environment. However, while its practitioners are reflective and sophisticated, its basic logic cannot escape (like that of all other epistemologies in the humanities) the fact that its practitioners have to make ontological pre-judgements about the nature of their own and other people's social existence and society's mechanisms for change. They intervene in these ways while still insisting on a realist epistemological position. As ought to be clear, no historian can escape making ontological choices about what is 'good' to believe about how the world works and, I am arguing, it is those choices that ultimately make the differences in history because ontological choices translate into attitudes toward the role of concept and social theory. Hence, it seems clear that the social ontological choices of historians like Geoffrey Elton, Jack Hexter, Arthur Marwick, Deborah Symonds and the editors of *Reconstructing History* (1999), Elizabeth Fox-Genovese and Elisabeth Lasch-Quinn, place their modernist emphasis upon the role of agency and intentionality and even assumptions about 'human nature' in explaining historical change.

For such historians, agent intentionality is viewed as the best explanation of both individual and group behaviour. Let me be clear about what I am saying here. These decisions are personal. They are moral and ethical choices which have nothing to do with the nature of past, present or future reality. These ontological preferences, though disguised by being couched in epistemological terms, are used to account for society structured according to patterns of individual choice. This pre-judgement about the structure of social reality founded on the assumption of the primacy of individual choice is then turned into a particular version of 'the good society'. In the case of the editors of *Reconstructing History*, for example, the principles of property rights is assumed to legitimately flow from a belief in agency. Agency cast as choice within an economic context effectively legitimises a belief in the economic and social system of capitalism. While it is acknowledged this may provoke 'class tensions', the let-out is the belief that historical agents can resolve them. As the reconstructionist historian Martin J. Sklar claims, in the 'American liberal democratic political system' historically such tensions are invariably navigated and resolved (Sklar in Fox-Genovese and Lasch-Quinn 1999: 306). Clearly, Sklar's social ontology has directly influenced his historical analysis in a particular way. He concludes that American corporate capitalist society has worked over time to promote equal rights, equal liberties and equal opportunities which goes far in explaining why there is no socialism in the United States (ibid.: 319). What I am suggesting is that any meaning history has flows not just from the data but also from in this instance Sklar's ontological preferences. What starts his historical thinking, epistemology or ontology? I believe it is the latter.

Now, if we assume, say, that the ontology of individualism is replaced by some kind of holistic (i.e., structural) view of how the world works, then individual events and agent intentionality recede in causal significance. Historical individuals and their choices (agency) don't entirely disappear, of course, but they are seen as determined more often than they are determining. People are now viewed as being acted upon at least as much as they act for themselves. This view holds that modernist society is a complete human, social, cultural and material environment in which causation is a structured interaction of individuals and institutions, classes and other social groups, races and genders, contending ideological positions, individual human decisions and material processes.

Social structures are thus viewed by constructionists as knowable realities, the operation and existence of which tend to explain how human beings act, think and achieve and which can be taken, in turn, as explanations (causes) of agent self-awareness and personal behaviour. According to this totalist or structural social ontology, rather than consciousness determining our social being, society determines our consciousness. This late-modernist ontological position, while it originated in the nineteenth century with Marx (who emphasised the totalising social and personal effects of economic structures) and is in the work of all later generations of Marxists, is also located in the histories of those who chose other forms of totalist social explanations, most notably the French Annaliste school that emerged in the 1920s. This continues in many different forms.

With science as the model, new styles of social history produced what became the signature epistemological approach and methodology/practice of historical study of the twentieth century. This is what was proclaimed as the objective factual investigation of change over time based on the detailed research of specific 'problems' or 'themes' utilising generalising concepts and empirical-analytical methodology. This late-modernist epistemology can be seen not only in the *Annales* in France, but in social and economic history in Britain and the New History in America and all later historical movements through to the last twenty years or so. These constructionist histories (mainly social, cultural and gender) very largely replaced individualism (human free will, agency, intentionality or contingent events) with social structure (various kinds of determinism like class, culture, race, imperialism or nation) as the causal factors. This is 'factor' rather than 'actor' history.

The most recent variant of this late-modernist thinking is interesting in as much as it has been theorised as a reflexive or 'third way' out of the 'factor-actor' dichotomy that tries to combine both forms of ontological pre-judgements: the totalising with the individual. Since the early 1980s this was variously attempted in support of the liberal humanist argument that history is best understood as the result of the combination of agency and structure. This is mostly associated with the 'structuration' theories of the sociologist Anthony Giddens as translated into history thinking by the 'structurist' economic historian Christopher Lloyd (Giddens 1984, 1996, 1998; Lloyd 1993). Essentially, 'third way' ontological choices view the historical agent as a creature both acting and acted upon. For Giddens, structure and agency are mediated by those social practices associated with epistemology, i.e., practices of knowledge production. But, of course, this is just one more ontological preference and, as such, has no priority as a mode of historical analysis.

Giddens elects to walk the middle road between the extremes of Marxist determination and conservative rational action theory and it has been influential particularly in British political circles ('Blairism'). Actors are, so Giddens argues, formed by the social structures that they also play a central part in creating. As the commentator Lloyd says, rather than seeing agency and structure as opposites (historical explanations are *either* acts of human agency *or* social or institutional structure) they are better viewed as a pairing. And the link between the pair is knowledge. Thus, what and how we know becomes as important as what we know. Knowledge is not just a matter of information gathering, it is also a matter of our experience and 'being'. This approach is interesting, therefore, because it tries (but fails, as it must) to resolve the conflict between the ontological and epistemological.

Medieval heiresses and the construction of historical meaning

Nevertheless, the gains of theory, concept and both forms of inference (deductive and inductive) are apparently so immense that very few historians today would claim to be simply reconstructionist in their approach. Just collecting documentary data and inferring what they mean (i.e., inductively) is not good enough and probably never was. Given that the fundamental aim of most historians is to justify what they think the sources are telling them, the method of justification deployed by constructionists, as I have suggested, is to make a generalisation about a category of people or events by reference to a set of examples. How does this work in practice? While illustrations of this are vast in contemporary history research and writing, I have selected one at random from an edition of *The Economic History Review*. In an article in the August 2001 issue the historian S.J. Payling has attempted to evaluate the distribution of landed property in late medieval England by examining 550 baronial marriages compiled from one particular source that refers to the parliamentary peerage (Payling 2001: 413–429).

On the assumption of a third way ontology (that combines agency with structure) Payling sets out to challenge the foundational premise or hypothesis that explains the aggregation of landed estates among fewer and fewer owners in the medieval period in England. He does this by arguing (in a classic constructionist way) for the replacement of the established theory/

explanation of land aggregation with another more convincing (or so he claims) hypothesis. Accordingly his new hypothesis 'endeavours to describe the limitations placed upon land aggregation by the complex interaction of motivation and opportunity that governed the dispersal of heiresses' hands' (ibid: 414). Agency (motivation) and structure (opportunity) are evaluated in tandem.

As is the case with all constructionist history the author starts by sketching the established and presently widely accepted explanatory hypothesis and the supplementary hypotheses or assumptions upon which it depends. The established primary or core hypothesis as Payling explains holds that rules of inheritance were such as to concentrate estates into ever-smaller numbers of male ownerships (patrimonies). The supporting supplementary hypotheses include the rule of primogeniture (the first born male inherits everything); that land dispersal through sales to the non-landed was strictly limited; that the subversion of primogeniture by fatherly affection for younger sons was not enough to affect the land aggregation process; and female inheritance assisted in this aggregation of estates as new men did not enter the land-owning elite through marriage because heiresses customarily married men who were equally wealthy or wealthier.

Now, in pursuit of his replacement hypothesis that landed families were not intent on expanding their estates indefinitely through heiress marriage, Payling deduces several supplementary hypotheses to account for the fact that heiresses were not married within narrow social confines. These supplementary hypotheses include the argument that monetary gain was not the main consideration of the father in choosing a groom for his daughter; that often fathers wanted to retain the historic nature of their patrimony separate from a larger one; the cost of the settlement to the groom's father of marriage to an heiress as well as the 'portions' that had to be paid; and the widespread preference of fathers to marry their younger sons to heiresses because the dower was smaller.

In order to make these new supplementary hypotheses defensible (and be adequate supports for his new hypothesis) Payling draws on the evidence of the 550 marriage contracts and other sources culled from various County Record Offices, parliamentary rolls, the Public Record Office, and private letter collections, to support or reject his supplementary hypotheses. In his search for supporting examples he quotes from 154 first marriages contracted by peers in the first half of the fourteenth century of which apparently only 15 were to heiresses or heiresses-apparent at time of espousal, and 93 of the higher peerage between 1300 and 1499. He also uses well in excess of a dozen named examples of marriages among the landed. The creation by

Payling of several supplementary hypotheses allows for more evidence to be brought to bear in support of the new core hypothesis and enables him to turn what might seem at first blush not to be relevant data into useful support. Payling thus claims to challenge the prevailing interpretation that heiresses married into greater wealth and so, given the significance of this, the ownership of land was not, in fact, narrowed. Broad conclusions such as Payling's about the nature of historical change based on a few hundred examples taken from one source may not sound very scientific, and it isn't. But it is the nature of explanation in constructionist history.

The balance of probabilities

So, what is the nature of constructionist history today? It is reflected in examples like Payling's construction of his article's argument. Despite the methodological sophistication of constructionist history (as demonstrated in Payling's study), such history remains within the modernist epistemological argument that the past is ultimately knowable and that we can get pretty close to the truth not only of what happened and, therefore, what it all means, but also that we can describe it more or less accurately. As I suggested in Chapter 4, correspondence and correlation theories of truth continue to attract reconstructionist historians while coherence and consensus theories of truth appeal to constructionists and, hence, we have the broadly accepted notion of truth in history pivoting around correlation and coherence.

In effect, constructionist historians always work with the balance of probability though it may be based on what seems a relatively narrow range of data. As Miles Fairburn, one of the most lucid contemporary commentators on the practice of social history, argues, the nature of that balance is constrained by the burden and diversity of the examples and supporting instances culled by the historian from what is available in the archive (Fairburn 1999: 61). Certainly Payling does this with his examples. This method of investigation is that we have already encountered as hypothetico-deductive thinking, or argument to the best fit. As the heiress example illustrates, as a process of historical analysis it requires the historian to generate a series of propositions or hypotheses (core and secondary) and, by a mix of deduction and empirical investigation, seek out that one which seems to be the best at explaining what the data plausibly means.

The use of the hypothetico-deductive method is not, of course, any guide to the reliability of an explanation to the best fit. The fact that a hypothesis tidily takes into account the available evidence does not guarantee the truth of its explanation. History isn't built for proof because, as I have been at pains to argue, as a body of knowledge it results from the relationship between the historian's personal existence and the cognitive system of concept and social theory they choose to deploy. That history is a social and theoretical construct must not be forgotten especially when the epistemological claim is made (as it usually is) that historians can only provide provisional descriptions that hold until, as the philosopher Karl Popper suggested, they are falsified by the discovery of fresh data (Popper 1959). Take the statement 'the most significant development for the English working class in the last decade or so of the nineteenth century was probably the growth of trade unionism among unskilled workers'. As a statement of historical interpretation, what is, in effect, a statement of likelihood based on the presently available evidence, it remains provisional. But this claim cannot avoid provisionality in another and deeper sense, that it also remains a constructed social, cultural and discursive (written linguistic) practice.

Nevertheless, believing in the truth of statements attested to in the evidence is reasonably justified for both reconstructionists and constructionists, as long as certain truth conditions are met. Apart from the belief that the hypothesis deployed explains more of the data than any other, and without going back on the historian's natural scepticism about the statements of other historians, as a statement of historical description it should also fit better than other statements into a pre-existing structure of explanations believed to be true. Furthermore, the best hypothesis should include fewer suppositions than any other. Clearly, even with such statements of deductive and inductive inference historians are not delivering logically true statements. Such statements remain assertions that are 'more or less' likely to be truthful when measured empirically.

In practice, then, as with the example of the medieval heiresses, constructionist historical (explanatory) generalisation(s) about a large group is (are) inferred from a small sample of that group. This hypothetico-deductive method is widely believed to overcome the problem that historians cannot write down everything about the past as it happened (for the very real constraints not only of lack of documentary sources but also other practical matters such as how long the publisher wants the article or book to be and how much time is at the historian's disposal). A historical judgement is thus based on probability, reasonable doubt, and the webs of theories spun by the historian. Within these constraints the aim is to confirm the probability of an explanation being true by positing an expanding fan or web of explanatory hypotheses and supportive evidence.

An old question revisited: is history 'science' or 'art'?

Given that our knowledge of the past is always second-hand (because the historian cannot observe it directly), that our knowledge is always incomplete, that our account is always hypothetical and imposed, and that our ontological preferences mean the whole exercise is inflected with our social values, it may seem odd that anyone should waste time on arguing over whether history is in any way scientific. The perennial question is that if the reality of the past can never be recaptured, can historians ever provide scientific explanations? As I have noted, philosophers Carl Hempel and William Dray in the middle to latter part of the last century and more recently Christopher Lloyd, Miles Fairburn, Clayton Roberts and Graeme Snooks have argued that historical explanation can be legitimately subsumed under a general or 'covering law' which is directed at finding the hidden structures of human society. Advocates of the covering law assume history is amenable to general rules that govern agency, events and constitute the forces that create structures. To illustrate this, take the historical problem of how a historian understands and then tries to explain a process as broad and large-scale as the European immigration into America in the late-nineteenth century.

The fact that people migrated from Europe to America at that time is explained by empirical testing in the evidence and its accuracy is accountable for by a general law of human behaviour. The premises for the explanation, known in philosophy language as the *explanans* (that which does the explaining – say the desire for economic self-improvement or to escape military conscription) require a known outcome as found in the empirical evidence. This is called the *explanandum* (that to be explained – immigration from Europe to America in the 1880s and 1890s). The *explanans* contains a covering law to which reference is made in order to demonstrate that the *explanandum* had to happen. This hypothetico-deductive type of explanation is claimed to allow the truth of propositions to be inferred. Such explanations are clearly empirical, referential, factual, leave little room for interpretation, are cause-effect in character, and sanction if not the correspondence theory of knowledge one of its weaker cousins, and are, therefore, quite possibly capable of being predictive. Under these circumstances we can be objective, pretty truthful and, most likely, we can learn from history.

Are Hempel and his constructionist supporters correct in their belief that this hypothetico-deductive inferential form of explanation is right for historical understanding? Can, in fact, individual events be subsumed under the covering law model and lead to the discovery of determining social, economic or other structures? It is often argued that with individual events covering law theory is inappropriate. Is it possible to explain the particular outcome of the Cuban Missile Crisis in 1962 or the role of Cavour's attitude toward parliamentarianism in establishing a unified Italy with reference to general laws of human behaviour? Lurking behind all this is an even more substantial question. Are there laws of history? Regardless of the society and culture, are there universal patterns in the processes beneath the surface patterns in human events? Most historians would probably not agree with Graeme Snooks that there are such rules given the cultural differences revealed in different societies not to mention the ontological choices made among historians. However, it is the continuing interest in the connections between agency, event, structure and meaning that has pushed some historians in the direction of the third way (Snooks 1998: 3) and still invests the debate over history as art or science with a continuing significance.

Constructionist historians regularly maintain that every event has to be explained, sooner or later, under a covering law, although they may – and usually are – constrained by both period and location. As William Dray argued in the late-1990s, historians invariably explain by using generalisations although their scope is limited in time and space. Dray calls these 'limited-law explanations' or, in the case of explaining the actions of individuals, 'individual-character explanations' (Dray 1997: 769). Although Dray is firm that these explanations are not strictly scientific (in philosophy parlance they are not deductive-nomological, i.e., laws of explanation that can be deduced from the evidence) they are still essential to the work of historians as reliable generalisations. However, the non-scientific anti-conceptual reconstructionist historian will still insist if there are no covering laws then surely any pretence to scientific-type history explanation must give way to another form of argument that is entirely source-based. This means high degrees of certainty can only be assured at the event level through the truth conditional statement (of fact). It is precisely at this point that the reconstructionist and constructionist historians diverge. The former will happily give up on all possibility of general explanations of individual events (as subsumed under general classes of explanation) while the latter will still insist on the need to generalise if only at the 'limited-law' or 'individual-character' level of explanations. As Dray points out, this has significant repercussions for the kind of history you believe in and feel you can practice (Dray 1997: 769–770). Is history 'science' or 'art'? I raise the question once more only to bury it. The answer depends entirely on the assumptions the historian makes about the nature of explanation which, in turn, is dependent in epistemological terms on either giving up on, or still actively pursuing, a 'social science turn' of explanation – being either a reconstructionist or a constructionist historian.

As I have argued, constructionist historians work from the principle that without theory there is no history. The root of this lies in what the Marxist theorist Alex Callinicos calls 'philosophical naturalism' (Callinicos 1995: 8). Admittedly Callinicos is unusual in that he is a deeply committed Marxist and a historian of ideas who thinks about doing history more than most historians. He works from the anti-Kantian (anti-idealist) principle that, as he says, human beings are 'continuous with the rest of nature' and he stresses 'the methods shared by the physical and social sciences' (ibid.). His fundamental materialism leads him to explain 'human thought, language and action' by placing them in their physical and social contexts (ibid.). This has several important consequences. It locates history in the reality of the past world. It defends social theory or science-like constructionism. It also insists that any effort to equate historical writing with story telling misconstrues the scientific nature of historical discourse (Callinicos 1995: 9). But, what is worse, such a position may well lead to scepticism about historical knowledge (loosely a postmodern orientation) that is, so he claims, neither intellectually nor morally defensible. What is more, such a position throws out the judgement (that Callinicos wants to make as a Marxist) that historical knowledge must recognise an appeal to 'larger-scale theories of history' (ibid.).

What this means is that history must not only use concept and theory and be somehow scientific, but it also recognises it must have – perhaps incompatibly – an ontological dimension. Callinicos' ontology, that produces his metahistorical position, is Marxism. What is refreshing here is Callinicos' openness about his historical materialism and that this is the prism through which he thinks all sensible historians should view the past. Unlike reconstructionists and those scientific constructionists who deny the role of ontological pre-judgements in doing history, Callinicos not only recognises from where he comes (and where he wants history to go) but celebrates that potent mix of historical fact and political and social theory that makes history the most powerful tool available for shaping our culture and for dissenting from the present dispensations of global economic and political power.

Callinicos approves of the sociological theorist Maurice Mandelbaum's judgement that history cannot work without the historian accepting a theoretical commitment (Callinicos 1995: 92). To the well-known social science mantra 'no fact without theory' we might now agree with Fulbrook's recent claim of 'no history without theory'. As Callinicos says, the only choice the historian has is between a self-conscious taking on of social theory and an unstated dependence on an unspecified concept or theory. Defining the ontological judgements the historian makes about social reality as their 'assumptions' is not just a cop-out, it is to endorse the belief in common sense or the folk psychology of theoreticians like Mark Bevir. It seems to be less an aphorism and more an essential working principle of doing history in this constructionist world, that to understand history you must first know not only where the historian is coming from, but also where they intend to take you.

This is not, as Callinicos correctly argues, too much to ask. The modernist science-inspired desire to know, after all, requires us to question our own beliefs and assumptions as well as those of others in the process of acquiring knowledge. Every genre of history carries within itself the pre-judgements of its practitioners. We cannot argue, therefore, there is only one pre-eminent ontological pre-judgement or metahistorical position to be adopted. The nature of knowing things about the past cannot claim one privileged route – 'science' or 'art' – above all others. But what we should expect is that historians are deliberately self-conscious about how they theorise the present as well as past reality. After all, even the most obscure historical exercises can be used to promote and defend the big issues concerning the nature and development of our culture. It is important that we know what is really being argued when a historian examines the hands of heiresses.

History in a theory

The Marxist choice is for a historian the most theoretically explicit they can make. As a genre of history it is probably the most well known. It is also the most potent device for critiquing society. By comparison, other genres of theoretically informed history often seem less obviously so politically intrusive. But to believe this would be a fundamental error. Endorsing the epistemological model, for example, is itself a potent political statement. It is the argument that leads not just to the conclusion 'that facts speak for themselves' but also that such knowledge equates with true meaning. While it may seem common sensical to endorse this view, as I hope you will be aware by now, such a judgement has little of importance to say in the study of the past. The past, no matter how factual it may seem, does not speak for itself.

Examples of twentieth century history cast within an explicit theoretical framework are numerous, as you might imagine. But it is important to remember the improbability of being able in practice to usefully distinguish between a theory of history and history cast within a theory that can be tested via the evidence. Theories of history are usually better regarded as philosophies of history. By this I mean the past is approached through an (or a set of) ontological pre-judgement(s) that form an opinion on the past according to some desired or believed outcome as to what it means. In the language of philosophy this is a teleological explanation: the meaning of the past event is located in its conclusion, what it seemingly leads to. In other words, the state of affairs in which the historical process apparently culminates provides the explanation. For example, being an epistemological sceptic or a materialist or politically a liberal or conservative, or an idealist, or male or female, a member of a minority cultural group, or whatever, will produce in the present that past reality you think history has provided you with. This is essentially thinking backward from the ontological present to what you choose to believe is the epistemologically provided past. In other words, before applying a theory of explanation – a history cast within a theory – there pre-exists a grand narrative in the mind of the historian that explains everything as judged from the possible future through the present back to an assumed beginning. I would suggest all historians have these grand narratives and are, therefore, subject to teleological thinking.

The important point is not the acknowledgement of this or the conclusion that it is 'wrong' in some way, but how does the individual historian translate such pre-judgements into their preferred theories/hypotheses and concepts of historical explanation (their history cast within a theory)? Equally, how can historians reasonably claim they can escape their teleological philosophies of history? Trying to achieve this is, in effect, an intellectual Houdini act by which their philosophy of history is made to disappear within a theory. Instead of teleology there is causation. Instead of starting with the meaning of history, they claim to begin with open minds even though they have favoured theories they wish to apply to the past about cause and effect, the origins and development of structures in society, agency, contingency, etc.

That the tides of history ebbed and flowed in the last century is indicated by the rising popularity and then decline of theories that were borrowed from adjacent humanities and social sciences. With each borrowing the assumption was that each theory would give history an enhanced analytical bite. The major early twentieth century development of this kind was the original turn from events-based history via the French *Annales* School, toward wholesale borrowings from the disciplines of geography and sociology. Founded in 1929 by Marc Bloch and Lucien Febvre, the journal *Annales d'histoire économique et sociale* published history that was explicitly and self-consciously theoretical. The new history advocated in the journal's pages was novel insofar as the editors encouraged its contributors to capture the big structures underpinning the surface events of historical change. This led to the first major confrontation with the reconstructionist way of doing history. The editors actively encouraged borrowing theories and approaches from other disciplines (especially but not exclusively geography and sociology). In rejecting political history as a genre and conventional modes of thought, the journal was the first major European landmark in constructionist history. After the Second World War the journal continued under the editorship of Fernand Braudel whose advocacy and pursuit of total history was reflected in his book *The Mediterranean World in the Age of Philip II* (1949). Its self-conscious intervention in the past through its vast comparative dimension and its three measurements of time – the long run (*la longue durée*), the medium term of structural social, economic and political change, and the short term encompassing the actions of men and women – became a signpost to the profession. Reconstructionists insisted, of course, that it pointed in the wrong direction.

By the time I became an undergraduate history student in the late 1960s historians had come under three broad influences: those of universal laws of explanation based on Hempel's Covering Law Model (1942), historical materialism, as well as the continued popularity of rational action theory. By the 1960s, the first two of these three influences had confirmed the radical social science turn in the study of history. From what had been an early twentieth century empiricism shaped by sceptical common sense, to a third quarter twentieth century empiricism informed by sophisticated conceptual-isation and hypothesis, testing produced a history that took many forms. There was a new engagement with labour and class based history or history 'from below' as it was called. Then women's history emerged and soon turned into gender history. The old institutional economic history then mutated into the New Economic History heavily indebted to cliometrics. Imperial history was soon turned into subaltern studies, and social history was almost imperceptibly rendered into (enormous varieties of) cultural history. As I write this (early 2003) cultural history has now moved beyond the linguistic turn into something called 'culturalist history'.

Today history is more eclectic than ever before, as the social and political stakes have changed. The words of the historian Ernest Labrousse about the *Annales*, that it was concerned with the history yet to be invented, now apply more widely. The needs of the present are in the forefront of historians as never before as history struggles with its empirical-analytical heritage within the context of globalised capitalism and the demands of a wide diversity of social groups. The existence of journals such as *History and Theory*, *Clio*, *Common Knowledge*, *The Journal of Interdisciplinary History* and *Rethinking History: The Journal of Theory and Practice* evidence the growing interest in the nature of contemporary history thinking and practice. Increasingly, historians see their engagement with the past as starting with their problems in the present, not with the documents. The development of feminist history is the clearest case in point. As a genre of history it has become the arch constructionist historical enterprise quite simply because it was created and pursued in the early 1970s as a deliberate attempt to change contemporary society. As pre-judgements abounded from which half the population were excluded – positivism, Idealism, materialism, nationalism, and imperialism – so the determination of a new generation of women historians to destroy old notions of sexual identity grew and the present was turned into history.

Today, the variety of history and the battle over the character of the historical consciousness is matched not only by the proliferation of history journals, but books on 'what is history' and series such as the one this book is introducing. But regardless of the venue in which the battle is engaged (journal, book or classroom for that matter) history cast within theory must, as Callinicos points out, continue to meet three criteria (Callinicos 1995: 98–109). Each history cast within a theory must offer a structural explanation of the society with which it is dealing. Second, it must account for how it changes over time. And, finally, it must possess a sense of direction or a belief in the shape of an unfolding pattern in the past. But because of his desire to promote his own historical materialist pre-judgements, Callinicos, unfortunately perhaps, continues to reiterate the claim made by reconstructionists before him, that we can distinguish between a *theory of history* (or philosophy of history) and *history cast within a theory*. He says historical theories and philosophies can be distinguished because the former can be empirically tested and, if found wanting, abandoned and, of course, they are not teleological. They don't have an inbuilt direction. In other words, they are insulated from any ontological pre-judgements. Constructionist history can, by this logic, be truthful and have meaning as long as it is distinguished from the philosophy of history. The extent to which you are convinced by this argument will, of course, depend on how you view the role of theory in history, Marxist theory in particular, and the extent to which you believe you can distinguish 'being' from 'knowing' as you turn the past into that written cultural and aesthetic discourse we call history.

Conclusion

Methodologically constructionists adopt and adapt theories and concepts from the social sciences as well as apply their deductive logic (as Lloyd has done with Giddens and vast arrays of Marxists with Marx). Such activity suggests that the limits of nineteenth century empirical thinking have been reached (though its vestiges remain in reconstructionism). It seems very clear to most historians these days that the study of past societies cannot go on without the use of what they deem to be appropriate theory and concept and the power of inference both deductive and inductive and which many claim is scientific-like in approach. The adjunct to this is a critique of modernity that rejects the idea of any absolute knowing. But, as in Giddens' case, and it is probably the same for all late-modernists, the power of epistemology (exemplified in the logos and the correspondence theory) is still thought to ultimately conquer most of the epistemological errors conventionally associated with ideology and narrative-making. The argument remains that although we can only interpret reality through constructed knowledge, nevertheless, knowledge that is produced according to the basic principles of the epistemological model can overcome errors because such knowledge exists outside our mode(s) of inquiry. This, the residue of modernist thinking, remains not just active in constructionist or late-modernist thinking, but central to it.

Section Four

The-Past-as-History

Chapter 7

Narrative and representation

As the examples, among others, of Schama, Davis, Bisha and Gumbrecht have demonstrated, the main conclusion to be drawn from my brief introduction to the new historical thinking and practice is that our engagement with the past can only occur by understanding how we write and structure our historical narratives. My examination of the contending philosophies and epistemological approaches to history will conclude in this chapter and the one that follows with an outline of the structure of historical narrative. My key argument so far has been two-fold: that the study of the past cannot be insulated from the historian's ontological existence and that history is a form of representation. Because the conventional desire to maintain the distance between the historian and his/her history is not possible, I have argued that the historian must address that past within a much broader framework than simply that of the empirical-analytical. A pragmatic appraisal of the nature of history demands a recognition and understanding of its narrative-linguistic dimension as well. Even though historians may want to access past reality primarily as an act of empirical study it must remain essentially a function of their mind, their social existence and the narrative choices they make. In this and the final chapter I will explore the over-determining connections between the past, history and representation in pursuit of a wider understanding of how we can choose to think historically through the narrative construction of 'the-past-as-history'. I shall continue to argue that 'the past' will always remain integral to history. But, because history is *about* 'the past' it must always be epistemologically absent from it. An absent cause if you like?

The debate

The British social historian Lawrence Stone, as a good many social theory constructionists still do, once argued that those who endorse the linguistic or narrative turn imagine history is only about texts, with the reality of the past being crowded out. Such a referential-representationalist view is inaccurate and a misleading simplification. In another famous constructionist attack on narrative-making in history the Marxist historian Bryan Palmer described this linguistic turn as the descent into discourse. His point was that it was a dangerous emptying of the reality of the past out of history. Such concerns, he said, meant the fall from life into language and it was a choice we did not have to make. Palmer's belief (like that of Stone's) has, unfortunately, shaped the response of many historians both reconstructionist as well as constructionist to the linguistic turn.

One of the most well known and populist recent defences of the standard epistemological model, that of Richard Evans in his book *In Defence of History* (1997), is by a mainstream constructionist historian who thinks epistemological scepticism (he refers to it loosely as postmodernism) is irrational and is likely to lead to moral bankruptcy. It is the kind of thinking that believes, for example, film is nothing like history in its manufacturing process and is, because of that, always going to be an ersatz form of history. The confusion among such historians results from their assumption that there is an autonomous foundation of reality which *of itself* determines that literary production we call history and which, in turn, results in the conflation of 'the past' with 'history'. Such a category error leads them to the odd belief that the postmodernist's 'past' is the result of a rhetorical construction when, of course, it is 'history'. Palmer, for example, regrettably misleads us when he quotes Trotsky at the start of his book, that the beginning (of history) is the deed and the word is its phonetic shadow (Palmer 1990: 3). Whether Palmer, Evans and Stone like it or not, as a written language *about* the past and not its determined product, historical narratives are not 'in fact' lived the first time around. Reality may not possess a given narrative structure to be described as 'the story' of the actions of people in the past. If there is any benefit in this epistemological scepticism, it is the realisation that written history is not automatically coincident with the meaning of the past even though we may wish it were.

The reason why history is not truthful in the epistemological sense (of truth being the correspondence or correlation of word and world) is because all we have of our past reality is that which is known to us *through* its representation. To argue this is not, as Palmer tries to suggest, anti-realist and, therefore, anti-historical. According to Palmer's referentialist position, language must, at a basic level, be reflective of the knowable past. Language has to be the vehicle for conveying not just ideas but given meanings. But I would counter that language is not the written (or speech) equivalence of past reality. Language, among the many things it does, not only represents (and often it is pretty poor at that) but it also constitutes the cultural meanings of the past in the emplotments available in the present. Keith Jenkins has even gone so far as to argue (given these kinds of misunderstandings) that it might be better to do away with organised history and start afresh (Jenkins 1999).

But we do not have to do that. As the historian Robert Rosenstone has argued, whatever its empirical dimension history is '. . . a struggle in the present that we fight on the grounds of the past' (Rosenstone 1998: 142). In other words, our understanding of past reality is not through its *accurate* representation as a justified and propositional written rendition of that *thing* that once was, but is the result of negotiation of what it might mean through its pre-existing narrative meanings that are open to us now. History is not determined by 'the past' but is a far more complex process of over-determination that implicates the historian at its centre. Recognising this allows us to face up to history's state of undecidability and narrative indeterminacy (as for any written narrative).

If history is indeed an unavoidable process of narrative-making (as I choose to believe it is) two matters need to be examined. They are first (in this chapter) how we as narrative-making creatures organise what is our indeterminate interface with the past and why we should be happy to view the empirical-analytical dimension to history as part of a bigger over-determined narrative-making process. Then (in Chapter 8) we must assess the linguistic and textual (specifically the figurative) production of what we think the past means. What is important to historians now, or it should be if it isn't, is the connection between mind and past reality viewed, as Rorty says, as the relation between representation and what is represented (Rorty 1992: 371).

History turns: culture, discourse and narrative

While constructionism depends upon the quality of the analytical as well as the empirical connection made by the historian between action/event and structure, it also depends, like all genres of history, on the historical imagination and the construction of its form, that is, its literary representation. For epistemologically sceptical historians (like me) the early- to mid-twentieth century turn from reconstructionism into constructionism was and is not a particularly important matter. Whatever position was and is now occupied by the individual historian on the 'empirical to analytical' spectrum, ignoring the role of making narratives means (literally) only half the story is being told. In other words, even the most sophisticated constructionists – like Stone, Palmer and Evans – remain disappointingly epistemologically naïve because they never dispute the status of the once real in relation to its eventual incarnation in narrative. To put this as plainly as I can, they do not explore the distinction between the 'real object' and what it becomes 'as knowledge'. If they did then they may well become aware of the impossibility of 'discovering the real meaning' of 'the given past'. Not being epistemologically naïve means recognising the multiple determinations – empiricism, analysis, argument, ideology and narrative – through which we appropriate 'the past' or the once real in/as history.

As I have indicated, the key beliefs of those committed to the epistemology of 'know the past know the history' are referentiality, inference, the corres-pondence theory of knowledge, and of dualities such as those of subject and object, content and form, fact and fiction and knower and known. Of equal importance is the faith placed in the propositional truth conditional statement and the belief that this equals 'getting the story straight'. In other words, it is held that *the* narrative exists 'back there'. Specifically, it is to be 'found' embedded as Bevir says within agency and/or structure. The historian (aka the knowing subject) who can be epistemologically objective and who can generate mind- and language-independent knowledge can thus discover *the* story. And finally, this knowledge can be represented accurately as history (with language as the mirror of the past). Epistemological sceptics question all these beliefs. We argue that the epistemological position that insists we can represent the reality of the past results from not fully appreciating the nature of representation and its most essential characteristic, that of the unavoidable overlap of subject (historian) and object (the past) and the indeterminative nature of history.

Despite the views of Palmer, Stone, Evans etc, it is important to recognise that increasing numbers of historians have accepted this 'postist' position. The shift from the empirical-analytical paradigm toward the narrative-linguistic had its origin in the epistemological scepticism located in European decon-structionist and post-structuralist intellectual circles in the 1960s. For history the message (slow though it was to get through to the world of Anglo-American empiricism) was that this (the) epistemological model of history had ceased to be convincing in all of its particulars. In the past twenty years, therefore, increasing numbers of constructionists have begun to move beyond the debate over intentionality or social theory and even beyond the third way. They have begun to shift their idea of history as a construction, toward knowledge of the past that is predicated upon what may yet turn out to be a new paradigm – the new culturalist history. While still seeking something they might call meaning in the past, such historians recognise that historical reality is not just assembled from its empirical fragments, but it is a literary construction all through.

While it seems 'new histories' tend to arrive every generation, this latest 'new history' is different because through its stress on the over-determining and indeterminate connections between the past, language and social theory it acknowledges those changed conditions for knowing we have been experiencing in the age of late-(or post)modernism. As might be expected, a number of commentators and historians have cast this new situation of/for knowing in terms of the crisis that has recently developed in social history. Geoff Eley, for example, in the mid-1990s argued that the old social history with its claims to knowable social structures had given way before the recognition of the discursive nature of all cultural practices (Eley 1996). Among the growing though still minority list of constructionist historians willing to be epistemologically disobedient (in Keith Jenkins' provocative phraseology) are those like Patrick Joyce, Greg Dening, Richard Price, James Vernon, Simon Schama, Robert Rosenstone, and Joan Wallach Scott, and those less well known who may well constitute a further noncompliant generation such as Paolo Palladino, Wolfgang Ernst, Jon Walker, Patrick Finney, and Bryant Simon (all published in the journal *Rethinking History: The Journal of Theory and Practice*). None of these (to my knowledge) would call themselves postmodern historians as such but all are intellectual transgressors. All recognise that the hegemony of the epistemological paradigm should be confronted (at least upon occasion) because of its inability to account for the role of figurative and symbolic thinking in doing history.

Perhaps more challenging to many conventional historians than the work of Joyce, Dening, Schama, Rosenstone etc, was the foray of history into its graphic form with Art Spiegelman's *Maus I* and *Maus II* (Spiegelman 1986, 1991). Spiegelman's Holocaust narrative is told through the memories of his father as mixed allegory, style, and figure. Using the non-academic genre of the comic strip or, as it has been called, the graphic novel, Spiegelman defamiliarises the reader through many disruptive metaphoric techniques (the Nazis become cats and the Jews mice) and the drama and trauma is compacted and dislocated through the use of varieties of contrived imagery and dialogue boxes, family photographs, crematoria designs, etc. The trivial is mixed with the significant, big and small narratives intertwine, and there is a clear self-consciousness about the creation of the text with at one point a text-within-a-text reminiscent of Schama's use of René Magritte's 1933 painting *La Condition humaine*. The Spiegelman combination of serious topic and apparently flip form is a potent deconstruction of the concept of history as a formal representation of the past as it really was. Historians who want to confront established notions of historical genre are increasingly exploring these issues and what are its limits (Frey and Noys 2002).

Although he uses a more conventional form of written representation, among my list one of the most (in)famous practitioners of the new social history (or postist or post-social history) is the British social historian Patrick Joyce. Rejecting crude economic determinism but also moving beyond the popular dalliance with the relative autonomy of the social sphere and discarding the angst that still pervades much social history over either agency or structure, Joyce has moved outside the conventional conceptual categories (especially class) to a concern with the epistemological foundation of what he sees as the categories of social identity (Joyce 2001: 378). To this end he continues to disobediently explore '. . . the linguistic turn in terms of the relationship between the social and narrative' after the cultural turn (ibid.). Joyce's work reveals how some historians are shifting their gaze from the social and its structures to culture and its practices. This is the mediation (or practical result if you prefer) of what, at the epistemological level, is the turn from the empirical-analytical desire for 'the answer' through distanced objectivity, to the narrative-linguistic forms of competing and uncertain positions that result from our subjective perception and representation.

Lest there be any confusion, the culturalist turn is not to be confused with the study of the history of culture. It is not to be mixed up with the history of art, music, kinship relations, ideas, costume, manners or literature. The culturalist turn, for those (now post-constructionist?) historians involved, it is a matter of epistemology and it resulted from what a range of post-1960s historians, philosophers and critical theorists had noted: the return of history to a concern with narrative, symbol and representation as recognised in both the activities of people in the past and in 'doing history' in the present. For such historians, whether they still call themselves constructionists, or post-constructionists, deconstructionists, post-history historians (or have no label), or who self-consciously play with form like Spiegelman, they have not abandoned the empirical-analytical or the archive but they have moved into an exploration of the universe of representation and its rejection of one-to-one causal connection between 'the past' and 'history'. Once such historians began to question that the past worked according to structure (economic, political, social) or human action (motive, decisions) or some (more or less) complex combination of the two, they moved on to question the available forms of history and specifically the separations of subject and object and content and form. In other words, they wanted to explore what happens when they re-cast their engagement with the past to examine the symbolic or figurative negotiation between agency and structure, historian and the past.

While being mindful of the third way constructionist approach but not to be confused with it, this history turn toward culture has had the effect of revitalising both agency and structure. Social historians in particular are still seeking material causes while accepting that what agents thought at the time remains central to our understanding of change over time. The new culturalist history thus pays homage to the subjectivity of human agents in their own time and their own ontological-epistemological engagements. It recognises that human beings act in response to the concepts and those contemporary narrative representations – texts – through which they apprehended their reality. A further consequence of this new culturalist history has been a revival and re-theorising of biography as a historical genre. No longer regarded as 'history lite' biography has appropriated several methodological as well as epistemological orientations, not least the Marxist Antonio Gramsci's theory of the intellectual, Hayden White's theory of historical/literary forms, and a variety of biographer-historians have explored the collapse of subject and object as well as content and form (Edel 1984; Marcus 1994; Munslow 1992; Nadel 1984; Nora 1987; Olney 1972; Pachter 1981; Steedman 1986; Weiland 1999; Young-Bruehl 1998).

Using this text analogy – that historical actors existed as we do in a social universe of textual representation and narrative-making – we might wish to study the late nineteenth and early twentieth century American race leaders Booker T. Washington and W.E.B. Du Bois for their intellectual critique of as well as contribution to American race relations. In so doing the historian may see them as both working within as well as against a dominant white bourgeois enterprise culture (Munslow 1992: 110–147). For the American culturalist historian it might be imagined that the American age of corporatist industrialism created narratives within which such intellectual agents existed, negotiated, struggled against and complied with. Such a historian might then consider whether, if the logic holds that history is a narrative constructed in the here and now, it would have been thus in the past. Narratives defined as cultural discourses must clearly have an existence in the past, just as history as a cultural narrative does today. In other words, historical agents would have created their own meanings as they imagined their own cultural stories in the same way historians do.

As Roger Chartier has claimed, even when it is cast in its most severely structural forms history 'belongs fully to the realm of narration' (Chartier 1993 [1988]: 62). Indeed, for Paul Veyne historical explanation only exists when we emplot our history narrative (Veyne 1984 [1971]: 87). So, is it a matter of *either* empiricism/analysis *or* narrative? If we think both worked together in the past then they are likely to do so today as we write history. We write history no differently to how everyone else – past and present – wrote their way to an understanding of the world in which they exist(ed). It seems reasonable, then, to epistemological sceptics like me, to do away with the false opposition between historical knowledge and the narrative. Once this is done the question becomes one of understanding how individual historians deploy different types of narrative (and form) in their writing as well as how they may locate pre-existing historical narratives if they believe they can be found.

If they choose to believe the meaning of reality is created by the sign and signifier relationship that exists within (say) cultural or class or gender formations, then viewing the past as a sign system makes viewing history (as a cultural product of the historian) tenable in the same way (Jenkins and Munslow *The Nature of History Reader* 2004 forthcoming). And here we are brought back squarely to their ontological pre-judgements about how they see the connections between agency and structure (not to mention right and wrong, good and bad). It seems clear to epistemological sceptics that the preference for one history form over another will produce differing historical meanings. To put it in terms that should be familiar to you by now, choosing the form of the history will throw into relief the different ways in which the content and sources are selected, used and given meaning.

So here is the 'reality' of history. Reference to the sources, for most historians, guarantees that the past is knowable as it was. Hence the belief that we can be in touch with the reality that produced the evidence, and the typescript hard copy we eventually create can, if done honestly and with judicious balance, bring it back with substantial accuracy. In other words, the given story of the past exists behind history, which is only to be viewed as its expression/representation. This, realists argue, is what makes history not an invented story and certainly not a graphic novel, film or experiment. But, once it is admitted that history is a narrative constructed about other narratives then, in White's famous phrase, history can be seen as what it really is, a literary artefact, a fictive construction that is produced as much by the figurative imagination of the historian as its archival referent. We now have again to face the usual problem. Is history not merely indirect and heavily mediated, and perhaps even a fictive knowledge, or can it be truthful correspondence? A better understanding of the nature of representation and the structure of the historical narrative should help us with this question. To reach an understanding of the work of history – and by that I mean the over-determined construction and architecture of indeterminate historical narratives – the contribution particularly of Hayden White and Frank Ankersmit needs to be properly understood. But before considering the insights of White and Ankersmit, I want first to further reflect upon the legacy left to them and to us by Collingwood.

R. G. Collingwood and the historical imagination

The most potent tool available to the historian is his or her capacity to imagine metaphorical connections. Even though it was most clearly formulated by Hayden White, this isn't a new idea. R.G. Collingwood in the early part of the last century, in his famous sceptical discussion of the historical imagination, argued the historian would naturally take into account 'the ready-made statements of his authorities' (the sources), but what they believe to be true is 'not given in this way but constructed by his *a priori* imagination' (Collingwood 1994 [1946]: 243). Although believing in inference as the logic of history he argued the sources could not be viewed as the origins of inference. Instead Collingwood was driven to the conclusion that historical facts are nothing more than 'a pattern or black marks on white paper: not any historical fact at all, but something existing here and now and perceived by the historian' (ibid: 244) and what he called the 'web of imaginative construction' is something that is 'far more powerful than we have hitherto realised' (ibid.). He believed that ultimately we rely on our 'web of imaginative construction' for our history. Collingwood argues

> It is thus the historian's picture of the past, the product of his own *a priori* imagination, that has to justify the sources used in its construction. These sources are sources, that is to say, credence is given to them, only because they are in this way justified. [However] . . . Freed from its dependence on fixed points supplied from without, the historian's picture of the past is thus in every detail an imaginary picture, and its necessity is at every point the necessity of the *a priori* imagination. . . . The resemblance between the historian and the novelist . . . here reaches its culmination. (ibid.)

For Collingwood, historians should not address the content of the past expecting by its verification and the use of correspondence theory to generate its truth and meaning as a historical narrative. While we do not abandon the concept of truth by accepting the linguistic turn from epistemology, we create intellectual space for a history that emphasises the figurative basis for the emplotments, arguments and ideological modes of explanation upon which we are reliant for the meaning we ascribe to the past. This means a rejection of that unobtainable epistemological dogma of 'objective' explanation that privileges itself above all others. What Collingwood called 'the constructive imagination' of the historian creates a picture of the subject of their research. He claimed that this picture or mental image that appears specifically as a web of imaginative construction '. . . stretched between certain fixed points' of the documentary sources (Collingwood 1946 [1993]: 242). For him the historian's web of imagination depends for its validity not just on 'the support given by facts' but that it 'serves as the touchstone by which we decide whether alleged facts are genuine' and what they can mean (Collingwood 1946 [1993]: 244). As he says 'the truth is to be had not by swallowing what our authorities [the sources] tell us', but the fixed points themselves must be arranged, and our interpretation will eventually justify those sources used. While the historian stays unequivocally attached to the data, *making sense of what it means* requires it must be cast 'in every detail' as an 'imaginary picture' (Collingwood 1946 [1993]: 245).

As Collingwood insists, the resemblance between the historian and the novelist should be as clear as it is close. Each one constructs a mental picture that is a narrativised sequence of events, a description of situations, an analysis of agent intentions and motives, the proposal of structures and a study of characters. All of these elements are organised into a coherent narrative structure that encompasses strategies of explanation that will be conceptual in nature, based on argument and/or ethical judgements, and which seems plausible given the evidence selected. The novel and the history must both possess meaning and include that which is appropriate to making the story convincing or plausible. This means both the novel and the history are self-explanatory and, ultimately, self-justifying. This is because they are the products of the writer's and historian's *a priori* imagination. In other words, we cannot judge the narrative only by reference to the facts that supposedly live outside it.

This has been vividly illustrated in the work of reflexive historians like Greg Dening, Richard Price and particularly in Robert Rosenstone's two books *Mirror in the Shrine* (1988) and *The Man Who Swam into History* (2002). In *Mirror in the Shrine* Rosenstone is clear that the book (about the encounter between America in the shape of three American nineteenth century visitors to Meiji Japan) is also about the concerns of the author and his relationship to the story he is telling and how the past and present interpenetrate, 'an act of reconstruction and representation' (ibid: xi). In *The Man Who Swam into History* Rosenstone tells the story of his family over several generations using mixed voices and multiple tenses. This is not conventional history and, as the author admits, though factual, the story may not be true. There are, after all, many stories about the same past. This doesn't matter as long as they convey meaning. As this book demonstrates very clearly, creating an empathy with the past is surely at least as, if not more important, than any flawed attempt to resurrect the past under the belief that it comes back to us as it really was. Rosenstone's books make your imagination work, make you 'feel the-past-as-history'.

Price has long been associated with historical anthropology and his reflexive excursions into the nature of his own narratives. Recognising the cue provided by the 'godfather' Clifford Geertz, Price has variously explored the rhetorical aims of ethnographic based history, and the fractures that have begun to appear in the epistemological foundations of ethnography. Acknowledging that having tenure might have something to do with it, Price felt free to begin 'experimenting with narrative' from the late 1970s (Price 2002: 354). He began to argue and demonstrate how different historical and ethnographic situations lent themselves 'to different literary forms (and vice versa)' approaching each potential book by searching out 'or even inventing a literary form that does not come pre-selected or ready-made'. Best known of his experiments are *Alabi's World* (1990) in which he used different type-faces to represent different perspectives/voices, *Enigma Variations* (1995) in which truth and fiction are merged in order to explore fact and verisimil-itude, and *The Convict and the Colonel* (1998) in which 'the new ethnography' emerges. The point of all this is, of course, to explore the constructedness of narrative and how what we might call the new history is taking shape. The new history as demonstrated in this book is a liberating and potent mix of the past, personal memoir, indulgence in elegant writing, inventive form, defamiliarisation, a re-working of chronological time (flashbacks, cuts for-ward), is ideologically self-conscious (at one point using parallel columns for left and right wing sources), and de-privileging of 'key figures' that would characterise more usual histories of Martinique (the ostensible subject of the book). The book is an exercise in what Price calls 'postcarding' (ibid: 362).

Dening's reflexive history illustrates how casting the past as a performance highlights how the historian generates meaning through 'true storytelling' (Dening 1998; Dening 2002). Dening's history is performative – for himself and for others. The historian performs for others and the past performs for him/her. We can work in archives, discuss in disciplined discourse, reflect, observe, read, claim referential authority but ultimately we can only persuade through our story-making and telling (Dening 2002: 5–6). And for Dening this is the essence of our postmodernity. We must use our imagination to perform/tell even our true stories. By imagination he means the apt metaphor, defamiliarising the clichéd, working fictions 'in our non-fictions the better to be read' (Dening 2002). Dening insists to be historians we must begin by fine-tuning our imagination by describing our present – which for him is infused with the metaphor of the beach (Dening 1998: 146). As we soon realise, this suggests that everything we 'discover' about the past was the subject of somebody else's reflective discourse. Everything we know as historians begins with our own contemporary talk and the fictions in our own language and our own existence. Rosenstone and Price know that. And I am beginning to. Because we cannot experience the past, we have to dream it before we can tell it.

This Collingwoodian notion of providing the historical imagination with substance comes very close to White and Ankersmit's later narrativist arguments. No honest historian wants to construct a picture of things as they were not, or events as they did not happen and then pass them off as reality. But, it bears repeating, and as Rosenstone and Dening demonstrate, this is not the main issue. What is, is the role of the imaginative dimension in creating historical meaning. To respond to this concern demands understanding the active role of our human troping ability in creating meaning and conveying the plausibility of historical narratives.

What is of importance is that in representing the events and processes of the past historians make the same basic imagined connections between language and life (the word and the world) that all human beings do when they translate their thinking into narratives. Although he did not use the language of metaphor or figurative troping, Collingwood understood how we 'see' the connections (his 'webs of imagination') between objects. They are always in terms of part-to-whole and whole-to-part. This determines how we explain them. Troping, as the linguistic creation of meaning through comparison is, consequently, the only way historians can make past relationships visible – Dening's beach. We do this by establishing cause and effect relations through analogy and contrast. The tropes, understood as varieties of metaphor, provide the bond between knowing and telling. As Ricoeur suggests 'to instruct by suddenly combining elements [of reality] that have not been put together before' (Ricoeur 1994 [1978]: 33) is the function of metaphor and it is the essential mechanism by which the historian brings together (to colligate, imagine, mediate or emplot) the historical field they see before them in their own time and in their sources.

Figures of thought: the foundation of history thinking

As we shall see in this and the next chapter, the contribution of White and Ankersmit has been two-fold. In the case of White it was to use and apply literary theory. Initially in a Kantian way, White developed the theory of the tropes to capture past reality. Later, in a substantial epistemological shift to the construction of the history text as a form of representation that can only acknowledge the sublime or ineffable, he happily accepted the ultimately inexplicable nature of the past. Ankersmit's contribution was to take on the mantle of this later White and explore the production of the whole text from a non-Kantian position. So, while he acknowledges metaphor as central to the act of representation, he argues that we expect far too much from our representations of the past if we anticipate they will tell us what it really means.

Both White's and Ankersmit's insights will be pursued in the next chapter, but for the present any rounded view of how history works has to start with White's argument that we must understand the way in which realist literature works. All historians ought to possess an understanding of how figurative language creates the meaning we ascribe to the real world past or present. Assuming history – though dreamed – is indeed a realist literature, then knowing how to construct a narrative is just as important to the historian as knowing one's way around the evidence or understanding the nature of argument and concept, or having a sense of social responsibility. Indeed, sophisticated realists have few difficulties in addressing the truthful character of metaphoric descriptions. But, as realists, they have perforce had to claim that language can carry past reality onto the present written page. Hence it is that, for McCullagh and Ricoeur, truth can be a function of the use of metaphor in explanation. But, ultimately, this can only be based on adequate inference from the data even though it can only be carried to the page through analogue, resemblance, or substitution (McCullagh 1998: 75–82; Ricoeur 1984: 3, 1994 [1975]: 56). For others like me, and I suspect Dening, Rosenstone and Davis, this makes no sense. Once the move is made to the narrative level then rational and plausible explanation can certainly take place, but truth and objectivity as recognised by epistemology must be left behind. Representation, by its nature, cannot splice together reference with *its* presumed truth and meaning.

Historians need not accept that past reality and its traces exist and that they can be understood only through the historical narrative, but that even when based on the sources there is no given narrative in the past to be discovered and, therefore, represented accurately. There are, in other words and by example, many narratives in the same 10,000 factual statements of any history book. Of course, most historians know the narratives they write are not accurate pictures of past reality, yet most write them on the determinist assumption that the past is an object that is given and independent of the discourse through which it is appropriated and about which knowledge is created. The realist Ricoeur dryly observed: 'If history is a construction, the historian instinctively would like his construction to be a reconstruction'

(Ricoeur 1984: 26). Although the historian is implicated in what they write, convention insists he or she is not permitted by epistemological Canonical law to intrude *in any way* on the factualism of the past and from this the further assumption is made that historians can in some way opt out of history and into the past. The important issue is the deliberate disregard of the figurative or tropic modalities in which the historical imagination is framed. The result is the attempted degree zero writing of most historians, the effort at transparent and far from indeterminate textualism where the imaginative architecture is buried and ignored.

My argument is, therefore, rather straightforward. It is to point out what has generally escaped the attention of reconstructionists and constructionists, that the structure of the history text *is* a structure and, as such, it has a logic of its own. Its logic is not that of reflection of the empirical essence hidden in things in the past but, rather, as a form of explanation its power resides in its own structure – structure which is always more than the sum of its parts.

Collingwood, White and Ankersmit (plus a raft of others including Ricoeur, Arthur Danto, Peter Munz, Louis Mink and Jenkins) all seem to be agreeing with Rosenstone, Davis, Schama and Dening that *how* and, therefore, *what* historians think about the events of the past is undertaken through the structured use of figurative language. That is, historians, like everyone else, use (various forms of) metaphor to fix a meaning for the past. Although we can safely assume events occurred, our effort to understand what they mean can only be done through an act of representation engineered by our figurative language use. The history text, while it is clearly referential in nature in that it cites a real past, is a literary structure because its explanations are figuratively conceived and imagined. By definition, therefore, past reality can only be constructed as we imagine it rather than as we can vicariously experience it through the sources. It is this lack of direct sensory experience that language with its metaphoric basis can try to overcome if the historian so desires, but which it must also transgress and may turn out to be inadequate – indeterminate – for the creation of plausible meaning.

One reason why historians choose to ignore their metaphoric thinking is not just a woeful lack of basic training in the nature of representation but more importantly their logocentric desire for original meaning (which probably dictates their lack of knowledge about the nature of representation). Even those realists who have addressed what is usually (and over simplistically) called 'style' have not been able to move beyond the idea of the 'translation of reality into prose'. Peter Gay, for example, in his book *Style in History* (1988 [1974]) recognised that the historian was a professional writer, but while 'he must give pleasure' (sic.) Gay insisted it must be 'without compromising truth' (ibid: 4). Clearly, Gay works on the principle that truth can be 'found' and transferred into the medium of narrative. At the end of his detailed analysis of the style of historians like Gibbon, Ranke, Macaulay and Burckhardt, he still believes that the historian's 'use of elevated diction . . . synecdoche, anaphora, or whatever other devices he may use, perform reportorial functions' (ibid: 216). History thus remains a science in method and it corresponds to the past in outcome. For Gay there is no 'thea' in history, no place of seeing, only demonstration.

McCullagh, in a similar vein, feels it is safe to say that if the '. . . salient features of a metaphor *really do resemble* those of the subject of the metaphorical statement, then we commonly say that *the metaphorical statement is true* (my italics)' (McCullagh 1998: 77). By the same logic he maintains that metaphorical statements are false if there is no resemblance. This compounds Gay's mistake in not appreciating the nature and complexity of metaphor and representation. The point is that once logocentrism is challenged it becomes much easier to understand that the history narrative is not just a collection of single referential statements, but is rather an autonomous structured literary artwork the meaning of which, whether we like it or not or whether we realise it or not, is imagined rather than discovered. But, what is more, as the literary critic Northrop Frye argued almost half a century ago, literary meaning is always hypothetical. It has an assumed relation to the external world, and this assumption 'is part of what is usually meant by the word imaginative' (Frye 1967 [1957]: 74). Hence, as Rosenstone *et al.* know, what distinguishes different histories is as much dependent upon the form of the narrative, composed as it is of trope, argument, emplotment and ideology, as the content referred to.

If the shift from a simple factual statement to the level of conveying meaning is one of the essential functions of language then clearly that function is situated in what the philosopher Stephen C. Pepper called the root metaphors of thought and White has recently referred to as figures of thought – metaphor and its primary variants of metonymy, synecdoche and irony (Pepper 1970 [1942]: 84–348; White 2000: 393–394). These fundamental building blocks provide first for cognition, then understanding and, finally, meaning. Although they are manifested (in our texts) most obviously as our figures of speech or tropes, root metaphors or figures of thought literally '*pre-figure*' and thereby make the connections between historical events (the empirical) in Collingwoodian webs of construction cast as the three main strategies or modes of explanation adopted by historians, *viz.* emplotment, argument and the ideological or moral implications of these prior aesthetic acts. As White famously recognised when providing this, his model of the historical imagination in his book *Metahistory* (1973), there are two levels, the primary tropic or figurative level, and the determined level of explanation. The tropic or metaphoric level is comprised of the four elemental kinds of metaphor/webs of imaginative construction noted above. The level in which explanation takes place has three distinct aspects: those of emplotment or the story form chosen by the historian, the form of preferred argument or inference, and the ideological or moral stance the historian chooses to take in explaining how past reality works. It is here that their ontological prejudgements most clearly operate.

The logic of language, history and the historian

Even now, thirty years after the publication of *Metahistory*, many historians still find it difficult to accept three particular corollaries of the narrative-linguistic position of the new history. First, the emplotment does not pre-exist in the evidence. Second, the logic of inference (explanation via induction and deduction and the assigning of knowable intentionality) is secondary to the figurative capture and representation of the content of the past. And finally that a moral judgement is crucial to how we provide a meaning for it. In other words, that the metaphoric form which results from the exercise of the historian's imagination in which they first secure the past by choosing a period, a theme, a problem, an event, an intention, the wish to 'know things about' and their 'meaning', has a powerful pre-shaping authority over our historical knowledge, its interpretation and, therefore, the final meaning we 'find'.

At present the majority of historians are unprepared to accept that the mechanisms for this narrative-linguistic capture of the past (its content, our objects of study) are the figures of thought with which all human beings are endowed. Though these figures of thought are our thinking control mechanisms, the fact that they become manifest as various kinds of figurations when we speak or create written narratives seems a trope too far. Nevertheless, these figures constitute the images and connections between them that serve to signify a reality (past and present) that can only be imagined rather than directly perceived. The historian Carolyn Steedman chose to entitle her 2001 study of the role of the archive in doing history *Dust*. Herbert Butterfield in *The Whig Interpretation of History* (1973 [1931]) concludes his thoughts on history likening it to 'a harlot and a hireling' (p. 94). The historians Anna Green and Kathleen Troup give their book the title *The Houses of History*

(Green and Troup 1999). History could not exist as a form of cognition without our capacity for metaphoric thought. What this means is that history cannot be determined in its final instance by the empirical alone. There is always something other than 'the past' at work. That this is increasingly recognised does not mean it is either fully understood or adequately theorised.

As history is a performative discourse written *about* the past we always have several narrative options when we describe past happenings. It seems the only problem is to choose which mechanism is most appropriate for deciding what is 'the best option'. This issue has caused enormous conflict among historians. White was roundly attacked in the debate over whether events like the Nazi Holocaust could be emplotted in ways other than as a tragedy. Surely, given the nature of certain events there could only be one given emplotment? This argument relies upon the empirical-analytical belief that 'the facts' determine 'the meaning' of an occurrence. In other words, 'the facts' referee between meanings. Hence, through their comparison and verification, 'the facts' will 'tell us' what they most likely mean. Though this sounds convincing it does not recognise the complexities of turning the reality of the past into that written cultural discourse we call history. From the narrative-linguistic perspective 'the facts' are 'in fact' ultimately a function of the ontological pre-judgements made by the historian about events.

This is illustrated by the contemporary history of life in the French occupied zone internment camp at Gurs near the Spanish border by Pnina Rosenberg (Rosenberg 2002). Between 1939 and 1943 thousands of foreign nationals, both male and female, were interned in Gurs. The internees were determined to maintain a cultural life as can be seen in the large number of paintings and drawings that survive, especially the portrayal of daily life in the graphic booklets of Horst Rosenthal. Rosenberg uses the small booklet produced by Rosenthal called 'Mickey Mouse in the Gurs Internment Camp' to illustrate how the horror of life could be addressed at the time but also now as a commentary on the graphic novel genre of historical analysis. In Rosenthal's booklet charming illustrations of Mickey Mouse are interleaved with raw ironic texts. The source raises the question for Rosenberg whether only a fictional character could manage such a vicious reality. In turn this raises the poignant question of why the historian cannot do something similar. What necessary constraints are there? Not only would this challenge accepted thinking and practice (not in itself necessarily a 'bad thing'?) but far more significantly satirise unthinking historical epistemological conventionality. The only question is whether irony is, after all, a legitimate emplotment for all forms of narrative. Or are there some historical subjects above irony? If so, are some above other forms of emplotment? The answer is yes, but only if you choose to believe in a given story with a given meaning and, hence, a given ethic. And if this is so then we have a severe case of the epistemological tail wagging the dog. And Mickey could never be sent to Gurs.

Strictly speaking the logic of history conceived of as a narrative-linguistic as much as an empirical-analytical enterprise dictates that, uncomfortable though it may be to some historians, we are free to choose the form our history can take in just the same way we can elect to apply one social theory or another, or choose to believe in contingency and agent intentionality, or some more or less complex combination of those things. We can elect to cast any set of single referential statements 'of fact' into an imagined and aesthetically preferred and tropically in*form*ed narrative as we pursue their collective meaning. The implication is that beyond the referential sentence narrative plausibility – narrative truth – is the primary measure of history. If the narrative is now constitutive of the empirical (not its existence but what it means) it raises the matter of the comparative compulsions of the real and its narrative representation. In effect this comes down to the same perennial question that arrives in the wake of the rejection of the model of the physical sciences for history. This is the re-definition of truth in history through the conflation of subject (historian) and object (the past as history). It is because narration is the natural environment for history that the new history is seen as primarily an interpretative activity rather than an explanatory one. Narration is at once the way in which a historical interpretation is realised and it is also the mode of discourse in which a successful understanding of the past is represented. We can reach an understanding in history, but we cannot explain as scientists do.

What, then, is the reality of historical representation? It exists somewhere in the links between language, history and the historian. Given their ontological existence it is impossible to easily distinguish the historian from what they write. What this means is that it is only when the historian writes history that he or she exists as a self-conscious entity engaged with the past. When the historian connects with the reality of the past they are also speaking to and creating themselves. Many historians have written self-consciously like this, in what several commentators have referred to as the middle voice. As Rosenstone has argued, one way to circumnavigate the limits of representation in order to engage with the past and what it might plausibly mean is to tread a path between the voice of distanced and objective scholarship and the subjective voice of poetry and fiction (Rosenstone 1996: 216). Originating in Greek grammar it refers to those verbs that designate an effect on the subject instanced by the action expressed in the verb. Thus, in history what is going on is equivalent to the historian saying 'I am providing the testament of the past'. This suggests the active participation of the historian through the writing of the historical narrative. In other words, the form, rationality and meaning of events result from the historian's narrativisation.

It is this realisation that led White (and others who tend to publish in journals like *Rethinking History: The Journal of Theory and Practice*) to argue that certain modernist events cannot be understood within the conventional conceptions of historical representation. In other words, trying to maintain the fiction of the distinction between subject and object will never permit the historian to 'get close to' the meaning that may exist within certain 'modernist events' (like total war and technologically and scientifically organised genocides). Understanding the past (by the subject) means working through the collapse of subject and object. To put it very plainly, our ontology is central to our epistemological wants. Only in this way can history *really* function to grasp *the* meaning of the past if, lamentably, we insist there is one. It is only when the historian defines themselves in relation to the past by overtly writing themselves into it, that any knowledge about the past can be derived.

White has had cause to experience a great deal of personal and professional abuse, especially from reconstructionists like Arthur Marwick and Geoffrey Elton, because of his claim that the past can only be appropriated *through* history and the associated argument that most historians (especially reconstructionists) cherish – the unobtainable goal of historical truth. The reason it is unobtainable is that there is no direct access to a pre-tropic or pre-figurative past reality. The great irony in all this is that White has, of course, been the most realistic of historians because he has had the conviction to point out the problems with the epistemological approach. As I have also argued, the reality of doing history is that it is a literary as much as it is an empirical and an analytical activity. While historians acknowledge that the past and history are not the same thing, they generally fail to pursue what this logic leads to. The logic requires us to consider that because history is a literary creation it allows us to inventively and innovatively explore the consequences of the unavoidable collapse of subject (author) and object (their history narrative).

Conclusion

In the absence of propositional correspondence truth in narrative representation, what is good for us to believe about the past becomes of central importance. In the absence of truth defined in such a way we must rely on our ethics, generosity toward and respect for the views of others, personal integrity, political awareness, and as strong a sense of social responsibility as we can muster. If we believe meaning in history is not found but is produced as much by our narrative construction as the archival sources or our inferences, then writing about the past is an ontological matter through and through. While the single propositional sentence may be justified, the step into narrative takes us beyond the epistemological, and it demands we understand the structure of narrative for it is only in this way that any claim to truth concerning the past can be made. I will turn to this in the next and final chapter.

Chapter 8

History is historiography

In this chapter I shall explore the consequences of the argument that the new history is characterised by the rejection of empirical foundationalism. The idea that history is ultimately determined by 'what happened' in the essentialist sense that it possesses its own given meaning, is giving way to a much more sophisticated engagement with the past. It has been said that in history all judgements are challengeable and all conclusions are provisional (Lamont 1998: xi). Well, of course they are, but not just for the reasons normally given. It is never only or just a matter of combating the dominant interpretations of individual historians or even schools of history by debating the use of historical sources or by bringing new evidence to bear. What remains unacknowledged in such a belief is the deep-seated epistemological issue of history as an over-determining process of figuration, narrative-making and emplotment, analysis and argument, ideological and moral explanation, *as well as* empiricism.

Let me be clear on this point. I am arguing that history is historiography because historiography is, in its essence, the making of narratives. In other words my description of the historical enterprise as 'the-past-as-history' signifies history's status as a narrative about the past. If all we have is reality and language then history should be seen as what it manifestly is: a written discourse about the past and pre-existing narratives. Strictly speaking, then, there is no history only historiography defined as what we write about the past in order to understand it. The implication is that – ironically – history defined as the analysis of sources ceases to be a useful definition of what it is that historians mainly do. Obviously, historians still examine and refer to sources, but that activity takes place within the over-determined process of narrative-making. The primacy of the empirical is, therefore, replaced by the discursive. This 'saves' history from the simplification of determinism and places the philosophy of history back on the agenda.

Given this I will now briefly examine the implications of the idea, a central plank of White's and Ankersmit's analyses of history, that there is no useful cognitive distinction to be made between history thought of as a series of complex *representations* of the past and *representations* of imaginary events. By foregrounding the fabricated and narrativist nature of our acquaintance with the past, the process I have called the-past-as-history, we have seen already how the implications for conventional notions of reference, the distinctions of form and content as well as between subject and object, and truth, objectivity, and the origin and production of meaning are radically challenged. The final question is, therefore, what does the structure of the-past-as-history look like?

Description and representation in the historical narrative

I have been suggesting that in history truth and meaning derive not simply from the raw data. The idea that knowledge of facts will give you knowledge of what they mean because they contain a given meaning, even if it were correct, ignores the further fact that we are narrative creatures with an impulsion to both create narratives and to interpellate or call others into subject positions through them. This is not to fall into the 'epistemic fallacy' whereby objects/things are reduced to discourse. It is, however, to argue as I have done, that while single factual sentences are propositional and work through inference, history narratives are not like that. The narratives we create allow us to move beyond epistemology just as painting and sculpture moves us beyond what they represent and they allow us to constitute our social existence as well. As Ricoeur, White and Ankersmit collectively remind us, the representation is only a substitute for what it represents but that process of representation carries within it a whole framework of power and meaning creation (Ricoeur 1986 [1978]: 216; White 1987: 1; Ankersmit 2001).

I have suggested that knowledge of how narrative works will help historians to better understand the full reality of the translation of knowing into telling and they should start by appreciating that a representation is not the thing-in-itself; it is a replacement or proxy for it derived for a purpose. I have set myself against the extremes of idealism and empiricist factualism being in favour of the pragmatism of a structured linguistic mediation that acknowledges the historian's ontological existence. As Hegel's insight has it history denotes what happened, the contemporary narratives of those happenings, and then the historian's later re-narrativisation. But it is more than even this. When we narrate the-past-as-history we are requiring not just closure but also moral meaning (White 1987: 21). This moral meaning is potent in direct proportion to the strength of the claim to the objectivity of the text defined as the discovery of *the* story in much the same way that realistic painting can be claimed to be an accurate rendition. The American Edgar Cameron's 1884 painting *Niagara Falls in Winter* can be seen as a rendition of this sort which tells us what it was like and invokes a meaning for us. But as a representation we are also free, if we choose to be, to generate our own sense and meaning of the majesty of Niagara Falls in winter. This can be viewed as a form of truth if we want. The fact that it isn't the thing-in-itself nor a facsimile, that its individual brush strokes do not correspond to actual floating ice, is irrelevant to the process of creating its meaning. And we don't worry about it. We enjoy it for what it is and for what it can tell us within the confines of its form. It is, in other words, a narrative truth – a truth created by the nature of the construction of narrative – rather than its reflection of reality.

Surely, we are told, this cannot apply to history. Even though it is the overall effect of the historical text that gives the past a meaning, aren't the single truth conditional statements in every history text meant to be (unlike Cameron's brush strokes) an accurate representation of past reality and cannot be regarded as a substitute? But once it is 'put together' the historian's picture can, like the painting, be epistemologically only *true to itself*. While both the painting and the history text do, of course, possess referentiality, they become and exist only as representations, as historiography. Like a painting the historical text is always an exercise in the historian's imagination, in 'seeing' patterns in the past (for the painter such patterns would be made up of light and dark as they observe the vista before them). While sentence-length descriptions are meant to refer directly to what happened (the vista), the substance of narrative descriptions functions to propose plausible relationships between them – not of light and dark but of actions and decisions by historical actors, social and other structures and the historian's judgements about the character of social change and his/her ethical decisions.

Narratives are, in Ankersmit's phrase, literary *theses* about promising ways of organising the past. Language must, thereby, substitute for reality like a painter's brush strokes that are composed into an effect. As soon as the historian has chosen their subject matter the next choice is how to convey the idea of interpretation of the past as a narrative. With each sentence a judgement is made about whether the new piece of information connects to what has been previously said and whether it takes the history in the direction required. Context, like the tonality of the painting, is created to produce an overall effect of time and place. Explanations are then sketched bearing in mind the constant shift from specific to general and back again. Histories, like paintings, evolve in their creation. Rather than copying what they observe in crude empirical fashion, historians normally look to their subject matter initially with no idea how they are going to describe it. But then they will think and write, write and think. Because of this, every history is personalised and written in the middle voice. Just as the painter's brushwork provides the stylistic signature of a painting, so the historian's powers of representation and figuration personalise their histories.

As painters recognise, an edge in a painting is the meeting of two forms, which carry different meanings. An orange fruit will have a soft edge because it represents a curve; the corner of a building has a sharp edge because it represents 90-degree converging planes. Similarly, historians construct their representations by locating foreground and background and use sources in different ways to lend depth and perspective, the curves and planes of meaning. Again like a painting, just as the brushstroke is a representation of shape, light and form, the narrative construction of the historian is not a literal translation of the subject matter. Just as the painter might use a palette knife to create terrain textural effects, a historian will select an apt metaphor to create a textual effect. In history all this constitutes the realistic effect. This is not dangerous for the past or demeaning to the people who lived in it because like the naturalist painter, most historians assume the effect is a realist one. But, we must always remember that history is not the same as the past. Like the painting, it is the historical narrative's substitution or 'aboutness' which clues us to history's proper status as a secondary form of manufactured knowledge. It provides narratives with their fictive truths.

The logic of the narrative is, as we know, that it is more than a (large) collection of descriptive propositional/truth conditional sentences. As Collingwood suggested, empty data have to be used by us to build up more or less complex historical *descriptions*, or what Ankersmit calls 'narrative substances'. Examples would be 'The Tudor Revolution', 'The Pequot War', 'The Gupta Empire', 'The Tragedy of Vietnam', 'Margaret of Austria', 'The Strange Death of Liberal England', 'The Velvet Revolution', 'The Age of Improvement', 'The Battle of Britain' and so on and so forth. Like Van Gogh's *Sunflowers* or Picasso's evocation of the Minotaur, the imaginative constitution of these substances takes us from the sources/data to the created 'historians' facts' and on to historical descriptions that soon become full-fledged generalisations within larger narrative structures. These are the layers within a narrative just as subject matter, toning the canvas, sketching in the subject, blocking in, brushwork and handling edges are in painting. From the point that the historian deems it appropriate, he or she shifts a gear to the explanation of their understanding of what it all means. This is the narrative layer of the composition of their historical interpretation.

Take the following list of what would be regarded by most US historians to be sentence-length truthful statements (of fact) that can be empirically justified:

- Two US resident Italians called Nicolo Sacco and Bartolomeo Vanzetti were arrested for payroll robbery and murder on May 5th 1920
- The US Immigration Act was passed in 1921
- Hiram Wesley became the Imperial Wizard of the Ku Klux Klan in 1922
- In 1922 the US writer Sinclair Lewis published a book called *Babbitt*
- In July 1925 the US ex-Secretary of State William Jennings Bryan was the prosecuting attorney in the trial of John T. Scopes when the latter was charged with breaking a Tennessee law that forbade the teaching of the theory of evolution in its schools
- Nicolo Sacco and Bartolomeo Vanzetti were executed in the electric chair in August 1927
- H.L. Stimson was appointed President Herbert Hoover's Secretary of State in 1929

All of these statements are *true* in the sense that they accord/correspond with the available evidence of things that occurred in time and space, and no historian who values their professional reputation disputes their (f)actuality. Such statements cohere with the past upon which most historians agree. It is true, according to the coherence theory of truth, for example, that Constantinople fell to the Turks in 1453 because most historians agree on the truthfulness of that statement (Stanford 1994: 124–125). Thus it is that, according to conventional empiricist thinking, only by providing new data that falsifies a hitherto accepted statement can new interpretations or meanings be produced. What this means is that description can only operate at the single sentence level. 'Nicolo Sacco and Bartolomeo Vanzetti were executed in the electric chair in August 1927' is a justified description. It contains referentiality (Nicolo Sacco and Bartolomeo Vanzetti) and it states a property the speaker is justified in believing it has (both were executed in the electric chair in August 1927). This subject-predicate state of affairs, because it does not apply to the level of historical narrative representations, must cast doubt on the philosopher John Searle's argument that there is a knowable past reality independent of our representations. Even though they accept that our representations are relative to an arbitrarily selected set of concepts, most historians still work according to the belief that the ultimate arbiter remains 'it really happened or it didn't' in the creation of meaning (Searle 1995: 161). Accordingly, there can only be dispute with inaccurate single propositional statements. Ultimately, it would seem, only right or wrong facts count and what they mean is beyond language. But this is a dangerous, unwise and unwarranted belief when writing history.

It is both dangerous and unwise if we want to give a meaning to America in the 1920s (and its importance to us today). It is unwarranted once we begin to understand the literary constructedness of history. What this means is that the historian has to create a narrative in which he or she composes their preferred list of propositional factual statements (from the millions available to them) *in a particular way*. What is at issue is not the epistemological status of those statements that most historians agree upon according to the evidence (e.g., the US Immigration Act was passed in 1921). The issue is how such descriptive statements (the facts) or others that are constituted by one historian's 'reading' of the archive, are ordered and 'put together' through the mechanisms of emplotment, argument, use of concepts and ethical judgements to form a coherent and plausible structure of historical interpretation of the events to which they refer. The past world – which is dead and gone – is indifferent to how we choose to represent it.

Because the new history is not foundationalist it admits all it knows about the past is fallible but not only in the sense of empirically falsifiable. The new history recognises that its statements of meanings are always located in discourse even when a claim is made to the so-called extra-discursive. As I hope will be clear by now, what I am saying is that the act of writing a meaningful historical narrative is where the historian's own ontological beliefs and decisions about how the present and the past are turned into the realm of the epistemological. The historical narrative, rather than presenting the 'findings' of the archive, is the site where different strategies of explanation operate, not least the aesthetic and moral as well as the empirical and the rational. While the real past may not alter, what is knowable and believable about it, and what it means as history, can never be fixed except within and by the architecture of the historical narrative.

F.R. Ankersmit: from epistemology to narrative

Assuming that what the past means is not determined by what the past was like, but by the language used by the historian as he or she speaks about it in the present, then clearly history must be subject to the ontological considerations of *our* being and existence. Echoing White, Ankersmit contends historical knowledge is made as much by the historian's language as it is 'found' in the sources (Ankersmit 2001: 30). This does not mean you can't be an empiricist and/or cannot be analytical. Historians have to be referential, rational but also representational. However, the argument of many historians that they can endorse a particular version of a realist epistemology *and* accept convenient bits of the narrative-linguistic argument is, plainly, wrong. This is the position of those empirical-analytical historians who say something like 'postmodern history usefully reminds us of the role of language in doing history even so we must stick to basic epistemological principles'. Such thoughts reveal an elementary misunderstanding of how history works through the distinction between sentence-length description and narrative representation (Tosh 2001; Evans 1997; Windschuttle 1995).

In Chapters 2 and 4 I talked about the correspondence theory of knowledge and the nature of truth, I challenged not only the crude realism that still lurks in the minds of some historians but also the referential-representational thinking of most historians. While accepting that past reality once existed independent of our minds and writings, I rejected the notion of its accurate representation (and by implication the correspondence or even the correlation theory of truth). I suggested it is impossible for the historian to escape from narrative into the past. I also argued that being an anti-representationalist (as I am) is not the same as being anti-realist. The question I was raising (and which is one important reason for writing this book) is whether, when we make narratives, we can remain in touch with past reality beyond the single propositional or truth conditional statement. In their different ways I invoked Kant's idealism, Rorty's pragmatism and Ankersmit's representationalism in support of my judgement that what is really important about history is how we construct it as a form of literature beyond the level of the single descriptive and referential sentence. While the content of the past is our external reference point, how we construct its meaning (our interpretation) is as much about writing as it is about empiricism and analysis.

The provocation to the epistemological model of accurate and frictionless representation comes today from those philosophers of history whose thinking has supported the new culturalist history. In other words the justified historical description championed by McCullagh, Bevir, Bunzl etc, has been confronted even by those like Zagorin, Iggers and Chartier who, while they do not accept the mirror of nature as the metaphor that best suits the history project, nevertheless accept justified belief about 'the given event', the accurate understanding of causation, the match of the word and world, the logos, 'the truth'. Chartier has even gone as far as trying to outline the rules of 'truthful narration' as he calls it in his pursuit of the accurate representation of the real external referent or object (Chartier 1993 [1988]: 63–67). The first Chartier rule is to become aware of the factors that govern the 'discursive practices of representation' akin to Foucault's so-called genealogical study of what brought our textual sources into existence. Described in his books *The Order of Things* (1966) and *The Archaeology of Knowledge* (1969) Foucault points to the connections between discourses, habitual and customary practices, discipline-based ways of thinking and those dominant representations that characterise historical epochs or epistemes as he prefers to call them.

Chartier eventually hedges his bets in much the same way as do Appleby, Hunt and Jacob with their practical realism, and Bevir, Bunzl, Iggers and McCullagh in their own ways. While Chartier at least recognises the problematic nature of the relationship between representation and the practices represented, at the end of the day he still endorses the epistemological model by insisting that historical statements must be capable of being checked for their accuracy against the evidence and that this will clue us to what it all means. Although he acknowledges historians have moved decisively from a conception of language and narrative as just mimetic activities, this acknowledgement has not freed him from the idea of history as facsimile. This is because of his ultimate inability to let go of the belief in the mimetic power of representation. Like the novice swimmer he is afraid that without the empirical-analytical buoyancy aid he will drown. Well, I suppose you might, but only if you panic.

The leading thinker on the nature of representation in history today is Frank Ankersmit. Working from the belief 'that language is the principal condition for the possibility of all knowledge and meaningful thinking' Ankersmit has subjected the history text as a whole to its most searching analysis (Ankersmit 1983, 1989, 1994, 1995, 2000, 2001, 2002). As he points out, history is what most people think of as truthful representation *par excellence*. Consequently, its failings in this respect are all the more difficult to accept. His analysis of 'narrativism', by which he means the study of the historical text as a whole in order to distinguish it from the single descriptive statement, is at the centre of his investigation.

Conventional thinking focuses (as we saw when discussing McCullagh in Chapter 3) on the propositional truth conditional statement. The unstated assumption is that history consists entirely of such statements. This thinking precludes examination of the narrative substance of the text as a whole. As I have argued, how historians represent an event or action is highly significant when the single historical statement of cause and effect is embedded within

the overall text(ual representation). While the effort of historians is expended producing the research-testable propositional statement of what happened, the textual level remains forgotten and is still viewed as mere report. Once again, epistemological history thinking misses the point. The translation from past reality to a sentence, while it has the appearance of being a statement of the real, can only possess *meaning* when it is embedded in a discursive text. Indeed, as Peter Munz has pointed out, many descriptive sentences in themselves are actually interpretative and, therefore, not amenable to strictly empirical verification (like saying 'Montezuma was Cortés' puppet', or referring to the period of the late eighteenth century in US history as 'an American Renaissance'). The point is very simple. It is not a matter of arriving at the factual sentence (i.e., the event under a description) and then assuming this somehow becomes objective history when lots of them are put together. The problem is *how* are the factual sentences put together? How this is done not only constitutes meaning and the 'narrative truth' of history, but it also directly affects what facts are used and why. And these decisions are normally made early on in the historical 'investigative' process.

Historians have a real problem here as Ankersmit, with admirable relentlessness, points out (Ankersmit 2001). We can't stop at factual statements. We must create a narrative out of them as the intellectual space where the imaginative and interpretative acts take place. But the process of making these narratives is barely acknowledged. Few historians explain (or are aware of?) their figurative assumptions or emplotments, not to mention their ontological pre-judgements. If they are self-conscious about their arguments and ideological positions they still remain oblivious to how these are mediated in *and* precede their narratives. The reason for this ignorance can only be their training. Historians are not made aware in history boot camp that their narratives, the vehicles for interpretation, meaning and explanation, cannot be verified in any epistemological sense. Hence historians are condemned to remain silent on the cognitive nature of their narratives. If the logic of proof does not apply to history then neither, as I have argued, does the idea of discovery – and certainly not at the narrative text level.

The correspondence theory of truth cannot apply to the historical narrative in the way it applies to the propositional truth conditional sentence. Truth defined in correspondence terms can only be said to exist (if it does at all) in history at the sentence/statement level. Texts and narratives on the other hand are imaginary. They are fictive constructions and cannot, by definition, be epistemological entities. Every narration carries meaning but unfortunately it also suppresses and disguises the mechanism by which it legitimises knowledge. It is important to any adequate understanding of the work of history – and by that I mean the construction and architecture of historical narratives – that the contribution of Ankersmit and White is properly understood.

Ankersmit (not to forget a further long list of epistemic sceptics like White, Pepper, Ricoeur, Kellner, Mink, Munz, Jenkins, etc) has pointed to the need for a comprehensive theory of representation that takes into account the reality of the past *and* its translation into the discourse of history. Ankersmit has shown historians how to do this in his recent work, much of it being collected in his book *Historical Representation* (2001). In this explanation of the nature of representation he has forced historians to address a new agenda. Working from the well-established position that the chances for the accurate representation of the past are slim primarily because of doubts over the theory of correspondence as the link between reality (the represented) and language (representation), this becomes impossible once we work up to the level of the work of art, painting, history, etc. This is put as the doubt that what exists in the one has a counterpart in the other. Because of the categorical difference between language and reality, to be realistic in our understanding of history we must abandon ideas of truth cast solely in epistemological terms (Ankersmit 2001: 275).

Ankersmit is insistent that there can be no descriptive counterpart in representation to that which is represented. His logic is that correspondence demands that if our 'description of the represented were false for its representation (or vice versa), there would be no correspondence between the represented and its representation' (ibid: 276). Hence correspondence and truth would require that the past and history 'are identical if and only if they are identical under each description of the two' (ibid: 276). Ankersmit quotes the philosopher Nelson Goodman to the effect that an 'object resembles itself to the maximum degree, but rarely represents itself' and as Virginia Woolf is reported as saying 'Art is not a copy of the world; one of the damn things is enough' (ibid: 276).

What makes Ankersmit the most significant historical thinker today is the nuanced nature of his argumentation. He reasons that our postmodernist age is exemplified by the attack on representationalism. Further he argues that reality and language will always differ and correspondence cannot work. However, it is this that makes representation what it is. I would interpret this as saying that the space that exists between the represented and its representation is filled by historiography. The epistemological gap between the represented and its representation is the site of history or, to be more precise, the-past-as-history. It is the site of its figurative processes, its emplotments, arguments, theories, and moral meanings. Because a narrative is not just a collection of subject-predicate descriptions of events, its architecture of strategies of understanding function to create a meaning that while it lacks correspondence, it is as I have argued more than the sum of its referential parts. The historical narrative provides a value added dimension to the past. This calls our attention (or it should do) to its narrative truth characteristic. Narrative truth I define as that meaning which we construct in lucid, rational, cogent and well-argued referential narratives and is not dependent on correspondence theory. This is plainly because the predominant feature of even the most realistic/referential of narratives remains their historiographic nature: their fictive and figurative construction. It is this literary architectural design that produces the narrative truth that is the essential characteristic of history as a discipline. It is not a matter of anti-truth but of which kind of truth you want to endorse and adopt.

Hayden White: figuring the past

If Ankersmit is right in assuming the historical narrative is not propositional then its logic must be figurative. Our stories, arguments and moral positions are the mediations that result from how we figuratively connect those separate fragments of reality that are presented to us (the historical field before us). This argument is encapsulated in White's now famous epigram that we should be concerned with the content of the form. If we want to seriously address how historians think and work then we cannot continue to operate only at the level of the document, the concept, and the inference. We must also address the tropic or figurative construction of thought. This, not referentiality, is the key to a realistic appraisal of the architecture of our history thinking and practice as it is in all non-scientific narratives. It is by our power of figuration that we make the connections between cause and effect, agency and structure, and address matters of epistemological scepticism, relativism, political power, and the improvisational in doing history.

You will recall how I have defined the empirical-analytical or epistemological model of history as comprising a belief in reality as known through its sources, correspondence, intentionality and inference. I cast doubt on the logic that holds the last three principles necessarily follow from the first two and, in addition, that this model fails to make space for the narrative-linguistic constitution of meaning. The-past-as-history, therefore, has a layered and interlocking structure of composed narrative that has several elements: single descriptive statements of justified empirical belief, the logic of the trope, an emplotment that gives sense to the passage of time and our inference of the meaning of human actions, an argument about the relationship between agency and structure and cause and effect, other explanatory concepts and theories and, of course, an ideological freighting/value-ladenness. Like White and Ankersmit I am arguing that the historical narrative, as the site of meaning creation, requires that the historian when designing their narrative will deploy several strategies of understanding in addition to that of the empirical-referential. The basis and starting point for any analysis of the structure and functioning of historical thinking and practice, is located in White's model of the historical narrative (White 1973, 1978, 1987, 1992, 1998, 2000) which is itself a synthesis of ideas culled from Pepper, Frye and Mannheim (for recent commentaries on White see Munslow 1992, 1997, 2001 and Jenkins 1995, 1998a, 1999).

Briefly, White describes three strategies within the narrative that historians establish to explain what the past means. These are explanations (explanatory strategies to be precise) through emplotment (constructing stories about change over time), argument (generating causal relationships between acts and events) and ideological preference (offering ethical positions and value judgements about the nature of reality). Each of these strategies is articulated in one of four modes. Following the literary critic Northrop Frye (and basic literary theory) White argues emplotments may be constituted as a Romance, Comedy, Tragedy or Satire. Borrowing from Pepper, White maintains the historian's arguments can be cast in the modes of Formism, Organicism, Mechanism and Contextualism. The ideological implications of these two (prior) aesthetic categorisations or layers he derives from Mannheim's 'ideal type' classification of arguments. These are Anarchism, Conservatism, Radicalism or Liberalism (Frye 1967 [1957]; Pepper 1942; Mannheim 1947 [1936]). White claims the specific combination of modes put together by the individual historian constitutes the historian's historiographical style. The connections between these strategies and modes White describes as 'elective affinities' that possess a rhetorical logic, which is also culturally and ethically influenced. White's gloss on this is that ultimately the historian can put them together as they wish. This is reflected in Ankersmit's contention that rep-resentation leaves the necessary space for the historian to do his or her work. From the perspective of White's structure of figuration, emplotment, and argument and their ideological implications we can ourselves establish our historiographical space.

Underpinning the four explanatory strategies of narrative-making is the universal figurative mechanism all human beings employ to make connections within the empirical and intellectual worlds, that is, the process of troping.

There are four key tropes: metaphor, metonymy, synecdoche and (white adds) irony.

Figure 1

Trope	Emplotment	Argument	Ideological implication
Metaphor	Romantic	Formist	Anarchist
Metonymy	Tragic	Mechanist	Radicalism
Synecdoche	Comic	Organicist	Conservatism
Irony	Satirical	Contextualist	Liberalism

Source: Hayden White (1973) *Metahistory: The Historical Imagination in the Nineteenth Century*, Baltimore, Johns Hopkins University Press.

It is White's judgement that the tropes constitute the logic of historical thinking and they are best thought of as foundational forms of historical consciousness. The tropes are what Pepper refers to as the four root metaphors or figures of thought and which are familiar as the four key tropes (Pepper 1942: 84–114). The dominant tropological mode, whichever it happens to be in any given historian's narrative (or school of history for that matter) is the 'metahistorical' base of the(ir) historical narrative. In other words, the dominant linguistic trope provides the shape or form through which objects are initially grasped or understood and then explained. The singularly important feature of troping is that it does not occur after the data has been investigated. Prior even to the emplotment there is the mode of linguistic consciousness through which the historian (like all human beings) presupposes or prefigures the processes and events that existed in the past. In other words, historians possess a dominant linguistic predisposition toward the historical subject matter to be 'investigated' just like the artist will approach their subject matter with a preferred form in mind. It is this figurative or tropic preference that characterises the nature of every historical understanding.

Like White the linguistic philosopher Max Black and the psychoanalyst Gemma Fiumara also argue the tropes must be elemental to pre-empirical construction of our narratives. Tropes, as the primary forms of consciousness, make connections between objects and concepts through the mental processes of 'seeing' substitution and/or association and/or differentiation (Black 1979: 19–43; Fiumara 1995: 98–99; Ricoeur 1994 [1978]: 44–64). This must, of course, also apply to the connection between 'the past' and the cultural discourse of 'history'. When, for example, we 'turn' our selections from the data stream of, say, black history in America in the 1920s into the Harlem

Renaissance, we are making a straightforward metaphoric connection. In this case the analogue is with another metaphor, that of the European Renaissance in the fifteenth and sixteenth centuries. This is because we think there are – comparatively speaking – shared elements in both. Indeed, the Harlem Renaissance has become so entrenched in historical thinking that it is now, effectively, a dead historical metaphor in much the same way as the 'Industrial Revolution', the 'Cold War', or 'The Era of Good Feelings'. But the point, of course, is that dead historical metaphors become the reality of the past – at least until another culturally preferred metaphor comes along. It is this way entire schools of history are also formed. Historians take up where other historians have left off working in an invented and sedimentary historiographical tradition.

What should be clear by now is that this narrative-linguistic foundation to meaning and truth gives pre-eminence to ideas about the past and their expression as words. It should by now go without saying, that the data remain the raw material of history, but of equal importance is how we stitch them together to create a meaning, which we are happy to believe, is truthful. So, what exactly is the structure of this narrative truth? As the basic unit of historical analysis, the figure or trope recognises, describes and permits the re-description of relationships between past things as well as the historical concepts that our minds construct. In his explanation of this Ricoeur points to Pierre Fontanier's key treatise *The Figures of Discourse* (1830) in which Fontanier first identified the three foundational forms of relationships that we figuratively construct between ideas as ones of figurative correlation and/or correspondence.

The first of these foundational forms of figurative thinking is the reference we make to an object or a person by naming and, in effect, reducing it to an essence or key attribute we think it possesses. This is the reductionist trope or figure of metonymy. An example would be to imagine/interpret steel magnate Andrew Carnegie's social vision as one that reduced America, through a presumed relationship of correspondence or contiguity, to its most important part, which in Carnegie's case could be interpreted as the pioneering entrepreneur. America thus went forward thanks, as Carnegie saw it, to the power and authority of the new class of late nineteenth century businessmen. Metonymy here is the connective understanding of events, actions and processes in the past in the mode of part-to-part relationships where one part is reduced to a correspondence function or manifestation of another through contiguity (is 'caused' by it). Given 'metonymic thinking' we would 'imagine' or 'understand' the past as being inhabited by agencies and structures that are often hidden but which extrinsically determine change over time. Metonymic thinking is thus central to all reconstructionist and constructionist history because of its implication of correspondence and the epistemological theory of truth and representationalism associated with it.

The second of Fontanier's figures is the integrative connection made when a constituent part or parts are named to represent the whole. This is the trope of synecdoche. A synecdochic connection would view (we might still say the historian 'imagined' or 'understood') Carnegie (while still appealing to the same body of evidence as in the above example) as rejecting a reductionist vision of society because it carried with it the tragic possibility of social conflict. Class conflict, between the new class of entrepreneurs and, say, the immiserated workers, could be averted assuming all the parts (the two major social classes) were brought together. Interpreting Carnegie as wanting social harmony reveals a synecdochic integrative approach on the part of the historian (who imputes it to the mind of Carnegie) and they may elect to infer that the age in which Carnegie lived was one where the predominant mode of thought was itself synecdochic. Here the historian is advancing or imposing his or her narrative truth as that of the historical agent. It cannot, of course, be otherwise.

In this example, by defining synecdoche as describing a whole-to-part relationship where qualitatively the whole is more than the sum of its parts demonstrates the historian's organic vision of integration as the key to explaining change over time. While they will seek empirical support – and find it – for this 'understanding' it remains their own. The historian is thus transposing his or her 'interpretation' of Carnegie into Carnegie's vision of himself and his world. Both these tropes constitute an ontologically inspired figurative visualisation of the data or content of the past, and which prefigure its 'discovery' in the archive. Hence it is that the figurative paradigms we deploy necessarily precede the evidence we study.

The same logic applies to the application of Fontanier's third key figurative form, that of metaphor. Through this a reference is made to one thing as another (correspondence) through an assumed resemblance (mimesis). The historian's intention here is a comparison/resemblance of character or quality between whole objects. Continuing with the example of Carnegie the historian is always free to interpret him metaphorically. The historian would do this by arguing that, say, Carnegie saw the Republic as an express train that thunders by in comparison to Europe, which crawls at a snail's pace. This is, in fact, what Carnegie himself said in his own discussion of wealth-creation in America. Carnegie's preferred metaphor is thus happily appropriated as a useful starting point before the historian sets about a further and more sophisticated tropic reconfiguration.

These three basic forms of explanation (in which all refer to one thing through correspondence, connection or resemblance to/as another) have been recognised by philosophers since Aristotle. Many since Fontanier have also explored them and it fell to White to remind us of their central role in doing history (White 1973). As I said above, in addition to metaphor, metonymy and synecdoche White adds irony to constitute the fourth key trope or mode of explanation used by historians. This, he claims, is the master trope of our present postmodern age as it allows for our scepticism about correspondence truth and the inexplicable paradoxes in the conditions under which we generate cultural knowledge. The naïve modernist can still use the other prefigurative forms in the belief that language can still corres-pond with past reality. However, once correspondence has been abandoned (as it must given our postmodern existence?) we can cast all our connections ironically through the use of semantic inversions like oxymoron (essentially a compacted paradox). One of my favourite examples of oxymoron is 'truthful interpretation' which, for me, encapsulates the problem with epistemology. Another I like is the 'minor crisis' in historical studies.

There are, of course, a great variety of other tropes. Variations in metaphor include simile, which is the explicit comparison of one thing with another, and personification, which is reference to objects as though they had human qualities. There is periphrasis, which is the connection made by the sub-stitution of a descriptive word/phrase for a proper name or a proper name for a quality linked to it. Exaggeration and understatement also makes connections and create meaning as with hyperbole (exaggeration for effect) and litotes (understatement for effect). The tropes operate, therefore, by the redescription of (what is an already textualised) reality with the aim of prefiguratively grasping its meaning. Hence it is that the historian's narrative design in which emplotment, argument and ideology/values work, operates interpretationally as an extended figure of one kind or another. The logic of this, and a logic which makes it so awkward for reconstructionist and constructionist historians to accept (wedded as they are to correspondence or correlation theory), is that discovering new data does not necessarily make any difference to its tropic prefiguration or to what, ultimately, the historian thinks is meaningful about it. Hence 'empirical truth' is oxymoronic when the same data has diverse meanings for different historians.

Emplotting the past

So, what happens in the historical narrative that our tropic thinking both prefigures and predicates? Ricoeur maintains that the primary conceptual medium for explaining change over time resides in that element in the narrative where we give a form to sequences of events that occur over time – the story or emplotment. Although White agrees with this, unlike Ricoeur he does not accept events and actions have the same structure as narrative. Unlike Ricoeur White believes the historian's narrative structure is imposed on past events and so we cannot find history's story or emplotment (*muthos*). But, in a view that he does share with White and Ankersmit, Ricoeur insists that 'telling' in history is more than the recounting or describing 'what happened'. Ricoeur argues that the historical narrative is far more than the sum of its truth conditional statements. It is, instead, through the language and the structure of the historical narrative that the past gains its meaning.

The first element or layer of the historical narrative, and which in itself can give the past *a* meaning, is its emplotment. To emplot is to linguistically turn a chronological flow of events (a chronicle) into a story with an assigned explanation of causes and effects. This normally takes the form of a Romance, Tragedy, Comedy, Satire or some combination. For White, as I have just suggested, these emplotments do not pre-exist in any given corpus of data. There has been something of a debate on this. Other narrativist philosophers of history like David Carr disagree. Carr argues the narrative form is imposed but still insists it is a reflection of the true nature of events (Carr 1986a). Alternatively, the evidence can be seen as being provided with *a* meaning by emplotting it. Historians don't interfere with the factual, but they must arrange it in varying ways to provide it with (*an* emplotted) meaning. In a romance, for example, the protagonist or hero (which may be a person, class, nation, tribe, physical building, race, mode of transport, gender, etc) transcends their world of experience – they 'win out'. In a tragedy they don't. For Ricoeur tracing action is the key to emplotment. To emplot is, as he suggests, not merely to re-arrange 'human action into a more coherent form', but it is a structuring 'that elevates' action, that is, gives it a meaning (Ricoeur 1994 [1978]: 40). Other historians might elevate social structures. But whatever the mechanism you choose, as Kant said, and Ricoeur and White agree, history has to deploy emplotments.

Although explanation through emplotment is the result of figurative creation or the 'seeing' of resemblance or imitation, it nevertheless lends itself to the idea of the mimetic (mimesis). As I have pointed out, the epistemological model allows history to aspire to the truth of the past through correspondence. Rhetorically speaking, this is mimesis and imitation (usually in the metaphoric form of metonymy). Much confusion exists among historians precisely because they mistake mimesis/metonymy for correspondence. But the historian's emplotment is not just the result of a figurative mental act, for, while it is primarily poetic/imaginative (using figures) and symbolic (using linguistic signs and symbols, i.e. words) it acts mimetically. It is used with the intention that it shall be representational. Thus, for most historians, it is undertaken as an honest effort to represent *the* causes that they believe must link events together. The historian who believes this does so because he or she assumes the act of writing a narrative mimics the intentional act of the historical agent or the 'discovered' structures of historical (social, cultural, economic) change. Ricoeur endorses this through his 'big assumption' that people in the past always constructed their lives as narratives with plots. Historians, according to Ricoeur, are thus able (with hindsight and according to the evidence) to discover *the* story shape of the past that occurred in the minds of historical 'actors' and which dictated their intentions and actions.

As White is happy to acknowledge, Ricoeur's invaluable contribution to historical thinking and practice is to emphasise the centrality of narrative-making (White 1987). This is a major advance on the epistemologies of naïve reconstructionism and even the most sophisticated constructionism with their shared assumption that conflates correspondence with mimesis. However, where Ricoeur still seeks to discover *the* story (in the action or the structures that the narrative can mimic) White does not. Taking Ricoeur's belief in the subjective element in history to heart, that it is the mind of the historian that provides the meaning in the narrative, White draws a different conclusion. Endowing the past with meaning by writing historical narratives, White insists, means prefiguring the object of study (objects like 'the French Revolution', 'feudalism', 'Ben Franklin', etc) imaginatively rather than taking it as simply existing and, therefore, carrying an inherent emplotted meaning (White 2000: 393). White is adamant that imaginative prefiguring means objects are always created or constituted within the mind through figurative processes that are more comparable with literature than any empirical 'science' (White 2000: 394).

Arguing with the past

In White's model the historian's imaginative/aesthetic emplotment strategy is supported by at least two other conceptual schemes of explanation. These are the argument or cognitive operation and the unavoidable moral/ethical or ideological strategy of explanation. If we assume history is a 'narrative meaning production process' rather than only or even primarily an act of empirical discovery and inference, it is reasonable to assume the historian is already likely to possess a preferred explanation of how the world works today and, therefore, how it worked in the past. As I have suggested, this is derived entirely from his or her ontological presuppositions about the nature of existence. The historian's ontology is particularly evident in the kinds of arguments and moral positions he or she invokes to explain how the world fits together. These cognitive conceptual and ethical/ideological strategies for explanation, which form part of the epistemological assumptions of the historian, directly influence the kinds of history eventually produced. Like the painter choosing their genre, the historian selects their form (biography, general survey, diplomatic history, labour history, etc), their arguments and the moral meaning they believe derives from their ideological orientation.

In addition to the explanatory level of emplotment ('what happened to whom/it') in the narrative historical account, is explanation by formal argument or the answer to the question 'how does everything work together?' (see Figure 1 on p. 169). Because of the historian's ontological presuppositions about what they think are the laws of historical explanation that best describe the nature of cause and effect, the argument layer of narrative understands events (pre-shaped in the form of an emplotment) usually in a deductive-nomological fashion whereby a premise leads to a conclusion (see Chapter 6). This means invoking premises (or *explanans*), a covering law, and the *explanandum*. Probably the most famous example is Marx's assumed relationship between the material base of society and the changes that occur in the social and intellectual superstructure. Using his base-superstructure figure, Marx explains how, as changes in the (economic) base occur over time so (logically) does the nature of the (social/cultural/intellectual) superstructure. Examples of logical arguments do, of course, abound in history and are integral to it. But they are often made without comment or examination, as 'assumptions' such as that stock market crashes are not permanent. Logically you can't have a permanent state of crash? Or another equally dubious argument is that the empirical-analytical model is the 'only way' to do history.

The problem with historical arguments is not just that historians rarely agree on which laws of causation to adopt in particular cases but, as this book demonstrates, not all historians accept the form or model of scientific explanation in history. White, following Pepper, points to the four primary modes of arguments, technically theories of, or assumptions about truth and verification that can be deployed by historians: Formist, Mechanistic, Organicist and Contextualist. It is important to remember that correspondence, correlation, coherence or consensus orientations to truth apply to the argument element of the narrative. Thus, the formist theory of truth, while it emphasises the unique character of events, may still be construed in a correspondence way. Even though mechanistic historians have a tendency to reduce explanation to determining causal laws and categorise events (as Marxists do), depriving them of their unique character, they are still free to believe they are seeking out the truth. The same applies to contextualists and those who prefer organicist arguments. The important point is that all arguments operate within the substance of the narrative and should not be seen as somehow unconnected to anything else in the process of meaning creation.

Valuing the past

Historical explanation is complex precisely because it is not scientific. It is complex because like all narratives it both constructs its interpretations and represents them. In other words, because history has no given story or pattern to be discovered, it is most important to recognise and understand that the study of the past cannot be insulated against ideology. The implications of this are wide-ranging, not least for those positivists who would prefer to view history as a science and essentially non-political, non-social, non-religious, etc. The great irony is that their preference can only be couched in philosophical terms. Hence the claim is made that ideology is a corpus of values and beliefs held by an individual historian for other than epistemological reasons. As a non-epistemic form of explanation ideology is what the historian thinks is good to believe about their ontological and moral existence. Just as the constructionist is likely to argue that history is theory all the way through, the deconstructionist will acknowledge it is ideological all the way through. This is only in part because adopting a theory is as much a political act as any other. It is also to do with how the historian's sense and sensibilities give meaning to their sources.

The usual question is how can a historian combine both an ideological or non-epistemic form of explanation with the idea of objective inquiry? Perhaps more interesting, however, is how can they reasonably prioritise one form over another? As we know, constructionists of various kinds insist they can overcome ideology through their claim to have provided a fully scientific history that reveals the patterns, covering laws or stories extant in the past. But this is not really the important question. It is, rather, not whether but what kind of political values does the historian inject into their history and how is this processed by their imagination? Plainly, while historians do history for many reasons, one of the most important is to create a moral meaning for the conduct of our lives today and this can only be done within the aesthetic of our narrative. Historical interpretations are based not merely on the data but on moral beliefs about what they really mean, and which are in turn informed by our taste and sensibilities and what we think constitutes the beautiful and the sublime.

In spite of it flying in the face of history as an aesthetic as much as a rational and empirical activity, many historians still seem to think that history must be free of ideologies. The worst theory in history is that tainted by politics as Sir Geoffrey Elton maintained. He believed that ideology and theory was essentially the same thing, noting that 'adherents of theory do not allow facts to disturb them but instead try to deride the whole notion that there are facts independent of the observer'. He concluded that the Marxist position 'was impressive' except that those who endorsed it usually failed 'to allow better knowledge to affect their theses' (Elton 1991: 20). As Elton said of the work of the British Marxist historian Christopher Hill, he was forced to strain the facts of history. Elton said Hill's history was dictated by his tainted political belief (cast as a theory) that the English Revolution must be termed bourgeois. Elton suggested that Hill, finding the urban and mercantile class not up to the task of bourgeois revolution, effectively ransacked the social groups that remained for their revolutionary intent, eventually settling on a small group of malcontents called Ranters whom, as Elton delights in pointing out (though he always said he was unhappy about it) did not really exist as such (Elton 1991: 20–21). The point Elton was making was that as a matter of fact there were no classes in Hill's Marxist sense in England in the seventeenth century, only powerful individuals. Classes only existed in Hill's fevered ideological brain. When fully into his stride Elton went on to attack feminist history and all forms of religious belief as dangerous impositions on the past. As he said, any comprehensive theory used to order the evidence is never actually tested in the evidence, but serves only to twist it in the required direction. Unsurprisingly, perhaps, Elton does not recognise his placing of the individual at the centre of his arguments is as much a construct of narrative as is class.

That there is a value-judgement dimension in every historical narrative is recognised in White's model as well as more generally (Harlan 1997). Although there is no doubt that ideology as a strategy for explanation derives from the historian's desire to pursue 'the truth', and part of the discovery of truth is the recognition that 'history' must have moral lessons. Hence it is that every history makes its claim to realism through its philosophy as much as the sources it quotes. For the deconstructionist historian, in part following the ideas of the moral philosopher-historian Emmanuel Levinas, this isn't at all problematic (Levinas 1991 [1961], 1981 [1973]). For the deconstructionist who has challenged the epistemological compulsion to truth as correspondence, morality and ethics become the instruments of what history should be about. In the-past-as-history, politics may mean recovering both forgotten or deliberately excluded groups of human beings, but it is also the way in which a sense of pastness can be used as the key vehicle for ethical living. History is located, as Levinas argues, in the trace of the past defined in our obligation to the rips and fissures in what we know about the past. It leaves space for our moral imaginings to emerge from that, which is not known.

In one sense there cannot be an explanatory priority between ideology/ ethics, argument or emplotment because they must all ultimately work together to provide morally convincing and plausible historical explanations ('what's it mean for responsible living?'). Following Mannheim's categorisation of ideology, but matching them cognitively to their tropic, emplotment and argument forms, White notes four key kinds of ideological implications that signify moral positions: Anarchist, Radicalism, Conservatism and Liberalism. Each one of these can (and usually does) make its own claim to representing the past accurately in the name of reason and realism. But, each form of ideological orientation is different, defined in the view each holds of the pace of change over time. Conservatives assume a natural rhythm to time, Liberals a socially constructed (usually cast in the form of a parliamentary) pace to change while Radicals and Anarchists view time passing in the form of a variety of cataclysmic transformations.

White concludes his analysis of the formal structure of the historical narrative by considering that its ethical dimension along with its aesthetic and cognitive elements work together to produce its truth-value. Thus, a historian can 'explain' what happened by locating the law(s) that governed a set of events emplotted as, say, a tragic story. Or he or she may 'become aware of' the tragic meaning of the story they have emplotted in the 'discovery' of the law(s) that regulates the structure of events. Indeed, although White does not argue this, it seems quite reasonable to suggest that the historian can make an ethical choice first and aesthetics and cognition work in consequence of this choice. Whichever way it happens, the particular functional combination of explanatory strategies (aesthetic, cognitive and moral/ideological) the historian deploys will determine the structure of their historical understanding. The way each historian arranges these functional layers and modes will produce their own historiographical or narrative style. It will, as I have suggested, also constitute a narrative truth for historical understanding.

Conclusion

Clearly, as significant as they are, the tropes do not in and of themselves constitute the whole of history thinking and practice. History is as much about the events and the sources, as it is about the composition and delivery of meaning. But equally, to ignore the literary constructedness of history is to neglect how the figures/tropes allow us to assemble stories, propose arguments and establish ethical positions as forms of explanation 'of what it all means'. What is more, clarifying the existence and functioning of the tropes is not to say history is 'linguistically determined'. It is rather to point out that history is not ultimately (and therefore) only 'data determined'. That we can choose our tropes (once we are aware of them and how they work) suggests 'the past', and 'the imaginative consciousness' determine historical meaning through their reciprocity.

Conclusion

I have tried to argue that history is best understood as a way of constructing narrative explanations. In examining the structural relationship between the empirical-analytical and narrative-linguistic characteristics of history I stressed that historians are not constrained by the epistemological foundations of conventional history thinking. Although referentiality remains a constant, I also acknowledged that history requires the use of theory and concept to assist our understanding of what the past means and, finally, I suggested we must address the figurative processes of representation through which we constitute historical meaning. By revisiting history's philosophically modernist assumptions that culminated in the epistemological model (reality, sources, correspondence, intentionality, inference) I have argued we may come to a more realistic understanding of how epistemological thinking has produced its reconstructionist and constructionist varieties, both of which continue to insist on the primacy of content (past events) over form (their organisation and representation by the historian).

Furthermore, I have maintained that it is because modernist epistemology requires that we see history as primarily an empirical activity that generates accurate 'matter of fact' statements that truthfully describe 'the past', history is viewed as being about source-based knowable reality and the analytical practices of drawing reasonable inferences. From this perspective the narrative-linguistic position is usually criticised for its emphasis on the role of figurative explanation that mediates and reflects the historian's ontological presuppositions and which suggests a dismissal of the empirical-analytical. But such a characterisation would be, I think, unfair. My argument has not been to reject the empirical-analytical but to draw attention to the other crucially important aspect of historical thinking and its practice as a form of representation. That such an emphasis raises important questions about epistemology suggests we should rethink its role, rather than abandon it entirely in our history.

However, there is no very straightforward or convincing way of distinguishing between empirical or synthetic and analytical truth in history even though the division between reconstructionists and constructionists is largely founded on this distinction. Both accept empiricism as the basis of their work but each views the connection between empirical content and its form differently. The one sees form as produced by the content. For the other content is the evidence plus the discovery of its given meaning through a preferred conceptual and/or theory form. The deconstructionist argument is that both ultimately fail to do justice to our narrative-making of meaning. This is the logic behind the suggestion made at the start of this book and which I have worked through, that historians would benefit from viewing the three practical components of history as working together – referentiality, the deployment of theory and concept, and the functioning of figuration and representation. In so doing we arrive at an understanding of what the past means when turned into what it plainly is, the-past-as-history.

The specific question I have posed is whether the epistemological mode of historical explanation is the only legitimate way to define the nature of the historical enterprise with its aim of 'discovering' the truth of the past. By revisiting the history of historical thinking and the debates over the relationship between epistemology and ontology, rationalism, empiricism, perspective and theory, and via my brief engagement with Hegel, Kant, Nietzsche, Vaihinger, and more recently White and Ankersmit, I have noted the constantly challenged nature of epistemological beliefs. I have suggested that because history is a text written about past reality and that we cannot know the past thing-in-itself, what we do think we know about the meaning of the past is as much to do with the nature of representation as it is the past itself. Indeed, only by ignoring figurative thinking and the nature of representation will historians continue to rely on the correspondence of the past world and the present word and not see beyond the notion of empirical falsifiability.

I have contended that any apparent inconsistency between the empirical-analytical and narrative-linguistic in history evaporates if we accept that history is shaped as much by the form or structure of the discourse we deploy as its content and our use of theory. From this perspective the logic of history centres on how we imagine 'what it means' rather than rely on accurate description of what happened which, it is assumed, will tell us what it means. 'What is the meaning of the French Revolution?' is a question epistemologically little different to asking 'What is the meaning of my next door neighbours?'. Truth-conditional statements alone can never provide the meaning. This does not, of course, do away with useful, interesting and important debates over what happened in the past (or living next door to my neighbours!).

Reference, truth and representation

From a deconstructive or post-epistemology perspective, it is not possible and, therefore, it cannot be the function of the-past-as-history to turn referentiality into meaning in a correspondence sense. Deconstructionist historians do not believe, as do reconstructionists and constructionists, that the webs of connections between events and agent intentions are a matter of knowable causes and effects that can be set out plainly in a historical narrative that is viewed as a report of findings. Reconstructionists and constructionists both forget that history is not the reflected past (though be it, as they are apt to claim, through a glass darkly) because they fail to fully appreciate the implications of it being a discourse that refers back only after an anticipatory and self-conscious and deeply authored representational act of narrative-making.

I have made a case, mainly by invoking the arguments of a wide range of narrativist philosophers, that to explain the meaning of the past, history must acknowledge the narrative form(s) in which it is cast. The consequence of this is to raise questions about the nature of epistemology, representation, argument, truth, objectivity, and the functioning of theory and meaning. In other words, we now define history as a substitution for what once was (a representation for that represented) rather than a reflection of or resemblance to it ('it' being knowable and describable past reality). That the epistemological model continues to be defended by a variety of reconstructionist and constructionist historians, even though it is regularly acknowledged by them that it is an unattainable vision, is testament to the continuing power of the logos, which insists history must be a 'true copy' of past reality. This oxymoronic effort, it turns out, militates against knowing the meaning of historical understanding because such thinking assumes almost any historical explanation has to be better than living with an unfathomable past. Unfortunately all that historians have are representations of representations, that is, historiography.

Paradoxically, then, to insist on knowing the meaning of unknowable past reality (the past-thing-in-itself) is to be unrealistic. Realism demands an 'after the event' grasping of the meaning of individual and group intentions with the objective of making truthful descriptive historical statements. Such statements are, of course, cast as provisional awaiting the arrival ('discovery') of new sources from the past, or better inferences and/or even more 'revealing' theories. Deconstructionists, because they view history as an anticipatory act whereby the attribution of meaning consists in the prefigurative shaping of the form their history will take, are, perhaps, rather more realistic in their appraisal of what is history. It is this view of 'the-past-as-history' defined as a cultural process of anticipatory narrative-making and representation that I have tried to describe in this book.

I have been suggesting it is *through* as well as *in* the historical narrative that the happenings of the past (call them events under a description, propositional/ truth conditional sentences, or just 'facts') are imagined, organised and endowed with meaning. Historical truth – that quality most prized and yet most misunderstood in history – I have defined as that explanation we think provides the meaning of the past under the circumstances of our figurative thinking and narrative-making as well as with all due deference to referentiality. If, as historians, we wish for a definition of 'the truth' then we know we can look in many directions (like correlation, coherence or consensus) but we also know, as realists like McCullagh and Bunzl insist, that most turn primarily to the truth conditional statement and assume correspondence to reality translates into its narrative substance. Because we make an empirical declaration that something happened at a particular time and place truth (defined as empirical truth), this becomes common and collective knowledge because it seemingly does not depend on one's perspective or situation.

Ancillary to this is the situation that while we accept truth conditional sentences have a role as statements of what happened in the-past-as-history, they cannot guarantee 'the truth' because there is no 'right meaning' to 'find', and no given stories to 'discover' and 'get straight'. This means that the only truth in history is that which results from the coherence of strategies of explanation and metaphoric structure within the narrative. Hence it follows that the meaning of a historical representation can only be known when compared with other representations of the same object. In effect this suggests that narrative representations cannot be true (or false) in any correspondence sense, but only be 'more or less plausible' in comparison to other representational texts.

As Ankersmit argues (as well as Ricoeur and White in their different ways), giving primacy to description of events as most historians still do – because this is how they think narrative works – assumes explanation derives from reference in a subject(thing)-predicate(meaning) fashion, but history, because it is a form of representation makes such a distinction impossible to sustain (Ankersmit 2001: 39–48). Hence I have re-stated Ankersmit's key argument that a description *refers* to reality (because of its subject-term) whereas a representation (the entire text) can only be said to be *about* reality as well as *about* other historians' representations (the historiography) (Ankersmit 2001: 41). As Ankersmit points out this isn't a problem. In fact, it is in this indeterminate space that historical thinking takes place and its practices are undertaken. This helps us understand why the linguistic turn offers a more realistic appraisal of how historical writing and research actually work. Not only do historians describe what happened, they also debate the meaning of their 'American Revolution' or 'Enlightenment' against that of others in a coherent and plausible fashion in terms that encompass far more than reference to the sources. Unless there is a legitimate debate on the veracity of a particular source as used by an individual historian, what is contested in history are the products of the historians' webs of imaginative connections and their concepts, not just their propositional sentences.

It is this narrative plausibility in terms of the creation of metaphoric webs of significance that gives rise to our conception of narrative truth. What I am suggesting is that we try to move beyond the either/or-ism of objectivity versus relativism to a far more complex appreciation of our engagement with the past. Unless you happen to be an unreconstructed reconstructionist, because most historians conflate objectivity with sticking to empirical (the facts of the situation) and analytical (reasonable inference plus theory) procedures, they accept that being a Marxist or a Whig doesn't automatically make you wrong. Equally, I would argue, self-consciously choosing your figurative orientation or emplotment should not be seen as a bar to being a 'good historian'.

The constructionist mainstream chooses to believe in the ascendancy of analytical truth (in the form of theoretically informed inference based on an empirical foundation) but, like reconstructionists, they too dismiss matters concerning the nature of narrative representation. The important point is that while reconstructionists represent the empiricist extreme both make the same fundamental assumption that *the* meaning of *the* story must pre-exist in the data. Hence it is *the* story of William Gladstone and *the* story of the French Revolution come to us through referential correspondence. Given their shared modernist commitment to the logos it is necessary that this be so. For such historians history *results from* epistemology and, for this reason, the discovered story through mimesis is of *the* story once experienced as it was. Inasmuch as it is then printed accurately on the page it may be judged to be a truthful report after the event. The historian has thus discovered and published the true story of what happened. That it may later turn out to be the wrong story has done no injury to the mechanism of epistemology. It has just been poorly practised or been based on thin evidence. Epistemologically

nothing has changed in that the narrative is the report while the interpretation is a reflection on what it most likely means (explanation to best fit). What matters to such historians is that the story as told replicated the story enacted by historical agents. In none of this is there a sense that the historical narratives are anticipated by being subject to the ideas of the historian and his or her own cultural presence/present or that there has been a self-conscious effort to deconstruct epistemology.

If a historian endorses empirical correspondence above everything else then not only must they assume there are real stories in the past but that ultimately there can only be one historical narrative which is the expression of its reality. Contrary to this I have been arguing that history is more (though not less) than an empirical-analytical activity because the datum cannot deliver or explain itself with the historian as some kind of contextualising agent or midwife or, using a different metaphor, just a reporter. Facts do not justify their own meaning even when they have been subject to the thinking of historians. Once we accept the role of historians as creators of meaning rather than as sophisticated messengers conveying the truthful despatch from the past (even though they have to interpret the message), it is easier to see how a historian can select one covering law over another, or one emplotment rather than another or cast their story in one trope rather than another. For the constructionist their theory opens up the true meaning of the past, for the deconstructionist history is the staging or performance of the documentary source as a scripting process – literally of the-past-as-history – by transferring it to a preferred figurative or expressive register.

What is more, I have argued that as long as epistemology continues to be regarded as the preferred *modus operandi*, the actual narrative choices made by the historian will always remain 'hidden from history'. History is not, as I have suggested, just the hunting of the referent, it is rather its re-phrasing, re-emplotment and imaginative representation with the aim of generating different meanings for different purposes that are always – rather than 'sometimes' (as is associated with 'bad' history) – ideological and value-laden. The supposed real, the figurative and the ideological interweave. The epistemological position (realist and representationalist) oversimplifies the question of the connection between knowing and telling, not least the incommensurability between the propositional sentence and the interpretational text. Overlooking this means forgetting that there is a difference between the object (that which is represented) and its representation. Just as constructionists tell us what the past means through their strategic choice of theory and ideology, so deconstructionists point to their choice of figuration and emplotment *as well as* theory and ideology. This highlights the ontological assumptions

dramatists

made by each individual historian about the nature of causation, agency, intentionality, etc, when they set about substituting history for the past.

Knowing and telling: the structure of the historical narrative

I have further argued that although 'doing history' must be empirical and analytical, it is also a representational process that is initiated and directly controlled by the act of figurative thinking and that this directs the narrative emplotting of past events, the historian's use of sources and arguments/ inferences as well as recognising their ontological pre-judgements. I have, in effect, endorsed White's emphasis on history as a literary artefact along with Ankersmit's analysis of the philosophy of language. Like them I have acknowledged the epistemological gap between reality (the world and its description) and representation (the narrative). It still seems odd to most historians to suggest they think figuratively and create emplotments. Surely, they say, poets, dramatists and novelists do that and, while they can also make appeals to rational argument, they don't have to. There is also no necessary impulse toward factual truth in novels and poems. Hence it is that novelists and poets start with the form they want and fill it with the content they invent. Historians, they insist, always start with the real content and move toward discovering its given form in the inherent meaning to human actions. Poets create stories while historians weigh, consider and make a case for actual rational/explicably irrational behaviour. If there is a model to be followed, so it is argued, it is from jurisprudence not literature.

I have been arguing throughout this book that history as a substitution form of representation has nothing to do with truth defined as correspondence or correlation in the way description has. When we move from the sentence-length referential description into the realm of representation, i.e., the 'about-ness' of history, we are undertaking a quite different intellectual activity. In this 'aboutness' or aesthetic world, I have suggested that it is in the imaginative and improvisatory narrative act on the part of the historian that a meaning for the past is provided. It is in 'writing about the past' that the historian's ontological presuppositions do their work. For example, to list the theories and explanations offered by historians for the causes of the American Revolution and then claim they added up 'to collective grievances that rose to a climax in a gigantic failure of British statesmanship' is to offer an interpretation that has clearly moved beyond statements of causes such as 'trade regulation', 'the burden of debts on British merchants', 'the growth of a national consciousness', 'the lack of representation in Parliament' and the 'evangelistic impulse' (Tindall 1988 [1984]: 217–218). 'The failure of British statesmanship' is a widely accepted interpretation among historians and as such is analytically true being a coherent conclusion based on the range of representational statements already available. But clearly, such an interpretative statement is not and never can be synthetically or empirically true. It merely indicates the historian's preference for a particular representation of that aspect of the American past he or she is addressing from the statements previously made.

Deconstructionist historians point out that as individual historians come up with different stories (based on different themes, heroes and heroines, inferences, events, figures of thought, emplotments, content, arguments, ideological preferences and ontological presuppositions) the notion of empirical-analytical truth as the ultimate judge of given meaning needs re-thinking. No historian believes that they can just list facts and expect they will explain themselves, yet epistemology works according to this logic. As I have argued, the truth of the narrative is not simply the function of the accumulation of data but of its composition within them. White upset so many historians and realist philosophers because he said the reality of history is that we all work within a formal grid of figurative choices, emplotments, arguments and ideological positions even though there were choices to be made within them. Now, while he may have been too rigid in his formalism, it seems reasonable to assume that as historians write literature, how that literature is 'put together' must affect what it means. Philosophers of language like Ankersmit help us out here, agreeing with White that in order to have a meaning content needs to be given a form, but disagreeing that the figurative or tropological element is necessarily predominant and that the conceptual, ideological and matters of representation may be no more important than the figurative.

I welcome Ankersmit's gloss that the richness of the content of the past demands that we recognise the connection of concept/argument to literary form in relating reality and language. Acknowledging the narrative-linguistic dimension as a whole (literary theory plus the linguistic turn) means opening up both the mechanics and the implications of the transliteration of reality into its representation. In other words historians need to understand both the nature and architectural design of narrative-making and the challenge to epistemology provided by the linguistic turn, in order to better grasp the fundamentals of historical thinking and practice. As Ankersmit argues, representation is beyond epistemology because it connects things to things (Ankersmit 2001: 11–12). How this operates to create the work of history is, as I have argued, through the key features of historical theory and practice: figuration, emplotment, and concept, argument, theory and ideology.

Figuration

The basic logic of history is that of figuration. This is the mechanism for that metaphorical shift from *the* past to *a* history, the-past-as-history. As we know, a number of narrativist philosophers and historians (following Ricoeur and White) agree that the structure of historical discourse is predicated on the process of troping. This suggests that history has, at the very least, a dual loyalty to both the empirical-analytical and the narrative–linguistic: on the one side to the sources and inference, on the other the act of figurative creation that produces an emplotment. Following Collingwood, Pepper, Ricoeur, White and Ankersmit, I have contended that the metaphoric construction of meaning through comparison provides for all understanding. What is most significant in this is that such acts of imaginative composition unavoidably precede (hence they prefigure) what we think we have 'found' in the sources. Even if the aim is to reconstruct the past as it actually was, or construct a pretty close facsimile through the applications of more or less complex social theory, we still prefigure reality and this directly influences how we narrate it. Indeed, it may even be that the logic of figuration determines the kinds of sources we try to 'find' in the first place and the particular array of truth conditional statements we deploy.

Following White's argument I have suggested that it is through the four main tropes that we metaphorically apprehend the content field of the past by means of resemblance (metaphor), continuity (metonymy), integration (synecdoche), and the self-reflexive recognition of the inadequacy of representation (irony). What the historian does, though in most instances it remains un-self-conscious, is project onto 'the facts' the emplotment that is generated by their creative engagement with one or other or more of the master tropes (White 1987a: 47). It is at this most basic level that the questions of historical truth and objectivity arise and are settled. The epistemological judgement is that explanations can *only* be to the best fit and, therefore, figuration is *necessarily* relegated to figures of speech. But what is forgotten is that if historical explanation is by its nature figurative it is allegorical in its form (White 1987: 48). Once truth is freed from its narrowest definition as correspondence, then history can be viewed as carrying a truth-value by virtue not just of its rationality and coherence but also its figurative constructedness. History is not simply something we (empirically) observe and draw inferences about, it is something we imagine by making figurative connections and establishing coherent relationships through metaphor. By the same token this does not exclude the deductive-nomological or law-like inclinations of constructionists if that is their preference. For me the figures of thought preside over historical explanation in much the same way as logic does the structure of argument.

Emplotment

The link between reference and its historical representation is emplotment. I have argued that truth conditional statements or events under a description do not of themselves justify the emplotments we give to them. I have argued for a logic that holds there are no special or peculiar empirical grounds for believing, say, British imperialism can only be emplotted as 'a moral tragedy' for its proponents any more than the invention of the hydraulic press by Joseph Bramah was integral to 'the romance' of British industrialism. There are no criteria available to historians to make such judgements. All we have is that for the individual historian these occurrences add up to one emplotment rather than another. To emplot is to represent action, agency, and structure through time. To emplot is not, therefore, to be mimetic. To establish causation in history demands the categorisation of emplotment. Narrative truth can only emerge through its establishment. Because objectivity and truth in an epistemological sense have no role to play in the process of narrative-making, it is very important to understand that it is the emplotment that lends the essential dynamic to historical explanation as the historian moves from recounting to understanding and, eventually, an explanation of meaning.

If we follow narrativist logic, *single events* (like the death of President Lincoln or the Lisbon earthquake of 1755) would be taken as the representation of *processes* that have a meaning when they are thematically emplotted. The emplotting of the facts into a coherent or plausible arrangement flows from the power of narrative to explain the meaning of its content. The historical narrative is not simply or solely a report of what happened and why according to inferred and theory-informed cause and effect relationships. It is now that peculiar discourse written by a historian that enfolds a whole system of beliefs constructed usually for the benefit of a specific class, culture, gender or other categories of people. The power of narrative also has another purpose beyond emplotting time. It also naturalises a certain view or philosophy of the world, a set of ontological presuppositions if you like. Modernist epistemologists, of course, refuse to see it this way.

With an architecture that encompasses philosophical and emplotment making activities the new history should allow historians to extend their understanding of the past beyond its reconstructionist and constructionist forms. The role of facts in the emplotment remains, for example, very straight-forward. Facts can only exist within an emplotment as they are invested with the representation (dramatic or otherwise) we think it demands. Historians make emplotments with whatever fragments and sources they have to hand and in response to the demands of their culture. In contemporary Western European culture, the twentieth century Nazi Holocaust is generally regarded as a human tragedy of peculiarly monumental and horrific proportions. While you may agree with this emplotment (as I do) this should not stop us admitting to the fact that this modernist event has been cast in a popularly acceptable emplot-ment. And, lest there be any confusion, we should note that such culturally determined emplotments are moral judgements rather than simply or only empirically and inferentially justified beliefs. As Ricoeur says, we *learn* to see a given set of events as tragic, as romantic and so on (Ricoeur 1990 [1985]: 185).

Concept, argument, theory and ideology

Even for the historian who proclaims history is only about the interaction of contingent events and human agency/intentionality, it is impossible to engage with the past without concept, theory, argument and moral/ethical belief. Although theory and concept may be reduced by the reconstructionist to the level of the 'historian's working assumptions' within all narratives there are always theories and covering laws being generated and tested, adopted, modified and rejected. This means the constructionist historian, in addition to inference and explanation to the best fit, also elects to invoke categories, structures and conceptual classifications that organise and explain past social activity. Constructionists also buy into the belief that they can be objective even though they know their knowledge is situated with reference to a con-ceptual or theoretical position. By acknowledging their own ontological frameworks existing in healthy competition with those of others, construc-tionists insist that objectivity can be attained in and represented through more than one theoretical idiom. Of course, the ultimate conventional test remains to judge each historian's theoretical or conceptual 'take' on the empirical grounds invoked to support it.

That Sacco and Vanzetti went to the electric chair in August 1927 is a propositional statement that accords with the available evidence and upon which most historians agree. However, to know what it means for our under-standing of 1920s America requires the deployment, within an overall nar-rative structure, of what the historian deems to be an appropriate set of categories and concepts available to them. Immediately he/she is presented with the difficulties of selection. For example, should he/she avoid concepts that resonate in the here-and-now? Or should they deliberately cast them in terms that make sense today—like putting Romeo and Juliet in modern dress? That we choose our history can be seen in the very act of selecting individuals (like Sacco and Vanzetti). This illustrates the existence of a particular relationship between structure and agency constructed and proposed by the historian.

History is not primarily, much less entirely, a matter of the hypothetico-deductive process and explanation to the best fit that finds causes and effects and generalises toward large-scale explanation. History is not just a choice of one large-scale theory over another (Marxist class over Weberian agency?). It is not only a matter of hypothesis modification according to the nature of the supporting evidence, *explanandum* and *explanans*, or determining structure, change and direction. It is all this cast within its larger narrative framework. Concept, argument and theory are constituent elements in a literary historical structure that has a logic in which the historian determines the patterns of the past. In other words, we can test the truth or falsity of propositions according to the available evidence and whether, in Ankersmit's phrase, the object possesses the property we ascribe to it (Ankersmit 2001: 13). What should be equally clear is that we cannot do the same for concepts, arguments and theories defined as representations or models of reality. While sentences can be true or false, concepts and theories cannot.

If we view social theories and arguments as essentially metaphors (as with Marx's base and superstructure metaphor, or Giddens' third way) then not just their integration and utility within the narrative become clearer but also how historians use their concepts. Pepper, Ricoeur, White, Black, Mary Hesse, Thomas Kuhn, and Ankersmit have all stressed the figurative association between metaphor and argument. As Pepper, Ricoeur and White insist, explanatory models are extended metaphors. In Ricoeur's words, in the historical space produced by the impossibility of obtaining a strictly deductive relationship between *explanans* and *explanandum* we fall back on metaphor.

It is Pepper's judgement that both argument and hypothesis construction are metaphoric. He describes this clearly in his analysis of root metaphors or analogies (Pepper 1970 [1942]). The four primary forms of argument, you will recall, all make claims to truth: formist, mechanist, organicist and contextualist. Each is associated with its own root metaphor: similarity and uniqueness, machine-like reductionism, synthesis and consolidation, and integrationism. Each shapes the nature of causation according to its own premises. All of these primary arguments generate explanatory hypotheses analogical/figurative in form. For Marx, for example, historical change was satisfactorily explained through a mechanistic argument founded on the form of comparison derived from metonymy rather than metaphor. Marx 'argued' that the relationship between men under industrial capitalism was one of contiguity and difference (classes). He then moved into another root metaphor to explain the outcome of or meaning to history. Socialism and communism he 'argued' would ultimately be victorious. His argument deployed a synecdochic (integrative) configuration through which the whole becomes greater than the sum of its parts (White 1973: 302). What must not be forgotten is that the four primary forms of argument/explanation always support ideological/ ethical positions. It cannot be otherwise given the ontology of history. Ideology and our belief as to what is 'good' or 'bad' in history is still too often regarded in Eltonian fashion as a mischievous and dangerous form of personal and group bias that is destructive to the truth locked in history's sources.

But, assuming (as I do) that we cannot escape our being-in-the-world, as we can't its representation, the truth of our historical narratives is that they are always ideological or moral and hence cannot be understood by their referentiality alone but by the use to which their referentiality is put. History is a matter of how we establish the relationship between the real and the good/bad meaning we ascribe to it. Perhaps it is only once we dispense with the idea of the word-world match that we can come to a more 'realistic' understanding of the unavoidably relativist/ideological and ethical nature of the-past-as-history text? To interpret in history is to bring to it an ideological and moral perspective. This is not something that can be avoided. Indeed, it is the prerequisite to any understanding of the past. All history is teleological at some level. Like Hill's Marxist seventeenth century, history always looks to and anticipates the future in the past.

In appearing to be a reflection (more rather than less) of past reality, the historical narrative builds into its structure the views of its client group claimed to be correspondence with reality. The historical narrative is – in effect – the most potent cultural vehicle for ideology we have because narrative is conventionally taken by its practitioners (and uncounted millions of consumers) to be primarily denotative rather than connotative. Its key concern is to denote or reference what actually was, and then connote or suggest what it meant. It is at the level of the connotative that ideology operates. In other words, historical narratives can state literally what happened but the interpretations of meaning are always undertaken through the creation of plausible stories that are (usually consciously though not always) ethically and morally inflected. It is for this reason that histories are thus always more plausible to a readership that shares the moral inflection built into them and less to those who do not. So, the question we should always ask about ideology, ethics, morality, position, situated knowledge etc, is not just how do historians establish their meanings factually but also ideologically.

Final remarks

Does all this mean that 'what the past really was' can only be judged by our aesthetics, by our forms of representation? In other words, is the truth of the past to be determined subjectively by the form we select, by our trope, emplotment, argument and ethical position? As one recent commentator argued, it is easy to see why many professional historians fear that arguments that openly recognise the aesthetic and ideological judgements that went into them can lead to 'abuses of scholarship, to simplistic and one-sided characterisations of the past' (Pihlainen 1998: 17–18). Such arguments are oversimplifications because they constantly work toward and demand a single truthful answer to all complex historical problems. Though it may well turn out to be very unfortunate for reconstructionists as well as disconcerting for constructionists, there is no way to ensure truth in historical writing. This is because there is no objective measure for truthful knowing in interpretative narratives.

The desire for 'the answer' (i.e., correspondence truth) recedes considerably when we accept that the historical narrative (like all realist narratives) is constructed through trope, emplotment, conceptualisation, and analysis and ideological and ethical position taking deployed as strategies for explanation. This realisation does not mean we cannot do history. It means we do it differently, anew. The significant point is that because history cannot give us the meaning of the past by bringing its writing to the forefront of our endeavours, we can better guard against the empiricists who tell lies, and those historians (especially reconstructionists) who are unwitting captives of their ontological prefigurations (usually manifest as their unacknowledged ideological or moral preferences). There cannot be a 'truthful story' in the same way as there is no 'truthful interpretation' or the 'given meaning' of an event. In the end all histories are, by their very nature, fictive constructions and epistemologically – whether we are happy about it or not – they cannot be either true or false. If we wish to see truth in history it is a function of the plausibility, internal consistency and moral worth of the story. It cannot simply, or even primarily, be a function of the data or its analysis.

My deconstructionist argument against the exclusive concentration on the epistemological model has run something like this. First, the basic building blocks of historical thinking are constituted in the figurative as much as epistemological or empirical-analytical processes. Second, historians should take seriously the consequences of viewing history as what it palpably is, a written discourse – the-past-as-history. Third, history must always be viewed as historiography (it is historians who write history after all and not the past). Fourth, any meaning we ascribe to the past derives ultimately from the onto-logical (authorial) intellectual engagement of the historian as he or she narrates the-past-as-history in the present, rather than simply produces meaning through the truth conditional sentence. Fifth, because it is a literary form, history is a perpetual challenge to any epistemological notions of mirror-like representation. Sixth, the epistemological demarcation between a history and its philosophy is always transgressed because every work of history contains its own set of ontological presuppositions. Seventh, history, because it is a literary representation, has no scientific status. Eighth, the priority of content over form in the creation of meaning ceases to have any useful epistemological worth. Ninth, history has a truth-value precisely because of its re-classification as a literature and not through correspondence. All this adds up to a widening rather than a diminishing of the possibilities for our engagement with the past.

The logic of history as I have described it, of course, comes at a price. It requires the rejection of the centred, all-knowing utterly self-reflexive omni-scient narrator and the epistemological pretence that the existence of the past must entail (despite it being hedged about) correspondence and or correla-tion theories of truth. While the past makes history texts possible, only in its representation can a meaning be created for it. What is more, the past cannot be understood unless it is recognised as being located within the horizon of our present expectations. The past may have happened but history has not yet occurred. History is, after all, always written for the future. History exists only in anticipation, in effect the 'as if' of its representation. While history's adequacy as a description can be judged rationally and within referentiality, what it means remains an aesthetic act of judgement for it is only in and through language that we can discriminate between history and the past.

History understood for what it is – a representation – is not a 'problem' to be 'overcome' or a 'useful reminder' that historians trade in words and style. The fact that history is a written substitution for the past suggests that his-torians might benefit from working out the consequences of their situation. The narrative-linguistic indeterminacy that is elemental to the condition of 'doing history' does not mean 'the end of history' much less the end of justified belief. No longer viewing history as the written/language mirror of the past does not mean that we cannot have a narrative form of truth, or that we must glumly accept that one form of representation must be as good as any other, or that we are obliged not to be rational, or that we have got to decline into a wretched moral decadence, or that we unavoidably open the flood gates to historians who lie and cheat. Such arguments are merely the last refuge of historians who can't respond openly to epistemological scepticism. Moving from empirical scepticism toward epistemological scepticism means expanding our ideas about what it is that history can do. I recommend that historians free themselves from their belief that the source dictates the form of its representation. Still looming large in much contemporary history thinking is the truly odd notion that little of cognitive importance happens on the road from evidence to text. What is even worse is the belief that all that really matters in 'doing history' is what happens on the trajectory between past reality and the source. I remain hopeful that only a very few historians could encompass both these ideas at once.

Guide to key reading

Because the historian writes 'the-past-as-history' as much through its historiography as anything else it may be helpful for readers to know what texts have influenced my thinking (both for and against). In addition, this brief guide highlights those sources to which you should turn for a more complete consideration of the issues I have raised. Although I believe history is an integrated form of knowledge, for ease of explanation I structured the book under four general headings which I took to be the essential aspects of the process of history thinking and practice – epistemology, referentiality, theory and concept and representation. I will do the same with this brief annotated guide. Inevitably some texts can be placed under one or more of these headings and so their location here signifies the particular utility I derived from them rather than necessarily the intentions of their author. If I am correct in my assumptions about the architecture of history thinking and practice the reason for the lack of clear boundaries between the four aspects should by now be plain. I have argued that as knowing creatures historians move through and live within a coherent universe of evidence and belief, doubt and justification, truth and objectivity, concepts and theories and narratives and representation. In practice they cannot be separated.

To start with historians should understand history as an epistemology. This requires a basic introduction to the nature and theory of knowledge itself. This is well provided in four books: Jonathan Dancy, *An Introduction to Contemporary Epistemology* (Oxford: Blackwell, 1985), Linda Alcoff, *Epistemology: The Big Questions* (Oxford: Basil Blackwell, 1998), Robert Audi, *Epistemology: A Contemporary Introduction to the Theory of Knowledge* (New York: Routledge, 1998), and David Cooper, *Epistemology: The Classic Readings* (Oxford: Basil Blackwell, 1999). While historians do not have to be philosophers beyond having a basic grasp of the epistemological issues in doing history they should have some idea about the nature of the connection between existence and knowledge. This can be approached through a broad understanding of ontology and specifically the historian's ontological commitments. These connect or relate the historian's beliefs about existence (and the theories and concepts that support such beliefs) and those things they take to exist in the past and present. It is common and useful, therefore, to talk about a historian's ontology (what they think happened) or the ontology of a theory they hold, which means the things that happened for their theory to be true. This is crucial to understanding the nature of all history. See Reinhardt Grossmann, *The Existence of the World: An Introduction to Ontology* (London: Routledge, 1992) and Chapter 2 in Robert Nozick, *Philosophical Explanations* (Oxford: Oxford University Press, 1981).

Moving beyond the epistemology and ontology, how we acquire knowledge and understanding about the past are addressed in a great many 'explanation in history' texts. Here is the first clear example of overlap between aspects. In this instance it is theory and concept. I would recommend the following as broad and intelligent evaluations of the nature of history: Paul Veyne, *Writing History, Essays on Epistemology*, tr. by Mina Moore-Rinvolucri (Middletown: Wesleyan University Press, 1984 [1971]), R.F. Atkinson, *Knowledge and Explanation in History* (London: Macmillan, 1978), Arthur Danto, *Analytical Philosophy of Knowledge* (Cambridge: Cambridge University Press, 1968), Alan Donegan, 'Explanation in History' in Patrick Gardiner (Ed.) *The Nature of Historical Explanation* (Oxford: Oxford University Press, 1961 [1952]), and two books by W.H. Walsh, *An Introduction to Philosophy of History* (Westport, Connecticut: Greenwood Press, 1984 [1967]) and *Substance and Form in History* (Edinburgh: Edinburgh University Press, 1981). There are also two useful texts by William Dray who over a long career has remained a leading philosopher of history, *Laws and Explanation in History* (Oxford: Oxford University Press, 1957) and *Perspectives on History* (London: Routledge, 1980). See most recently his 'Philosophy and Historiography' in Michael Bentley (Ed.) *Companion to Historiography* (London: Routledge, 1997, pp. 763–82). A comprehensive introduction to history as a discipline and practice is Michael Stanford's *A Companion to the Study of History* (Oxford: Basil Blackwell, 1994) and up to date and collected from the pages of the journal *History and Theory* is *History and Theory: Contemporary Readings* edited by Brian Fay, Philip Pomper and Richard T. Vann (Malden and Oxford: Blackwell, 1998). This is an outstanding selection of recent work on the nature of historical explanation. Also particularly useful as a starting point for modernist-postmodernist history is Joyce Appleby, Elizabeth Covington, David Hoyt, Michael Latham, and Alison Sneider, *Knowledge and Postmodernism in Historical Perspective* (New York and London: Routledge, 1996). Highly critical of postmodernism is the Marxist theorist Alex Callinicos. His *Theories and Narratives: Reflections on the Philosophy of History* (Cambridge: Polity Press, 1995) is, however, probably the most lucid response from a materialist available today.

Two articles by Chris Lorenz that are careful and considered responses to the postist position are 'Historical Knowledge and Historical Reality: A Plea for "historical realism"', *History and Theory*, 1994, 33: 297–327 and 'Can Histories be True? Narrativism, Positivism, and the "Metaphorical Turn"', *History and Theory*, 1998, 37: 309–29. More strident than Lorenz is Perez Zagorin, 'Historiography and Postmodernism: Reconsiderations', *History and Theory*, 1990, 29: 263–74 and 'History, the Referent, and Narrative: Reflections on Postmodernism Now', *History and Theory*, 1999, 38: 1–24. This is an all-out attack on Keith Jenkins that is fairly typical of its kind. Such attacks have been regular occurrences as Jenkins has carved a special place for himself since his first foray into the nature of historical explanation in the early 1990s in a series of militant anti-epistemology and philosophically self-conscious texts. The earliest blast and recently re-issued as a 'classic' text by the publisher was his *Rethinking History* (London: Routledge, 2002 [1991]). This was followed by *On 'What is History?'* (London: Routledge, 1995), *The Postmodern History Reader* (London: Routledge, 1997), *Why History? Reflections on the Possible End of History and Ethics under the Impact of the Postmodern* (London: Routledge, 1999), and *Refiguring History* (London and New York: Routledge, 2002). Introductions to the philosophy of history do not abound but three of the most highly accessible are B.A. Haddock, *An Introduction to Historical Thought* (London, Edward Arnold, 1984), Robert M. Burns and Hugh Rayment-Pickard, *Philosophies of History: From Enlightenment to Postmodernity* (Oxford: Blackwell Publishers, 2000) and Michael Stanford, *An Introduction to the Philosophy of History* (Oxford: Basil Blackwell, 1998). See also Richard Palmer, *Hermeneutics: Interpretation Theory in Schleiermacher, Dilthey, Heidegger and Gadamer* (Evanston, Ill.: Northwestern University Press, 1969). Virtually forgotten despite Hayden White's indebtedness to the book, but one of the key texts in the philosophy of history is Stephen C. Pepper, *World Hypotheses: A Study in Evidence* (Berkeley, California: University of California Press, 1942). Although clearly straddling several aspects of the history project is Karl Popper's three key texts *The Poverty of Historicism* (London: Routledge, 1957), *The Logic of Scientific Discovery* (New York: Basic Books, 1959) and *Objective Knowledge: An Evolutionary Approach* (Oxford: Clarendon Press, Rev. Edn. 1979). William

Dray has also produced *On History and Philosophers of History* (New York: Brill, 1989) and edited *Philosophical Analysis and History* (New York: Harper and Row, 1966). Much under-rated is William B. Gallie, *Philosophy and the Historical Understanding* (London: Chatto and Windus, 1964). This is an early effort at addressing the story-making properties of history. More recently Mick Lemon has analysed the nature of history's narrative-linguistic form in *The Discipline of History and the History of Thought* (London: Routledge, 1995) and in *Philosophy of History* (London: and New York: Routledge, 2003).

There are many other key thinkers on the nature of history who are worth reading. Particularly student friendly are edited texts like Richard Kearney and Mara Rainwater, *The Continental Philosophy Reader* (London: Routledge, 1996). A survey text that is suited to trainee historians (and probably most of those already trained) is Marnie Hughes-Warrington's *Fifty Key Thinkers on History* (London and New York: Routledge, 2000). Each entry is accompanied by a listing of the subject's own key works and a bibliography of further reading. There are entries for most of the significant figures in the history and philosophy of history ranging from Braudel, through E.H. Carr, Collingwood, Croce, Dilthey, Foucault, Hegel, Hempel, Kant, Marx, Oakeshott, von Ranke, Ricoeur, Vico, Walsh to White. But even in a text so wide-ranging there are omissions with no references to, among others, Ankersmit, Barthes, Derrida, Danto, Dray, Levinas or Rorty. Filling this gap somewhat is John Lechte, *Fifty Key contemporary Thinkers: From Structuralism to Postmodernity* (London: Routledge, 1994). But even here Rorty is missing. I recommend all historians read the key works of Richard Rorty. These include his attack on correspondence theory in the work for which he is best known, *Philosophy and the Mirror of Nature* (Princeton: Princeton University Press, 1979) but see also his *Consequences of Pragmatism* (Minneapolis: University of Minnesota Press, 1982), *Contingency, Irony and Solidarity* (Cambridge: Cambridge University Press, 1989), *The Linguistic Turn: Recent Essays in Philosophical Method* (Chicago: University of Chicago Press, 1992) and *Philosophical Papers*, Vols. 1 (1991) and 3 (1998).

Defences of historical realism, referentiality and associated analytical structures like correspondence and inference (the empirical-analytical or epistemological approach) are, as you would expect, abundant. Many of the general 'explanation in history' texts I have noted so far are, in fact, written as defences of realism and correspondence. Among the most interesting early texts are Carl Becker, 'Everyman His Own Historian', *American Historical Review*, 1931, 37: 221–36, Charles Beard's 'Written History as an Act of Faith', *American Historical Review*, 1933, 39: 219–31 and 'That Noble

Dream', *American Historical Review*, 1935, 41: 74–87. In these Becker
and Beard recognise the ineluctable relativism of history but do so with
the intention of rescuing the empirical-analytical approach with its desire
for objectivity and truth. The importance of their work is that it remains
epistemologically committed. This position has extreme longevity and is
found in Raymond Tallis, *In Defence of Realism* (Lincoln: University of
Nebraska Press, 1998) and has been seen in recent constructionist and realist
philosophical responses to the epistemologically sceptical as in C. Behan
McCullagh's *Justifying Historical Descriptions* (Cambridge: Cambridge
University Press, 1984) and *The Truth of History* (New York and London:
Routledge, 1998). The notion of objectivity has been given a detailed treat-
ment by Peter Novick in his *That Noble Dream: the 'Objectivity' Question
and the American Historical Profession* (Cambridge: Cambridge Univer-
sity Press, 1988). Students should also read the defences offered by James
T. Kloppenberg in his 'Objectivity and Historicism: A Century of American
Historical Writing', *American Historical Review*, 1989, 94: 1011–30, and
Andrew P. Norman, 'Telling It Like It Was: Historical Narratives on Their
Own Terms', *History and Theory*, 1991, 30: 119–35. This general position
has been popularised in texts such as Richard Evans' *In Defence of History*
(London: Granta, 1997), the hugely popular primer of John Tosh, *The
Pursuit of History* (Harlow: Longman, 2000 [1984]), Joyce Appleby, Lynn
Hunt, and Margaret Jacob, *Telling the Truth About History* (New York and
London: Norton, 1994), Lynn Hunt, 'Does History Need Defending', *History
Workshop Journal*, 1998, 46: 241–49, and her *The New Cultural History*
(Berkeley: University of California Press, 1989). Most recently it has been
given a firm constructionist turn by Mary Fulbrook in her *Historical Theory*
(New York and London: Routledge, 2002). And it has even been influential
on reconstructionists like Arthur Marwick in his *The New Nature of History:
Knowledge, Evidence, Language* (Houndmills: Palgrave, 2001), which is the
latest incarnation of his book *The Nature of History* (London: Macmillan,
1970). However, the Becker-Beard approach had little effect on unrecon-
structed reconstructionists like Sir Geoffrey Elton in his *Return to Essentials:
Some Reflections on the Present State of Historical Study* (Cambridge:
Cambridge University Press, 1991) and his now severely dated *The Practice of
History* (London: Methuen, 1967) as well as Jack Hexter, *The History Primer*
(London: Allan Lane, 1972). There is a greater recognition of the complex-
ities involved in authoring the past in Deborah A. Symonds, 'Living in the
Scottish Record Office' in Elizabeth Fox-Genovese and Elisabeth Lasch-
Quinn, *Reconstructing History* (New York and London: Routledge, 1999,
pp. 164–75) but ultimately correspondence, objectivity and truth win out.

Clearly, as this listing demonstrates, the emergence of postmodern and anti-representational criticism has prompted a realist counterattack in the past twenty years or so. Among the most thoughtful and considered responses are those that defend rational action theory and agent intentionality like John Searle, *Intentionality* (Cambridge: Cambridge University Press, 1983) and *The Construction of Social Reality* (London: Allan Lane, 1995). Also thoughtful are F.M. Barnard (1981) 'Accounting for Actions: Causality and Teleology', *History and Theory*, 1981, 20: 291–312, Mark Bevir (in his debate with Frank Ankersmit), 'Exchanging Ideas', *Rethinking History: The Journal of Theory and Practice*, 2000, 4, (3): 351–72 and *The Logic of the History of Ideas* (Cambridge: Cambridge University Press, 2000 [1999]), George Wilson, *The Intentionality of Human Action* (Stanford, California: Stanford University Press, 1989), Martin Bunzl, *Real History* (London: Routledge, 1997), and Geoffrey Roberts, 'Postmodernism versus the Standpoint of Action', Review of *On 'What is History?'*, by Keith Jenkins, *History and Theory*, 1997, 36: 249–60. A leading and highly sophisticated defender of the empirical-analytical position is Georg Iggers. See his 'Historiography between Scholarship and Poetry: Reflections on Hayden White's Approach to Historiography', *Rethinking History: The Journal of Theory and Practice*, 2000, 4, (3): 373–90 and *Historiography in the Twentieth Century: From Scientific Objectivity to the Postmodern Challenge* (Hanover and London: Wesleyan University Press, 1997). A useful survey is provided by Dorothy Ross, 'Grand Narrative in American Historical Writing: From Romance to Uncertainty', *American Historical Review*, 1995, 100: 651–77. For the more technically minded see John R. and Susan G. Josephson, *Abductive Inference* (Cambridge: Cambridge University Press, 1994), Peter Lipton, *Inference to the Best Explanation* (London: Routledge, 1993), and D.J. O'Connor, *The Correspondence Theory of Truth* (London: Hutchinson, 1975).

The best general overviews of mainstream constructionist history today that reflect the impact and predominance of theory and concept are provided in two weighty texts. The first is Kelley Boyd's two volumes, *Encyclopedia of Historians and Historical Writing* (London and Chicago: Fitzroy Dearborn, 1999) and Michael Bentley's edited *Companion to Historiography* (London: Routledge, 1997). The variety and sophistication of history work presently available is clearly reflected in these volumes. The rare appearance of contributions that address the narrative-linguistic in these works such as Peter Munz's chapter 'The Historical Narrative' in Bentley indicates the nature of this constructionist dominance. As I have argued, the debate over constructionist/scientific forms of explanation start with the covering law model. While few historians working today will have read Carl Hempel, I think it is worth going back to his original formulation. See his 'The Function of General Laws in History', *The Journal of Philosophy*, 1942, 34: reprinted in Patrick Gardiner (Ed.) (1959) *Theories of History* (Glencoe, Ill.: The Free Press, 1959).

Perhaps the most accessible writer on constructionist history is Peter Burke and his survey texts are excellent introductions to what is history today. See his edited *New Perspectives on Historical Writing* (University Park: Pennsylvania University Press, 1992), *History and Social Theory* (Ithaca: Cornell University Press, 1993) and *Varieties of Cultural History* (Oxford: Polity Press, 1997). A helpful introduction to the varieties of history available today is Anna Green and Kathleen Troup (Eds.) *The Houses of History: A Critical Reader in Twentieth Century History and Theory* (Manchester: Manchester University Press, 1999). Located more toward the social science end of the market is Murray G. Murphey, *Our Knowledge of the Historical Past* (Indianapolis and New York: Bobbs-Merrill, 1973) and also his 'Explanation, Causes, and Covering Laws', *History and Theory* (Themed Issue), 1986, 25: 43–57. An attempt at compromise and balance is Jerzy Topoloski, 'Towards an Integrated Model of Historical Explanation', *History and Theory*, 1991, 30: 324–38.

Uncompromising recent defences of social science history are to be found in Christopher Lloyd's *The Structures of History* (Oxford: Basil Blackwell, 1993), Clayton Roberts, *The Logic of Historical Explanation* (University Park: The Pennsylvania University Press, 1996), William A. Green, *History, Historians, and the Dynamics of Change* (Westport, Connecticut: Praeger, 1993), Graeme Snooks, *The Laws of History* (London: Routledge, 1998) and Miles Fairburn, *Social History: Problems, Strategies and Methods* (Houndmills: Macmillan, 1999). As militant in their own way as Jenkins is in any of his texts are the contributors to another survey edited by John Belchem and Neville Kirk, *Languages of Labour* (Aldershot: Ashgate Publishing, 1997). See also Alex Callinicos' *Social Theory: A Historical Introduction* (Cambridge: Polity Press, 1999). One of the primary areas of constructionist history and revealing of its location at the frontier with deconstructionist history has been women's history. An appropriate start can be made with Louise Antony and Charlotte Witt (Eds.) *A Mind of One's Own: Feminist Essays on Reason and Objectivity* (Boulder, Colorado: Westview Press, 1993). See also two key texts by Gisela Bock, 'Women's History and Gender History: Aspects of an International Debate', *Gender and History*, 1989, 1: 7–30, and 'Challenging Dichotomies: Perspectives on Women's History', in Karin Offen, Ruth Roach Pierson and Jane Rendall (Eds.) *Writing Women's History: International Perspectives* (Bloomington, Indiana: Indiana

University Press, 1991, pp. 45–58). Joan Scott is probably the most well-known feminist historian influenced by post-structuralism and literary deconstructionism. See her 'Gender: A Useful Category of Analysis', *American Historical Review*, 1986, 91: 1053–75, *Gender and the Politics of History* (New York: Columbia University Press, 1988), 'History in Crisis? The Others' Side of the Story', *American Historical Review* Forum, *American Historical Review*, 1989, 94: 680–92, 'After History', *Common Knowledge*, 1996, 5: 9–26, and *Feminism and History* (Oxford: Oxford University Press, 1996). Judith Butler's contribution in *Gender Trouble: Feminism and the Subversion of Identity* (London: Routledge, 1990) reveals the shift toward a deconstructive approach that is explored further in Mary Baker, 'Feminist Post-Structuralist Engagements with History', *Rethinking History: The Journal of Theory and Practice*, 1998, 2: 371–78.

What I have called 'the-past-as-history' – which acknowledges the deconstructive or postmodern take on history – is, as we know, essentially one of epistemological scepticism concerning the verities associated with the empirical-analytical position. These are primarily correspondence truth, inference, intentionality, and the difficult but necessarily objective-descriptive nature of history that clearly demarcates content from form, subject from object, fact from fiction, etc. There are several introductions to this disputed intellectual territory. See, for example, Beverley Southgate, *History: What and Why* (London: Routledge, 1996) and Alun Munslow provides succinct analyses of the narrative-linguistic position in two early editorials of the journal *Rethinking History: The Journal of Theory and Practice* (Vol. 1, 1997, 1–20 and 111–23) and in two recent books, *Deconstructing History* (London and New York: Routledge, 1997) and *The Routledge Companion to Historical Studies* (New York and London: Routledge, 2000). Two forthcoming books presently in process of being published are Robert A. Rosenstone and Alun Munslow (Eds.) *Experiments in Rethinking History* (London and New York: Routledge, 2004), a collection of innovative and experimental history taken by the editors from the journal *Rethinking History*, and Keith Jenkins and Alun Munslow, *The Nature of History Reader* (London and New York: Routledge, 2004), which frankly argues that history is literature.

But it is clear that the most significant contributions to the narrative-linguistic understanding of history as a form of representation have been made by a group of philosophers and historians that include Hayden White, Frank Ankersmit, Paul Ricoeur, Roland Barthes, Michel Foucault, Arthur Danto, Louis Mink and David Carr. White's key texts are *Metahistory: The Historical Imagination in Nineteenth Century Europe* (Baltimore: Johns Hopkins University Press, 1973), *Tropics of Discourse: Essays in Cultural Criticism*

(Baltimore: Johns Hopkins University Press, 1978), *The Content of the Form: Narrative Discourse and Historical Representation* (Baltimore: Johns Hopkins University Press, 1987), and *Figural Realism: Studies in the Mimesis Effect* (Baltimore: Johns Hopkins University Press, 1998). Ankersmit's contributions can be found in his *Narrative Logic: A Semantic Analysis of the Historian's Language* (Martinus Nijhoff: The Hague, 1983), *History and Tropology: The Rise and Fall of Metaphor* (Berkeley: University of California Press, 1994), *Historical Representation* (Stanford, California: Stanford University Press, 2001) and with Hans Kellner (Eds.) *A New Philosophy of History* (Chicago: University of Chicago Press, 1995). Paul Ricoeur has written on the role of narrative-making in history and the philosophy of history more broadly. His essential works are *Hermeneutics and the Human Sciences* (Cambridge: Cambridge University Press, 1981), in three volumes *Time and Narrative* trans. Kathleen McLaughlin and David Pellauer (Chicago and London: University of Chicago Press, 1984 [1983], Vol. 1), *Time and Narrative* trans. Kathleen McLaughlin and David Pellauer (Chicago and London: University of Chicago Press, 1985 [1984], Vol. 2) and *Time and Narrative* trans. Kathleen Blamey and David Pellauer (Chicago and London: University of Chicago Press, 1990 [1985], Vol. 3), *The Rule of Metaphor: Multi-disciplinary Studies of the Creation of Meaning in Language*, trans. Robert Czerny (London: Routledge, 1986) and *La mémoire, l'histoire, l'oubli* (Paris: Editions du Seuil, 2000). Roland Barthes' contribution to our understanding of the semiotics of history has been profound. See 'Le discours de l'histoire', *Information sur les sciences sociales*, 6: 65–75 (1967) trans. with an introduction by Stephen Bann, *Comparative Criticism – A Yearbook*, Vol. 3 (University Park: Pennsylvania University Press, 1981). Michel Foucault is one of the most controversial of historians for his flouting of many basic empirical-analytical assumptions. His main texts are 'The Order of Discourse', Inaugural Lecture at the College de France, December 2nd 1970, *The Archaeology of Knowledge* (New York: Harper and Row, 1972), *The Order of Things: An Archaeology of the Human Sciences* (New York: Random House, 1973), 'Nietzsche, Genealogy, History' in *Language, Counter Memory, Practice: Selected Essays and Interviews*, Ed. by Donald F. Bouchard, and trans. by Donald F. Bouchard and Sherry Simon (Ithaca: Cornell University Press, 1977, pp. 139–64), and *Power/Knowledge: Selected Interviews and Other Writings* (Brighton: Harvester Press, 1980). Arthur Danto's *Narration and Knowledge* (New York: Columbia University Press, 1985) is his major contribution to the debates. Louis Mink's argument that narrative can be viewed as cognitive is important. See 'History and Fiction as Modes of Comprehension', *New Literary History*, 1970, 1: 541–58 and 'Narrative

Form as a Cognitive Instrument', in R. Canary and H. Kozicki (Eds.) *The Writing of History: Literary Form and Historical Understanding* (Madison: University of Wisconsin Press, 1978, pp. 129–49). David Carr's input is most readily accessible in his 'Narrative and the Real World: An Argument for Continuity', *History and Theory*, 1986, 25: 117–31, and *Time, Narrative and History* (Bloomington, Indiana: Indiana University Press, 1986).

There are many other texts that address specific issues of a narrative-linguistic character. See for example Stephen Bann's 'Analysing the Discourse of History', *Renaissance and Modern Studies*, 1983, 27: 61–84 and *The Clothing of Clio: A Study of the Representation of History in Nineteenth Century Britain and France* (Cambridge: Cambridge University Press, 1984), Robert Berkhofer, *Beyond the Great Story: History as Text and Discourse* (Princeton: Princeton University Press, 1995), R. Canary and H. Kozicki (Eds.) *The Writing of History: Literary Form and Historical Understanding* (Madison: University of Wisconsin Press, 1978), David D. Roberts, *Nothing But History: Reconstruction and Extremity after Metaphysics* (Berkeley: University of California Press, 1995), Philippe Carrard, *Poetics of the New History* (Baltimore: Johns Hopkins University Press, 1992), Roger Chartier's *On the Edge of the Cliff: History, Language and Practice* (Baltimore: Johns Hopkins University Press, 1997), and Michel de Certeau, *The Writing of History*, trans. Tom Conley (New York: Columbia University Press, [1975] 1988). For more on metaphor in addition to Ricoeur see Max Black, 'More About Metaphor' in *Metaphor and Thought*, Ed. by Andrew Ortony (Cambridge: Cambridge University Press, 1979, pp. 19–43), Ann Curthoys and John Docker, 'The Two Histories: Metaphor in English Historiographical Writing', *Rethinking History: The Journal of Theory and Practice*, 1979, 1: 259–74, Gemma C. Fiumara, *The Metaphoric Process: Connections Between Language and Life* (London: Routledge, 1995) and Mary B. Hesse, 'The Explanatory Function of Metaphor' in Y. Bar-Hillel (Ed.) *Logic, Methodology and Philosophy of Science* (Amsterdam: North Holland, 1965). In addition to White, Ankersmit etc on the nature of representation see Hans Kellner, *Language and Historical Representation: Getting the Story Crooked* (Madison: University of Wisconsin Press, 1989), Kalle Pihlainen, 'Narrative Objectivity Versus Fiction: On the Ontology of Historical Narratives', *Rethinking History: The Journal of Theory and Practice*, 1998, 2: 7–22, Geoffrey Roberts, 'Narrative History as a Way of Life', *Journal of Contemporary History*, 1996, 31: 221–28 and his splendid collection *The History and Narrative Reader* (London and New York: Routledge, 2001). On filmic representation see Robert A. Rosenstone, *Visions of the Past: The Challenge of Film to Our Idea of History* (Cambridge,

MA.: Harvard University Press, 1995) and 'The Future of the Past: Film and the Beginnings of Postmodern History' in Vivian Sobchack (Ed.) *The Persistence of History: Cinema, Television and the Modern Event* (New York: Routledge, 1996, pp. 201–18).

Bibliography

Achinstein, P. (1983) *The Nature of Explanation*, New York: Oxford University Press.

Alcoff, Linda Martin (1998) *Epistemology: The Big Questions*, Oxford: Basil Blackwell.

American Historical Association (1995) *Guide to Historical Literature*, New York: Oxford University Press.

Ankersmit, F.R. (1983) *Narrative Logic: A Semantic Analysis of the Historian's Language*, The Hague: Martinus Nijhoff.

Ankersmit, F.R. (1989) 'Historiography and Postmodernism', *History and Theory*. 28: 137–153.

Ankersmit, F.R. (1994) *History and Tropology: The Rise and Fall of Metaphor*, Berkeley: University of California Press.

Ankersmit, F.R. and Kellner, Hans (Eds) (1995) *A New Philosophy of History*, Chicago: University of Chicago Press.

Ankersmit, F.R. and Bevir, M. (2000) 'Exchanging Ideas', *Rethinking History: The Journal of Theory and Practice*, 4, (3), 351–372.

Ankersmit, F.R. (2001) *Historical Representation*, Stanford, California: Stanford University Press.

Ansell-Pearson, Keith (1994) *Nietzsche and Modern German Thought*, London: Routledge.

Antony, Louise, M. and Witt, Charlotte (Eds) (1993) *A Mind of One's Own: Feminist Essays on Reason and Objectivity*, Boulder CO.: Westview Press.

Appleby, Joyce, Covington, Elizabeth, Hoyt, David, Latham, Michael and Sneider, Alison (1996) *Knowledge and Postmodernism in Historical Perspective*, New York and London: Routledge.

Appleby, Joyce, Hunt, Lynn and Jacob, Margaret (1994) *Telling the Truth About History*, New York and London: Norton.

Atkinson, R.F. (1978) *Knowledge and Explanation in History*, London: Macmillan.

Attridge, Derek, Bennington, Geoffrey and Young, Robert (Eds) (1987) *Post-Structuralism and the Question of History*, Cambridge: Cambridge University Press.

Audi, Robert (1993) *The Structure of Justification*, Cambridge and New York: Cambridge University Press.

Audi, Robert (1998) *Epistemology: A Contemporary Introduction to the Theory of Knowledge*, New York: Routledge.

Baker, Mary (1998) 'Feminist Post-Structuralist Engagements with History', *Rethinking History: The Journal of Theory and Practice*, 2: 371–378.

Bann, Stephen (1983) 'Analysing the Discourse of History', *Renaissance and Modern Studies*, 27: 61–84.

Bann, Stephen (1984) *The Clothing of Clio: A Study of the Representation of History in Nineteenth Century Britain and France*, Cambridge: Cambridge University Press.

Barnard, F.M. (1981) 'Accounting for Actions: Causality and Teleology', *History and Theory*, 20: 291–312.

Barthes, Roland (1983) *Empire of Signs*, Trans. Richard Howard, London: Jonathan Cape.

Barthes, Roland ([1967] 1984) *Elements of Semiology*, London: Jonathan Cape.

Barthes, Roland ([1981] 1967) 'Le discours de l'histoire', *Information sur les sciences sociales*, 6: 65–75 (1967) Trans. with an introduction by Stephen Bann (1981) *Comparative Criticism – A Yearbook*, Vol 3, University Park: Pennsylvania University Press.

Barthes, Roland (1957) *Mythologies*, London: Pan Books.

Barthes, Roland (1967) *Writing Degree Zero*, Trans. Annette Lavers and Colin Smith, London: Jonathan Cape.

Barthes, Roland (1972) *Critical Essays*, Trans. Richard Howard, Illinois: Northwestern University Press.

Barthes, Roland (1974) *S/Z*, Trans. Richard Miller, New York: Hill and Wang.

Barthes, Roland (1975) *The Pleasure of the Text*, Trans. Richard Miller, London: Jonathan Cape.

Barthes, Roland (1986) *The Rustle of Language*, Oxford: Basil Blackwell.

Barthes, Roland (1988) *The Semiotic Challenge*, New York: Hill and Wang.

Baudrillard, Jean (1976) *Symbolic Exchange and Death*, Paris: Gallimard.

Baudrillard, Jean (1983) *Simulations*, Trans. Paul Fosse, Paul Patton and Philip Beitchman, New York: Semiotext(e).

Bauman, Zygmunt (1997) *Postmodernity and its Discontents*, New York: New York University Press.

Bauman, Zygmunt (1998) *Globalisation: The Human Consequences*, New York: New York University Press.

Beard, Charles (1933) 'Written History as an Act of Faith', *American Historical Review*, 39: 219–31.

Beard, Charles (1935) 'That Noble Dream', *American Historical Review*, 41: 74–87.

Beck, Lewis White (Ed.) (1963) *Immanuel Kant: On History*, Indianapolis: Bobbs-Merrill Co.

Becker, Carl (1931) 'Everyman His Own Historian', *American Historical Review*, 37: 221–236.

Becker, Marjorie (1997) 'When I was a Child, I Danced as a Child, But Now That I am Old, I Think About Salvation: Conception González and a past that would not stay put', *Rethinking History: The Journal of Theory and Practice*, 1:343–355.

Becker, Marjorie (2002) 'Talking Back to Frida: Houses of Emotional Mestizaje', *History and Theory*, 41: 56–71.

Belchem, John and Kirk, Neville (Eds) (1997) *Languages of Labour*, Aldershot: Ashgate Publishing.

Bennett, Tony (1990) *Outside Literature*, London: Routledge.

Bennington, G. (1993) *Jacques Derrida*, Chicago: University of Chicago Press.

Bentley, Michael (Ed.) (1997) *Companion to Historiography*, London: Routledge.

Berkhofer, Robert F. (1995) *Beyond the Great Story: History as Text and Discourse*, Princeton: Princeton University Press.

Berlin, Isaiah (1997) *The Sense of Reality*, New York: Farrar, Straus and Giroux.

Bernauer, James and Keenan, Thomas (1988) 'The Works of Michel Foucault, 1954–1984', in James Bernauer and David Rasmussen (Eds) *The Final Foucault*, Cambridge, MA: MIT Press.

Bernstein, R. (1983) *Beyond Objectivism and Relativism*, Philadelphia: University of Pennsylvania Press.

Bertens, Hans (1995) *The Idea of the Postmodern: A History*, London: Routledge.

Bevir, Mark (1994) 'Objectivity in History', *History and Theory*, 33: 328–344.

Bevir, Mark (2000 [1999]) *The Logic of the History of Ideas*, Cambridge: Cambridge University Press.

Bisha, Robin (1998) 'Reconstructing the Voice of a Noblewoman of the Time of Peter the Great: Daria Mikhailovna Menshikova', *Rethinking History: The Journal of Theory and Practice*, 2: 51–64.

Black, Max (1979) 'More About Metaphor', in *Metaphor and Thought*, Ed. by Andrew Ortony, Cambridge: Cambridge University Press, pp. 19–43.

Bloch, Marc (1954) *The Historian's Craft*, Manchester: Manchester University Press.

Bloomfield, M.W. (Ed.) (1972) *In Search of Literary Theory*, Ithaca: Cornell University Press.

Bock, Gisela (1989) 'Women's History and Gender History: Aspects of an International Debate', *Gender and History*, 1: 7–30.

Bock, Gisela (1991) 'Challenging Dichotomies: Perspectives on Women's History', in Karin Offen, Ruth Roach Pierson and Jane Rendall (Eds) (1991) *Writing Women's History: International Perspectives*, Bloomington, Ind.: Indiana University Press, pp. 45–58.

Braudel, Fernand (1980) *On History*, London: Weidenfeld and Nicolson.

Braudel, Fernand (1995 [1963]) *A History of Civilizations*, Harmondsworth: Penguin.

Breisach, Ernst (1983) *Historiography: Ancient, Medieval and Modern*, Chicago: University of Chicago Press.

Bunzl, Martin (1997) *Real History*, London: Routledge.

Burke, Peter (1993) *History and Social Theory*, Ithaca: Cornell University Press.

Burke, Peter (1997) *Varieties of Cultural History*, Oxford: Polity Press.

Burke, Peter (Ed.) (1992) *New Perspectives on Historical Writing*, University Park: Pennsylvania University Press.

Burns, Robert M. and Rayment-Pickard, Hugh (2000) *Philosophies of History: From Enlightenment to Postmodernity*, Oxford: Blackwell Publishers.

Butler, Judith (1990) *Gender Trouble: Feminism and the Subversion of Identity*, London: Routledge.

Butterfield, Herbert (1973 [1931]) *The Whig Interpretation of History*, Harmondsworth: Penguin.

Callinicos, Alex (1995) *Theories and Narratives: Reflections on the Philosophy of History*, Cambridge: Polity Press.

Canary, R. and Kozicki, H. (Eds) (1978) *The Writing of History: Literary Form and Historical Understanding*, Madison: University of Wisconsin Press.

Cannon, John, Davies, R.H.C., Doyle, William and Greene, Jack P. (1988) (Eds) *The Blackwell Dictionary of Historians*, Oxford: Basil Blackwell.

Carr, David (1986a) 'Narrative and the Real World: An Argument for Continuity', *History and Theory*, 25: 117–131.

Carr, David (1986b) *Time, Narrative and History*, Bloomington, Ind.: Indiana University Press.

Carr, E.H. (1987 Second Edn) *What is History?*, London: Penguin.

Carrard, Philippe (1992) *Poetics of the New History*, Baltimore: The Johns Hopkins University Press.

Cassirer, E. (1981) *Kant's Life and Thought*, New Haven, Conn.: Yale University Press.

Caws, Peter (1997) *Structuralism: A Philosophy for the Human Sciences*, Contemporary Studies in Philosophy and the Human Sciences, Atlantic Highlands, NJ: Humanities Press.

Chartier, Roger (1993 [1988]) *Cultural History: Between Practices and Representations*, Cambridge: Cambridge University Press.

Chartier, Roger (1997) *On the Edge of the Cliff: History, Language and Practice*, Baltimore: The Johns Hopkins University Press.

Collingwood, R.G. (1994 [1946]) *The Idea of History*, Rev. Edn, Ed. Jan van der Dussen, Oxford: Oxford University Press.

Collingwood, R.G. (1940) *An Essay on Metaphysics*, Oxford: Clarendon Press.

Cooper, David E. (1999) *Epistemology: The Classic Readings*, Oxford: Basil Blackwell.

Cooper, John M. (1990) *Pivotal Decades: The United States, 1900–1920*, London and New York: W.W. Norton.

Corfield, Penelope J. (1997) 'History and the Challenge of Gender History', *Rethinking History: The Journal of Theory and Practice*, 1: 241–258.

Croce, Benedetto ([1917] 1968) *The Theory and History of Historiography*, Geneva: Droz.

Croce, Benedetto (1923) *History: Its Theory and Practice*, Trans. Douglas Ainslie, New York: Harcourt and Brace.

Culler, Jonathan (1983) *Barthes*, London: Fontana.

Curthoys, Ann and Docker, John (1997) 'The Two Histories: Metaphor in English Historiographical Writing', *Rethinking History: The Journal of Theory and Practice*, 1: 259–274.

Dancy, Jonathan (1985) *An Introduction to Contemporary Epistemology*, Oxford: Blackwell.

Danto, Arthur (1968) *Analytical Philosophy of Knowledge*, Cambridge: Cambridge University Press.

Danto, Arthur (1981) *The Transfiguration of the Commonplace*, Cambridge MA.: Harvard University Press.

Danto, Arthur (1985) *Narration and Knowledge*, New York: Columbia University Press.

Danto, Arthur (1997) *After the End of Art: Contemporary Art and the Pale of History*, Princeton: Princeton University Press.

Danto, Arthur C. (1965) *Analytical Philosophy of History*, Cambridge: Cambridge University Press.

Danto, Arthur (1998) 'Danto and His Critics: Art History, Historiography and After the End of Art', *History and Theory* (Themed Issue), 37: 1–143.

Darnton, Robert (1980) 'Intellectual and Cultural History', in Michael Kammen (Ed.) (1980) *The Past Before Us: Contemporary Historical Writing in the United States*, Ithaca: Cornell University Press, pp. 327–354.

Davidson, Donald (1984) *Inquiries into Truth and Interpretation*, Oxford: Oxford University Press.

Davies, Stephen (2003) *Empiricism and History*, Houndmills: Palgrave.

Davis, Natalie Zemon (1985) *The Return of Martin Guerre*, Harmondsworth: Penguin.

Davis, Natalie Zemon (1987) *Fiction in the Archives: Pardon Tales and Their Tellers in Sixteenth Century France*, Stanford: University of California Press.

Davis, Natalie Zemon (1995) *Women on the Margins: Three Seventeenth Century Lives*, Cambridge, MA: Harvard University Press.

de Certeau, Michel ([1975] 1988) *The Writing of History*, Trans. Tom Conley, New York: Columbia University Press.

Degler, Carl N. (1975) *Is There A History Of Women?*, Oxford: Clarendon Press.

Dening, Greg (1998) 'Writing, Rewriting the Beach', *Rethinking History: The Journal of Theory and Practice*, 2: 141–170.

Dening, Greg (2002) 'Performing on the Beaches of the Mind: An Essay', *History and Theory*, 41: 1–24.

Derrida, Jacques (1976) *Of Grammatology*, Trans. G.C. Spivak, Baltimore: The Johns Hopkins University Press.

Derrida, Jacques (1978) *Writing and Difference*, Trans. Alan Bass, Chicago: University of Chicago Press.

de Saussure, Ferdinand ([1916] 1959) *Course de Linguistic Generale*, Trans. Wade Baskin, London: Fontana.

Dilthey, Wilhelm (1976) *Selected Writings*, Ed. and Trans. H.P. Rickman with a Foreword by Isaiah Berlin, Cambridge: Cambridge University Press.

Domanska, Ewa (1998) *Encounters: Philosophy of History After Postmodernism*, Charlottesville: University Press of Virginia.

Donegan, Alan (1961) 'Explanation in History', in Patrick Gardiner (1961 [1952]) (Ed.) *The Nature of Historical Explanation*, Oxford: Oxford University Press.

Dray, W.H. (1995) *History as Re-Enactment: R.G. Collingwood's Idea of History*, Oxford: Oxford University Press.

Dray, W.H. (1989) *On History and Philosophers of History*, New York: Brill.

Dray, W.H. (1980) *Perspectives on History*, London: Routledge.

Dray, W.H. (1957) *Laws and Explanation in History*, Oxford: Oxford University Press.

Dray, W.H. (Ed.) (1966) *Philosophical Analysis and History*, New York: Harper and Row.

Dray, William (1957) *Laws and Explanation in History*, Oxford: Oxford University Press.

Dray, William (1997) 'Philosophy and Historiography', in Michael Bentley (Ed.) *Companion to Historiography*, London: Routledge, pp. 763–782.

Dreyfus, Hubert L. and Rabinow, Paul (Second Edn 1983) *Michel Foucault: Beyond Structuralism and Hermeneutics*, Brighton: Harvester Press.

Edel, Leon (1984) *Writing Lives: Principia Biographica*, New York and London: W.W. Norton.

Eley, Geoff (1996) 'Is All the World a Text? From Social History to the History of Society Two Decades Later', in T.J. McDonald (Ed.) *The Historic Turn in the Human Sciences*, Ann Arbor: University of Michigan Press.

Elton, Geoffrey (1991) *Return to Essentials: Some Reflections on the Present State of Historical Study*, Cambridge: Cambridge University Press.

Elton, Geoffrey (1967) *The Practice of History*, London: Methuen.

Ermarth, Elizabeth Deeds (1992) *Sequel to History: Postmodernism and the Crisis of Historical Time*, Princeton: Princeton University Press.

Evans, Richard J. (1997) *In Defence of History*, London: Granta.

Fairburn, Miles (1999) *Social History*, Houndmills: Macmillan.

Fay, Brian, Pomper, Philip and Vann, Richard T. (Eds) (1998) *History and Theory: Contemporary Readings*, Oxford: Basil Blackwell.

Finney, Patrick (1998) 'Ethics, Historical Relativism and Holocaust Denial', *Rethinking History: The Journal of Theory and Practice*, 2: 359–370.

Fiumara, Gemma C. (1995) *The Metaphoric Process: Connections Between Language and Life*, London: Routledge.

Forum, (1989) 'Intellectual History and the Return of Literature', *American Historical Review*, 94: 581–669.

Forum, (1991) 'The Objectivity Question and the Future of the Historical Profession', *American Historical Review*, 96: 675–708.

Foucault, Michel ([1975] 1977) *Discipline and Punish*, New York: Pantheon.

Foucault, Michel ([1976] 1979) *History of Sexuality*, Vol. 1, London: Allen Lane.

Foucault, Michel (1972) *The Archaeology of Knowledge*, New York: Harper and Row.

Foucault, Michel (1973a) *Madness and Civilization: A History of Insanity in the Age of Reason*, London: Tavistock.

Foucault, Michel (1973b) *The Order of Things: An Archaeology of the Human Sciences*, New York: Random House.

Foucault, Michel (1975) *The Birth of the Clinic*, New York: Vintage Books.

Foucault, Michel (1977) 'Nietzsche, Genealogy, History', in *Language, Counter Memory, Practice: Selected Essays and Interviews*, Ed. by Donald F. Bouchard and Trans. by Donald F. Bouchard and Sherry Simon (1977), Ithaca: Cornell University Press, pp. 139–164.

Foucault, Michel (1980) *Power/Knowledge: Selected Interviews and Other Writings*, Brighton: Harvester Press.

Foucault, Michel (1970) 'The Order of Discourse', Inaugural Lecture at the College de France, December 2nd.

Fox-Genovese, Elizabeth and Lasch-Quinn, Elisabeth (1999) *Reconstructing History*, New York and London: Routledge.

Frey, Hugo and Noys, Benjamin (2002) 'History in the Graphic Novel', *Rethinking History: The Journal of Theory and Practice* (Themed Issue), 6: 255–382.

Friedlander, Saul (Ed.) (1992) *Probing the Limits of Representation: Nazism and the 'Final Solution'*, Cambridge, MA.: Harvard University Press.

Frye, Northrop (1957 [1967]) *Anatomy of Criticism*, New York: Atheneum.

Fukuyama, Francis ([1991] 1993) *The End of History and the Last Man*, New York: Avon Books.

Fulbrook, Mary (2002) *Historical Theory*, New York and London: Routledge.

Gadamer, Hans-Georg (1998) *Praise of Theory: Speeches and Essays*, Trans. Chris Dawson, New Haven, Conn.: Yale University Press.

Gallie, William B. (1964) *Philosophy and the Historical Understanding*, London: Chatto and Windus.

Gardiner, Jane (Ed.) (1988) *What is History Today?*, London: Humanities Press International.

Gardiner, Patrick ([1951] 1961) (Ed.) *The Nature of Historical Explanation*, Oxford: Oxford University Press.

Gardiner, Patrick (1959) (Ed.) *Theories of History*, Glencoe, Ill.: The Free Press.

Gardiner, Patrick (1961 [1952]) *The Nature of Historical Explanation*, Oxford: Oxford University Press.

Gay, Peter (1966–69) *The Enlightenment*, New York: Knopf.

Gay, Peter (1974) *Style in History: Gibbon, Ranke, Macaulay, Burckhardt*, New York: Basic Books.

Geertz, Clifford (1973) 'Thick Description: Toward an Interpretive Theory of Culture', and 'Deep Play: Notes on the Balinese Cockfight', in *The Interpretation of Cultures*, New York: Basic Books, pp. 3–31, 412–454.

Geertz, Clifford (1983) *Local Knowledge: Further Essays in Interpretative Anthropology*, New York: Basic Books.

Giddens, Antony (1976) *New Rules of Sociological Method: A Positive Critique of Interpretative Sociologies*, New York: Basic Books.

Giddens, Antony (1984) *The Constitution of Society: Outline of a Theory of Structuration*, Cambridge: Polity.

Giddens, Antony (1990) *The Consequences of Modernity*, Cambridge: Polity.

Giddens, Antony (1991) *Modernity and Self-Identity*, Cambridge: Polity.

Giddens, Antony (1998) *The Third Way*, Cambridge: Polity.

Ginzburg, Carlo (1982) *The Cheese and the Worms: The Cosmos of a Sixteenth Century Miller*, Harmondsworth: Penguin.

Ginzburg, Carlo (1993) 'Microhistory: Two or Three Things That I Know About it', *Critical Inquiry*, 20: 10–35.

Goldman, A.H. (1988) *Empirical Knowledge*, Berkeley, California: University of California Press.

Goldstein, Leon (1976) *Historical Knowing*, Austin: University of Texas Press.

Goodman, Jordan (1997) 'History and Anthropology', in Michael Bentley (Ed.) (1997) *Companion to Historiography*, London: Routledge, pp. 783–804.

Graham, G. (1983) *Historical Explanation Reconsidered*, Aberdeen: Aberdeen University Press.

Green, Anna and Troup, Kathleen (Eds) *The Houses of History: A Critical Reader in Twentieth Century History and Theory*, Manchester: Manchester University Press.

Green, William A. (1993) *History, Historians, and the Dynamics of Change*, Westport, Conn.: Praeger.

Grossmann, Reinhardt (1992) *The Existence of the World: An Introduction to Ontology*, London: Routledge.

Gumbrecht, H.U. (1997) *In 1926: Living at the Edge of Time*, Cambridge, MA: Harvard University Press.

Haddock, B.A. (1984) *An Introduction to Historical Thought*, London: Edward Arnold.

Harlan, David (1989) 'Intellectual History and the Return of Literature', *American Historical Review*, 94: 581–609.

Harlan, David (1997) *The Degradation of American History*, Chicago: Chicago University Press.

Harris, James F. (1992) *Against Relativism: A Philosophical Defence of Method*, La Salle, Ill.: Open Court.

Harvey, David (1989) *The Condition of Postmodernity: An Enquiry into the Origins of Cultural Change*, Oxford: Basil Blackwell.

Heidegger, Martin (1962) *Being and Time*, Trans. J. Macquarrie and E. Robinson, Oxford: Basil Blackwell.

Hempel, Carl (1942) 'The Function of General Laws in History', *The Journal of Philosophy*, 34: reprinted in Patrick Gardiner (Ed.) (1959) *Theories of History*, Glencoe, Ill.: The Free Press.

Hesse, Mary B. (1965) 'The Explanatory Function of Metaphor', in Bar-Hillel, Y. (Ed.) *Logic, Methodology and Philosophy of Science*, Amsterdam: North Holland.

Hexter, J.H. (1961) *Re-Appraisals in History*, Evanston: Northwestern University.

Hexter, J.H. (1991) 'Carl Becker, Professor Novick, and Me: or, Cheer Up, Professor N.!', *American Historical Review*, 96: 675–682.

Hexter, J.H. (1972) *The History Primer*, London: Allan Lane.

Himmelfarb, Gertrude (1989) 'Some Reflections on the New History', *American Historical Review*, 94: 661–670.

Himmelfarb, Gertrude (1994) *On Looking into the Abyss: Untimely Thoughts on Culture and Society*, New York: Alfred A. Knopf.

Hirsch, Eric D. (1976) *The Aims of Interpretation*, Chicago: University of Chicago Press.

Hobsbawm, E. (1980) 'Some Comments', *Past and Present*, 86: 3–8.

Hoffer, Peter Charles and Stueck, William W. (1994) *Reading and Writing American History: An Introduction to the Historian's Craft* (2 Vols), Lexington: D.C. Heath.

Horwich, Paul (1990) *Truth*, Oxford: Oxford University Press.

Hughes-Warrington, Marnie (2000) *Fifty Key Thinkers on History*, London and New York: Routledge.

Hunt, Lynn (1989) *The New Cultural History*, Berkeley: University of California Press.

Hunt, Lynn (1998) 'Does History Need Defending?', *History Workshop Journal*, 46: 241–249.

Hutcheon, Linda (1988) *A Poetics of Postmodernism: History, Theory, Fiction*, New York: Routledge.

Iggers, Georg G. (2000) 'Historiography between Scholarship and Poetry: Reflections on Hayden White's Approach to Historiography', *Rethinking History: The Journal of Theory and Practice*, 4, (3): 373–390.

Iggers, Georg G. and von Moltke, K. (Eds) *The Theory and Practice of History*, Indianapolis, IN: Bobbs-Merrill.

Iggers, Georg G. (1997) *Historiography in the Twentieth Century: From Scientific Objectivity to the Postmodern Challenge*, Hanover and London: Wesleyan University Press.

Jenkins, Keith (1991) *Rethinking History*, London: Routledge.

Jenkins, Keith (1995) *On 'What is History?'*, London: Routledge.

Jenkins, Keith (1997) *Postmodern History Reader*, London: Routledge.

Jenkins, Keith (1998a) 'A Conversation with Hayden White', *Literature and History*, 7: 68–82.

Jenkins, Keith (1998b) Review of David Harlan, *The Degradation of American History* (1997), in *Rethinking History: The Journal of Theory and Practice*, 2: 409–412.

Jenkins, Keith (1999) *Why History? Reflections on the Possible End of History and Ethics Under the Impact of the Postmodern*, London: Routledge.

Jenkins, Keith (2002) *Refiguring History*, London and New York: Routledge.

Jordanova, Ludmilla (2000) *History in Practice*, London: Arnold.

Josephson, John R. and Susan G. (1994) *Abductive Inference*, Cambridge: Cambridge University Press.

Joyce, Patrick (1991) 'History and Post-Modernism', *Past and Present*, 133: 204–209.

Joyce, Patrick (1994) *Democratic Subjects: the Self and the Social in Nineteenth Century England*, New York: Cambridge University Press.

Joyce, Patrick (2001) 'More Secondary Modern than Postmodern', *Rethinking History: The Journal of Theory and Practice*, 5: 367–382.

Kammen, Michael (Ed.) (1980) *The Past Before Us: Contemporary Historical Writing in the United States*, Ithaca: Cornell University Press.

Kant, I. ([1781] 1933) *Critique of Pure Reason*, Trans. N. Kemp Smith, London: Macmillan.

Kant, I. ([1786] 1993) 'Conjectures on the Beginning of History', published 1786, in Reiss, Hans (Ed.) (1993) *Kant: Political Writings*, Cambridge: Cambridge University Press.

Kaye, Harvey J. (1996) *Why Do Ruling Classes Fear History?*, New York: St Martin's Press.

Kaye, Harvey J. (1995) *The British Marxist Historians*, New York: St Martin's Press.

Kearney, Richard and Rainwater, Mara (Eds) (1996) *The Continental Philosophy Reader*, London: Routledge.

Kelley, Boyd (1999) (Ed.) *Encyclopedia of Historians and Historical Writing*, 2 Vols, London and Chicago: Fitzroy Dearborn.

Kellner, Hans (1989) *Language and Historical Representation: Getting the Story Crooked*, Madison: University of Wisconsin Press.

Kenyon, J. (1983) *The History Men*, London: Weidenfeld and Nicolson.

Kloppenberg, James T. (1989) 'Objectivity and Historicism: A Century of American Historical Writing', *American Historical Review*, 94: 1011–1030.

LaCapra, Dominick (1983) *Rethinking Intellectual History: Texts, Contexts, Language*, Ithaca: Cornell University Press.

LaCapra, Dominick and Kaplan, Steven (1982) (Eds) *Modern European Intellectual History: Reappraisals and New Perspectives*, Ithaca: Cornell University Press.

Lamont, William (1998) *Historical Controversies and Historians*, London: UCL Press.

Lechte, John (1994) *Fifty Key Contemporary Thinkers: From Structuralism to Postmodernity*, London: Routledge.

Lemon, M.C. (1995) *The Discipline of History and the History of Thought*, London: Routledge.

Lemon, M.C. (2003) *Philosophy of History*, London and New York: Routledge.

Levinas, Emmanuel (1981[1973]) *Otherwise Than Being: or, Beyond Essence*, Trans. Alphonso Lingis, The Hague: Martinus Nijhoff.

Levinas, Emmanuel (1991 [1961]) *Totality and Infinity: An Essay on Exteriority*, Trans. Alphonso Lingis, The Hague: Martinus Nijhoff.

Lipton, Peter (1993) *Inference to the Best Explanation*, London: Routledge.

Lloyd, Christopher (1993) *The Structures of History*, Oxford: Basil Blackwell.

Lorenz, Chris (1994) 'Historical Knowledge and Historical Reality: A Plea for "historical realism" ', *History and Theory*, 33: 297–327.

Lorenz, Chris (1998) 'Can Histories be True? Narrativism, Positivism, and the "Metaphorical Turn" ', *History and Theory*, 37: 309–329.

Lyotard, François (1979) *The Postmodern Condition: A Report on Knowledge*, Paris: Minuit.

Magnus, Bernd and Higgins, Kathleen M. (Eds) (1996) *The Cambridge Companion to Nietzsche*, Cambridge: Cambridge University Press.

Mandelbaum, Maurice (1977) *The Anatomy of Historical Knowledge*, Baltimore: The Johns Hopkins University Press.

Mannheim, Karl (1946) *Ideology and Utopia: An Introduction to the Sociology of Knowledge*, New York: Harcourt, Brace and Co.

Marcus, Laura (1994) *Auto/biographical Discourses: Criticism, Theory, Practice*, Manchester: Manchester University Press.

Marshall, Brenda K. (1992) *Teaching the Postmodern: Fiction and Theory*, New York: Routledge.

Marwick, Arthur (1989 [1970, Third Edn]) *The Nature of History*, London: Macmillan.

Marwick, Arthur (1995) 'Two Approaches to Historical Study: The Metaphysical (Including Postmodernism) and the Historical', *Journal of Contemporary History*, 30: 5–36.

Marwick, Arthur (1998 [1993]) 'A Fetishism of Documents? The Salience of Source-Based History', in Henry Kozicki, *Developments in Modern Historiography*, Houndmills, Basingstoke: Macmillan.

Marwick, Arthur (2001) *The New Nature of History: Knowledge, Evidence, Language*, Houndmills: Palgrave.

Marwick, Arthur (2002) 'Knowledge and Language: History, the Humanities and the Sciences', *History*, Vol. 87, No. 285, January, pp. 3–17.

McCullagh, C. Behan (1984) *Justifying Historical Descriptions*, Cambridge: Cambridge University Press.

McCullagh, C. Behan (1998) *The Truth of History*, New York and London: Routledge.

Megill, Alan (1985) *Prophets of Extremity: Nietzsche, Heidegger, Foucault, Derrida*, Berkeley: University of California Press.

Mensch, James (1997) *Knowing and Being: A Postmodern Reversal*, University Park: Pennsylvania State University Press.

Mink, Louis (1969) *The Philosophy of R.G. Collingwood*, Bloomington, Ind.: University of Indiana Press.

Mink, Louis (1970) 'History and Fiction as Modes of Comprehension', *New Literary History*, 1: 541–558.

Mink, Louis (1978) 'Narrative Form as a Cognitive Instrument', in Canary, R. and Kozicki, H. (Eds), *The Writing of History: Literary Form and Historical Understanding*, pp. 129–149.

Momigliano, Arnaldo (1990) *The Classical Foundations of Modern Historiography*, Berkeley, CA.: University of California Press.

Munslow, Alun (1992) *Discourse and Culture: The Creation of America, 1870–1920*, London: Routledge.

Munslow, Alun (1997) *Deconstructing History*, London: Routledge.

Munslow, Alun (1997) Editorial, *Rethinking History: The Journal of Theory and Practice*, 1: 111–123.

Munslow, Alun (1997) Editorial, *Rethinking History: The Journal of Theory and Practice*, 1: 1–20.

Munslow, Alun (2000) *The Routledge Companion to Historical Studies*, New York and London: Routledge.

Munz, Peter (1997) 'The Historical Narrative', in *Companion to Historiography*, Ed. by Michael Bentley, London and New York: Routledge.

Murphey, Murray G. (1973) *Our Knowledge of the Historical Past*, Indianapolis and New York: Bobbs-Merrill.

Murphey, Murray G. (1986) 'Explanation, Causes, and Covering Laws', *History and Theory* (Themed Issue), 25: 43–57.

Nadel, Ira B. (1984) *Biography: Fiction, Fact and Form*, London: Macmillan.

Nora, Pierre (1987) (Ed.) *Essais d'ego-histoire*, Paris: Gallimard.

Norman, Andrew P. (1991) 'Telling It Like It Was: Historical Narratives on Their Own Terms', *History and Theory*, 30: 119–135.

Norris, Christopher (1990) *What's Wrong with Postmodernism?*, Hemel Hempstead: Harvester-Wheatsheaf.

Novick, Peter (1988) *That Noble Dream: the 'Objectivity' Question and the American Historical Profession*, Cambridge: Cambridge University Press.

Nozick, R. (1981) *Philosophical Explanations*, Oxford: Oxford University Press.

Oakeshott, Michael (1990 [1933]) *Experience and Its Modes*, Cambridge: Cambridge University Press.

Oakeshott, Michael (1983) *On History and Other Essays*, Oxford: Basil Blackwell.

O'Connor, D.J. (1975) *The Correspondence Theory of Truth*, London: Hutchinson.

Olney, James (1972) *Metaphors of Self: The Meaning of Autobiography*, Princeton, NJ: Princeton University Press.

Pachter, Marc (1981) *Telling Lives: The Biographer's Art*, University Park: University of Pennsylvania Press.

Palmer, Bryan D. (1990) *Descent into Discourse*, Philadelphia PA: Temple University Press.

Palmer, Richard E. (1969) *Hermeneutics: Interpretation Theory in Schleiermacher, Dilthey, Heidegger and Gadamer*, Evanston, Ill: Northwestern University Press.

Payling, S.J. (2001) 'The Economics of Marriage in Medieval England: The Marriage of Heiresses', *Economic History Review*, LIV, 3, pp. 413–429.

Payne, Michael (1997) *Reading Knowledge: An Introduction to Barthes, Foucault and Althusser*, Oxford: Basil Blackwell.

Pepper, Stephen C. (1942) *World Hypotheses: A Study in Evidence*, Berkeley, California: University of California Press.

Pihlainen, Kalle (1998) 'Narrative Objectivity Versus Fiction: On the Ontology of Historical Narratives', *Rethinking History: The Journal of Theory and Practice*, 2: 7–22.

Popper, Karl (1945) *The Open Society and Its Enemies*, London: Routledge.

Popper, Karl (1957) *The Poverty of Historicism*, London: Routledge.

Popper, Karl (1959) *The Logic of Scientific Discovery*, New York: Basic Books.

Popper, Karl (Rev. Edn 1979) *Objective Knowledge: An Evolutionary Approach*, Oxford: Clarendon Press.

Porter, Roy (Ed.) (1997) *Rewriting the Self: Histories from the Renaissance to the Present*, London: Routledge.

Poster, Mark (1997) *Cultural History and Postmodernity: Disciplinary Readings and Challenges*, New York: Columbia University Press.

Priest, Stephen (1990) *The British Empiricists*, London: Penguin Books.

Putnam, Hilary (1983) *Realism and Reason*, Vol. 3, Cambridge: Cambridge University Press.

Putnam, Hilary (1981) *Reason, Truth and History*, Cambridge: Cambridge University Press.

Putnam, Hilary (1987) *The Many Faces of Realism*, La Salle, IL.: Open Court Publishers.

Putnam, Hilary (1988) *Reality and Representation*, Cambridge, MA: MIT Press.

Putnam, Hilary (1992) *Renewing Philosophy*, Cambridge, MA: Harvard University Press.

Quine, W.V. (1990) *Pursuit of Truth*, Cambridge, MA: Harvard University Press.

Rabinow, Paul (1999) *Ethics, Subjectivity and Truth: The Essential Works of Michel Foucault, 1954–84*, London: Penguin.

Reiss, Hans (Ed.) (1993) *Kant: Political Writings*, Cambridge: Cambridge University Press.

Ricoeur, Paul (1981) *Hermeneutics and the Human Sciences*, Cambridge: Cambridge University Press.

Ricoeur, Paul (1984 [1983]) *Time and Narrative* (Vol. 1), Trans. Kathleen McLaughlin and David Pellauer, Chicago and London: University of Chicago Press.

Ricoeur, Paul (1984) *The Reality of the Historical Past*, Wisconsin-Alpha Chapter of Phi Sigma Tau: Marquette University.

Ricoeur, Paul (1985 [1984]) *Time and Narrative* (Vol. 2), Trans. Kathleen McLaughlin and David Pellauer, Chicago and London: University of Chicago Press.

Ricoeur, Paul (1986 [1978]) *The Rule of Metaphor: Multi-disciplinary Studies of the Creation of Meaning in Language*, Trans. Robert Czerny, London: Routledge.

Ricoeur, Paul (1990 [1985]) *Time and Narrative* (Vol. 3), Trans. Kathleen Blamey and David Pellauer, Chicago and London: University of Chicago Press.

Ricoeur, Paul (1991) 'Life in Quest of a Narrative', in *On Paul Ricoeur*, Ed. by D. Wood, London: Routledge.

Ricoeur, Paul (1996 [1995]) 'Intellectual Autobiography', in *The Philosophy of Paul Ricoeur*, Ed. by L.E. Hahn, Peru, IL: Open Court.

Ricoeur, Paul (2000) *La Mémoire, l'Histoire, l'Oubli*, Paris: Editions du Seuil.

Roberts, Clayton (1996) *The Logic of Historical Explanation*, University Park, PA: The Pennsylvania University Press.

Roberts, David D. (1995) *Nothing But History: Reconstruction and Extremity After Metaphysics*, Berkeley: University of California Press.

Roberts, Geoffrey (1996) 'Narrative History as a Way of Life', *Journal of Contemporary History*, 31: 221–228.

Roberts, Geoffrey (1997) 'Postmodernism Versus the Standpoint of Action', Review of *On 'What is History?'*, by Keith Jenkins, *History and Theory*, 36: 249–260.

Roberts, Geoffrey (2001) *The History and Narrative Reader*, London and New York: Routledge.

Rockmore, Tom (1995) *Heidegger and French Philosophy: Humanism, Antihumanism and Being*, London: Routledge.

Rorty, Richard (1979) *Philosophy and the Mirror of Nature*, Princeton: Princeton University Press.

Rorty, Richard (1982) *Consequences of Pragmatism*, Minneapolis: University of Minnesota Press.

Rorty, Richard (1989) *Contingency, Irony and Solidarity*, Cambridge: Cambridge University Press.

Rorty, Richard (1991) *Objectivity, Relativism and Truth: Philosophical Papers Vol. 1*, Cambridge: Cambridge University Press.

Rorty, Richard (1998) *Truth and Progress: Philosophical Papers Vol. 3*, Cambridge: Cambridge University Press.

Rorty, Richard (Ed.) (1992) *The Linguistic Turn: Recent Essays in Philosophical Method*, Chicago: University of Chicago Press.

Rosenstone, Robert (1988) *Mirror in the Shrine: American Encounters with Meiji Japan*, Cambridge, MA: Harvard University Press.

Rosenstone, Robert A. (1995) *Visions of the Past: The Challenge of Film to Our Idea of History*, Cambridge, MA: Harvard University Press.

Rosenstone, Robert A. (1996) 'The Future of the Past: Film and the Beginnings of Postmodern History', in Vivian Sobchack (Ed.) (1996) *The Persistence of History: Cinema, Television and the Modern Event*, New York: Routledge, pp. 201–218.

Rosenstone, Robert A. (1998) 'Editorial', *Rethinking History: The Journal of Theory and Practice*, 2: 139.

Ross, Dorothy (1995) 'Grand Narrative in American Historical Writing: From Romance to Uncertainty', *American Historical Review*, 100: 651–677.

Roth, Michael S. (1995) *The Ironist's Cage: Memory, Trauma, and the Construction of History*, New York: Columbia University Press.

Rowbotham, Sheila (1974) *Hidden From History: Rediscovering Women in History From the 17th Century to the Present*, New York: Pantheon Books.

Ruben, David-Hillel (1990) *Explaining Explanation*, London: Routledge.

Ruben, David-Hillel (Ed.) (1993) *Explanation*, Oxford: Oxford University Press.

Sachs, Sheldon (Ed.) (1979) *On Metaphor*, Chicago: University of Chicago Press.

Sahlins, Marshal (1981) *Historical Metaphors and Mythical Realities*, Ann Arbor: University of Michigan Press.

Sahlins, Marshal (1985) *Islands of History*, Chicago: University of Chicago Press.

Sahlins, Marshal (1989) *Boundaries: The Making of France and Spain in the Pyrenees*, Berkeley: University of California Press.

Schama, Simon (1991) *Dead Certainties (Unwarranted Speculations)*, New York: Knopf.

Schama, Simon (1995) *Landscape and Memory*, London: HarperCollins.

Schorske, Carl E. (1998) *Thinking With History: Explorations in the Passage to Modernism*, Princeton, NJ: Princeton University Press.

Scott, Joan W. (1986) 'Gender: A Useful Category of Analysis', *American Historical Review*, 91: 1053–1075.

Scott, Joan W. (1988) *Gender and the Politics of History*, New York: Columbia University Press.

Scott, Joan W. (1989) 'History in Crisis? The Others' Side of the Story', *American Historical Review* Forum, *American Historical Review*, 94: 680–692.

Scott, Joan W. (1996a) 'After History', *Common Knowledge*, 5: 9–26.

Scott, Joan W. (1996b) *Feminism and History*, Oxford: Oxford University Press.

Searle, John (1983) *Intentionality*, Cambridge: Cambridge University Press.

Searle, John (1995) *The Construction of Social Reality*, London: Allan Lane.

Sellars, Wilfred (1997 [1956]) *Empiricism and the Philosophy of the Mind*, Cambridge, MA: Harvard University Press.

Sheridan, Alan (1994) *Michel Foucault, The Will to Truth*, London: Routledge.

Shoemaker, Robert and Vincent, Mary (1998) *Gender and History in Western Europe*, London: Arnold.

Smith, E.E. and Medin, D.L. (1981) *Categories and Concepts*, Cambridge, MA: Harvard University Press.

Smith, Paul (1988) *Discerning the Subject*, Minneapolis: University of Minnesota Press.

Snooks, Graeme Donald (1998) *The Laws of History*, London: Routledge.

Sobchack, Vivian (Ed.) (1996) *The Persistence of History: Cinema, Television and the Modern Event*, London: Routledge.

Southgate, Beverley (1996) *History: What and Why*, London: Routledge.

Spiegel, Gabrielle M. (1992) 'History and Post-Modernism', *Past and Present*, 135: 197–198.

Stanford, Michael (1994) *A Companion to the Study of History*, Oxford: Basil Blackwell.

Stanford, Michael (1998) *An Introduction to the Philosophy of History*, Oxford: Basil Blackwell.

Stedman Jones, Gareth (1972) 'The Poverty of Empiricism', in Robin Blackburn (Ed.) *Ideology in Social Science: Readings in Critical Social Theory*, London, Fontana/Collins.

Steedman, Carolyn (1986) *Landscape for a Good Woman: A Story of Two Lives*, New Brunswick NJ: Rutgers University Press.

Stone, Lawrence (1979) 'The Revival of Narrative', *Past & Present*, 85: 3–24.

Stone, Lawrence (1991) 'History and Post-Modernism', *Past & Present*, 131: 217–218.

Stone, Lawrence (1992) 'History and Post-Modernism', *Past & Present*, 135: 187–194.

Stromberg, Roland N. (1994) *European Intellectual History Since 1789*, Englewood Cliffs, NJ: Prentice Hall.

Sturrock, John (Ed.) (1979) *Structuralism and Since: From Levi-Strauss to Derrida*, Oxford: Oxford University Press.

Symonds, Deborah A. (1999) 'Living in the Scottish Record Office', in Elizabeth Fox-Genovese and Elisabeth Lasch-Quinn *Reconstructing History*, New York and London: Routledge, pp. 164–175.

Tagliacozzo, Giorgio and White, Hayden (Eds) (1969) *Giambattista Vico: An International Symposium*, Baltimore: The Johns Hopkins University Press.

Tallis, Raymond (1998) *In Defence of Realism*, Lincoln: University of Nebraska Press.

Thompson, E.P. (1963) *The Making of the English Working Class*, Harmondsworth: Penguin.

Thompson, E.P. (1978) *The Poverty of Theory and Other Essays*, London: Merlin Press.

Thompson, John B. (1981) *Critical Hermeneutics*, Cambridge: Cambridge University Press.

Tindall, G.B. (1988 [1984]) *America: A Narrative History*, New York and London: W.W. Norton.

Toews, John E. (1987) 'Intellectual History after the Linguistic Turn: The Autonomy of Meaning and the Irreducibility of Experience', *American Historical Review*, 92: 879–907.

Topolski, Jerzy (1991) 'Towards an Integrated Model of Historical Explanation', *History and Theory*, 30: 324–338.

Tosh, John (2000 [1984]) *The Pursuit of History*, Harlow: Longman.

Tosh, John (2001) *Historians on History*, Harlow: Longman.

Turner, F.J. ([1893] 1961) *The Frontier in American History*, reprinted in *Frontier and Section*, Ed. by R.A. Billington, Englewood-Cliffs: Prentice Hall.

UTS Review (1996) 'Is An Experimental History Possible?' 2.

Veyne, Paul (1984 [1971]) *Writing History, Essays on Epistemology*, Trans. by Mina Moore-Rinvolucri, Middletown: Wesleyan University Press.

Vico, Giambattista (1968) *The New Science of Giambattista Vico*, Trans. Thomas G. Bergin and Max H. Fisch, Ithaca: Cornell University Press.

Walsh, W.H. ([1967] 1984) *An Introduction to Philosophy of History*, Westport, Conn: Greenwood Press.

Walsh, W.H. (1981) *Substance and Form in History*, Edinburgh: Edinburgh University Press.

Warren, John (1998) *The Past and Its Presenters: An Introduction to Issues in Historiography*, London: Hodder & Stoughton.

Weber, Max (1957, c1947) *The Theory of Social and Economic Organisation*, Trans. by A.M. Henderson and Talcott Parsons. Edited with an introduction by Talcott Parsons, Glencoe, Ill: Free Press.

Weiland, Steven (1999) 'Biography, Rhetoric, and Intellectual Careers: Writing the Life of Hannah Arendt', *Biography*, 22: 370–398.

Weitz, M. (1988) *Theories of Concepts: A History of the Major Philosophical Traditions*, London: Routledge.

White, Hayden (1987) *The Content of the Form: Narrative Discourse and Historical Representation*, Baltimore: The Johns Hopkins University Press.

White, Hayden (1973) *Metahistory: The Historical Imagination in Nineteenth Century Europe*, Baltimore: Johns Hopkins University Press.

White, Hayden (1978) *Tropics of Discourse: Essays in Cultural Criticism*, Baltimore: Johns Hopkins University Press.

White, Hayden (1978) 'The Historical Text as Literary Artefact', in Canary, R. and Kozicki, H. (Eds) *The Writing of History: Literary Form and Historical Understanding*, Madison: University of Wisconsin Press.

White, Hayden (1992) 'Historical Emplotment and the Problem of Truth', in Saul Friedlander (Ed.), *Probing the Limits of Representation*, Cambridge, MA: Harvard University Press, pp. 37–53.

White, Hayden (1995) 'Response to Arthur Marwick', *Journal of Contemporary History*, 30: 233–246.

White, Hayden (1998) *Figural Realism: Studies in the Mimesis Effect*, Baltimore: The Johns Hopkins University Press.

White, Hayden (2000) 'An Old Question Raised Again: Is Historiography Art or Science? (Response to Iggers)', *Rethinking History: The Journal of Theory and Practice*, 4, (3): 391–406.

White, Hayden (2000) 'The Postmodern Challenge: Perspectives East and West', *Postmodern Studies 27*, Ed. by Bo Stråth and Nina Witoszek, pp. 27–45.

White, Hayden (1996) 'The Modernist Event', in Vivian Sobchack (Ed.) (1996) *The Persistence of History: Cinema, Television and the Modern Event*, London: Routledge.

Williams, Raymond (1983 Edn) *Keywords*, Oxford: Oxford University Press.

Wilson, A. (Ed.) (1993) *Rethinking Social History: English Society 1570–1920*, Manchester: Manchester University Press.

Wilson, George M. (1989) *The Intentionality of Human Action*, Stanford, Calif: Stanford University Press.

Windschuttle, Keith (1995) *The Killing of History: How Literary Critics and Social Theorists are Murdering Our Past*, New York: The Free Press.

Wittgenstein, Ludwig ([1921] 1995) *Tractatus Logico-Philosophicus*, London: Routledge.

Wright, G.H. von (1971) *Explanation and Understanding*, Ithaca: Cornell University Press.

Young-Bruehl, Elisabeth (1998) *Subject to Biography: Psychoanalysis, Feminism, and Writing Women's Lives*, Cambridge, MA: Harvard University Press.

Young, Robert (1990) *White Mythologies*, London: Routledge.

Young, Robert (Ed.) (1981) *Untying the Text: A Poststructuralist Reader*, London: Routledge.

Yovel, Y. (1980) *Kant and the Philosophy of History*, Princeton, NJ: Princeton University Press.

Zagorin, Perez (1990) 'Historiography and Postmodernism: Reconsiderations', *History and Theory*, 29: 263–274.

Zagorin, Perez (1999) 'History, the Referent, and Narrative: Reflections on Postmodernism Now', *History and Theory*, 38: 1–24.

Index